Men of the Bible:
and What Made Them Great

by:

Woody Stieffel

January 2025

Olympus Story House

Contents

In Stieffel's work, a guide map is provided for today's man to follow, equipping readers with the tools to resist the vices and temptations that run rampant and embrace the greatness through the Lord that they were intended for. The author does a commendable job of weaving in his commentary and referencing modern-day anecdotes to help create a direct linkage between the particular biblical figure being discussed and how their story applies to the modern man. The result is a product with plenty of intrigue because of its ability to educate through the sharing of scripture while simultaneously showing each figure's human side, making them instantly relatable.

This anthology of short stories and commentary on men of the Bible begins with Jacob and a poignant yet timely verse from Romans 9:15: "I will have mercy on whomever I will have mercy." From the get-go, there is a clear understanding that the most recognizable names from the Bible are not infallible. In fact, men like Jacob are the ultimate recipients of God's mercy because he spent much of his early days committing treacherous acts and exhibiting an incredibly tenuous relationship with his brother. The scene where Jacob asks for Esau's birthright in exchange for some stew is mind- numbing yet perfectly captures Jacob's selfish nature at the time. Nevertheless, the author has a knack for highlighting how each figure comes full circle and fills his heart with the pure love of God.

Stieffel reflects on his own experiences with his four brothers, growing up playing ball, wrestling, etc., to demonstrate how a brother is meant to fight adversity, not be the adversity. This interplay between his own experiences and the connection to scripture adds a dynamic flow to the work that keeps readers turning the pages. What makes this work meaningful is that while readers stay engaged with strong storytelling, they learn a lot about the Bible without the denseness of reading it, prompting readers to want to read and learn more. MEN OF THE BIBLE And What Made Them Great Woody Stieffel For every figure described in the work, there arrives an inflection point, a moment where God's mercy is bestowed upon them in a way that changes their worldly and spiritual existence. For Jacob, it is meeting Rachel as she is tending her family's sheep. While he works for her family without any expectations of monetary payment, Stieffel highlights the modern generation's mindset of the "ends justify the means" and whether they get something out of it. The example he uses of healthy men declining to help with post-hurricane clean up because there's nothing in it for them is flabbergasting but also reality. Men today are in a spiritual slumber, with only dollar signs being their driving force. Yet, as the stories of Joseph, Sampson, etc. convey, when God is working through you, you are in your purest form and can rise above vices, prejudice, and short-sightedness. The author's recollection of helping someone at the gas station following a Billy Graham speech is especially thought-provoking. The author thinks he is doing such a great deed by helping a very needy man, but in reality, he realizes the greatness of man when God is working through him.

Prominent biblical passages such as David slaying the Philistine Goliath provide a strong sense of familiarity to readers, but within the various narratives, it is the "lessons to learn from this" portion that really becomes a unique opportunity to reflect and understand what the Bible has been trying to say all along in terms of the need for men to rise to greatness. Channeling both an author's talent for storytelling and resonating with today's modern man, Stieffel's work is a meaningful read that presents an ideal way for youth to connect to their faith and walk in the light of God. 10316 Sepulveda Boulevard, Mission Hills CA 91345 (818) 860-4130 www.olympusstoryhouse.com

— *Mihir Shah, US Review of Books*

Using highly factual Bible stories, author Woody Stieffel's book, Men of the Bible: And What Made Them Great, assesses the character of nine historical figures and illustrates what distinguished them from the rest. It also intends to highlight exceptional men who have gone unrecognized and God's encounters with them that resulted in incredible miracles.

Woody methodically discloses Jacob's background, demonstrating both his vile character and an extraordinary change in which he not only made amends with a sibling whom his mother liked less, but also cleansed himself of foreign deities and long-standing deception. He also discusses Samson, a foretold and incredibly gifted judge - a legendary one-man army, who epitomizes being filled with the Spirit and the incredible outcomes that resulted from it. He abandoned God, but God did not abandon him; rather, an unlikely incident taught him a lesson about God's mercy that he would never forget. He also looks at Mordecai, whose rise to prominence redefined grandeur, and David, whose popularity, while being tainted by filthy faults and blunders as well as brokenness and prayer, has endured to this day.

This book intelligently and courageously analyzes and reveals the positive and bad traits of well-known biblical figures while also providing an intimate glimpse into how their choices shaped their lives. By doing this, it invites the reader to envision and contrast their life with a preconceived idea of what God desires their current situation to become in the future. From a pragmatic standpoint, the author is able to highlight these well-known figures, not just their notoriety but also the circumstances which led to it and the preparations that some of them underwent. The reader may get a lot of knowledge, especially regarding relationships, from stories like Samson's and Solomon's, as he uncovers comparable flaws and consequences of their actions and decisions. The author's use of memorable Biblical events that make one think what they would have done differently is remarkable and provokes thoughtful contemplation.

Not only does Woody's thoroughly researched book provide a wealth of teachings, but it also has amusing word choices and humorous interludes. It draws indisputable findings and strong opinions that are sure to make an effect on the reader for a long time. With its distinct viewpoint and robust biblical worldview, the book surpasses expectations and is certain to change a reader's long-held beliefs and make them reevaluate their priorities.

One of the few works devoted solely to men's character development and spiritual advancement is Men of the Bible: And What Made Them Great. Perfectly grounded in biblical principles, it is a fitting companion for men of all ages, races, and origins. It is also deserving of being given as a Valentine's Day, birthday, or an anniversary gift.

This book is a thought-provoking read that offers timeless wisdom from the lives of biblical men. I would highly recommend this book for those looking to strengthen their own faith and gain a deeper understanding of biblical principles.

— *Ephantus M., Pacific Book Review*

PREFACE

"It is what a man is, more than what he has, that renders him truly great." (Matthew Henry)[1] Greatness does not belong to a man who wants it. In fact, the guy who wants it is probably undeserving of it. It's like chasing a butterfly. The more we pursue it, the more it flees from us. But when we finally give up, it comes and lands on our shoulder.

Generally, greatness consists of making other men better, such as a good leader. It belongs to the guy who does the most good, not who gets the most votes. A truly great man might not ever be considered for man of the year or other awards. He probably wouldn't even fill out the application.

Greatness usually starts off slowly and it is largely a work of God. He seems to take His time building and seasoning our character. We have a better chance of becoming a man of some worth if we yield to the fashioning hand of God. It would never have occurred to Joseph in prison, that God was building greatness in him. We may not recognize it as God's doing, such as when we have to change a child's diapers or when we get a flat tire at the worst possible time. What we do know is that our times are in His hand. For each of us, there are no accidents in life. God never says "Oops". And we know that **"all things work together for good to those who love God, to those who the called according to His purpose."** God surely pre-plans every detail of our

ix

lives, causing the events of our life to work refinement of character, purging of our lusts and greed, seasoning our soul with virtues, deepening our love, sharpening our skills, cutting away our excesses, filling up our lacking, beautifying our grace, softening our mercies, teaching us wisdom, improving our spiritual insights, perfecting our humility and steadying our steps as we walk with Him.

Of course, all the above is a life-long work. And a lot of life's lessons are re-runs. It feels like two steps ahead and one step backwards. But if we recognize what God is doing in us, we can make better progress by cooperating with His working and especially by praying for it. "OK, God, my driving was a little rude today. It's a good thing I don't have a Christian bumper sticker on my car. I'm sorry, Lord. There's no excuse for my behavior. Please help me to be in less of a hurry." This would bring more of a smile to God than the $125 offering on Sunday

Growing in God's grace will require some determination. Likewise for the man who wishes to "increase in wisdom and stature and in favor with God and man."

My intention in writing MEN OF THE BIBLE is to equip the men of America with the tools to build their own manhood. The entertainment element is just to keep you from falling asleep in the process.

The following studies of Bible men are not complete biographical sketches. Rather, they are excerpts taken from the Bible record to analyze their character and to highlight their greatness. This book is also an attempt to spotlight men that don't get as much attention as others. Please realize that there is a lot of excellent wisdom in the Bible regarding these men that is not included in this book. It is hoped that you will also read the entire Bible and drink in all the wisdom this book misses. MEN OF THE BIBLE is not just the stories of nine great men. It is also the story of a great God interacting among men, performing His wonders.

It is my hope that our ladies do not feel left out. MEN OF THE BIBLE would be just as good for ladies as for men. They might be pleased to know that a large part of this book is dedicated to men honoring the ladies in their life. Wives, daughters, sisters, mothers. From the beginning, God ordained that man is to take care of his women.

America needs a few good men to be the salt of the earth, a righteous remnant, who like Lot, are vexed in their souls from day to day with the perversions and disgrace of much of our society. May God make you one of them.

So men, let's get on with it.

---

1. *Matthew Henry Commentary, 1706*

JACOB: RASCAL REHABILITATED

I am not worthy of the least of all the mercies and of all the truth which you have shown Your servant. Jacob

The Holy Spirit writes in Romans 9:15, **"I will have mercy on whomever I will have mercy."** Lucky for Jacob. If God had decided to show mercy only to the righteous and deserving, Jacob would surely have been left out. And a number of people in his life would have whole-heartedly agreed. If he had died early in life, his gravestone would likely have read, GOOD RIDDANCE. Jacob was certainly a rascal early on, but God determined to work in his life and bring him to a new creation. Jacob needed a lot of rehabilitating. That may be why he lived so long. (147 years) Blessed is the man whom God has determined to work righteousness in his life no matter how long it takes. We can short-circuit the process with our stubbornness or we shortcut the process with our subjection and cooperation. Either way, we can **be confident of this very thing, that He who has begun a good work in you will complete it until the day of Jesus Christ."**

Why would God choose to do a good work in Jacob? Probably because of his Godly heritage: Abraham and Isaac. We know that Isaac married righteous Rebecca by faith. Fascinating story. So Jacob and Esau became twin sons of believing parents. And very wealthy parents. But Isaac and Rebecca had some flaws too.

Isaac once lied to king Abimelech, saying that Rebecca, who was exceptionally beautiful, was his sister. Isaac was worried somebody would kill him for his wife. No doubt they told their sons about the incident. Isaac got the idea from Abraham. Now when Abraham and Sarah pulled the same stunt, they said they were brother and sister, which was half true, and it worked out profitably for them. But when Isaac and Rebecca said the same thing, it was an outright lie. Unfortunately, our children tend to pick up our faults more easily than our qualities. But now both sets of Godly parents have a little deceit and trickery in their blood. So naturally, Jacob picks up on that and runs with it. He takes Dad's and Mom's sin and goes farther with it than they ever thought about. Well let's hear more about Jacob.

FAMILY FAVORITISM

The first thing we see happens when Isaac and Rebecca's twins seem to be in their teenage years. Esau, the elder twin, is the "manly" type, an outdoorsman who specialized in hunting. Jacob is introduced as "a mild man, dwelling in tents." In Genesis 25:28, we find that **"Isaac loved Esau because he ate of his game, but Rebecca loved Jacob."** This is not getting off to a good start. We have a flagrant case of parental favoritism. Maybe it can't be helped that a parent has a favorite child, but the parent should work at not letting it show. They should treat every child equally in showing affection and attention. Favoritism can hurt the less loved child with discouragement, which could hinder their personal development. It can also hurt the favored child by making him or her feel like they are

2

better than the other children. It can also set the children in a damaging rivalry. The neglected child could also harbor resentment against the parent. Favoritism is a very unhealthy family atmosphere. Favoritism can also foster favoritism. Remember Jacob later unabashedly showed favoritism toward Joseph. The ten older brothers of Joseph were so bitterly resentful that some were ready to kill him. Fortunately, they killed his coat of many colors instead.

But the sins of the First Family did not end there. It is a great pity that the two brothers did not grow up best pals. They had every reason to. There weren't too many other kids their age to play with. Each had a lot to offer the other. Esau could have said, "Jacob, come see this waterfall I found out in the woods. We can dive off this ledge!" Jacob could have said, "Come taste this stew I just cooked." They could have joked together, played catch together, wrestled together and insulted each other for fun. My four brothers and I did all that continuously. Fifty years later, we still playfully insult each other. Not so much with the romping and wrestling.

Recently, during a conversation with one brother, I said in a pretended exasperation, "Am I going to have to give you a piece of my mind?" His quick-witted reply was, "Well that won't take long." Although I am considerably older than my brothers, they have each done huge good things for me when I was in need. Things I would have no chance to ever repay. All I can do to show my gratitude is insult them. And they love it. **"A brother is born for adversity"**, but not to be the adversity.

Wise parenting by Isaac and Rebecca would have fostered good relations between the boys. Sadly, we are suffering the consequences of that failure to this day. (Jews vs Arabs) It's hard for anyone in a family to achieve greatness when they are constantly tearing each other down. High achievers almost always have family cheering them on. Jealousy and resentment have no part in a good family.

JACOB BARGAINS FOR THE BIRTHRIGHT

One day, Esau had an extra long day hunting and came home famished. The story continues in Genesis 25:30, "And Esau said to Jacob, **"Please feed me with that same red stew, for I am weary.** In v. 31, Jacob replies, **"Sell me your birthright as of this day."** How their lives and the world would have been different if Jacob had said, "Sure. Tell me how you like it. We've got plenty." It's not clear just how much the birthright included, but it certainly would have made Jacob inherit more some day. But would he be getting more of the inheritance at the cost of losing a brother? One thing that is clear is that Jacob was selfish. Esau is usually faulted for not valuing his birthright, but it is noteworthy that he really didn't care that much about power or wealth. Well Jacob got his wish, but ended up losing his brother.

On one occasion, a brother approached Jesus and said, **"Teacher tell my brother to divide the inheritance with me." But he said to him, "Man, who made Me a judge or an arbitrator over you? ... Take heed and beware of covetousness, for one's life does not consist in the abundance of the things he possesses."** Coveting is corrosive to happiness. And happiness does not always come with abundance of possessions. The best chance this brother had at happiness was having a good friendship with his brother. Notice that Jesus declined to be judge or arbitrator for them. That's because it's for people to decide for themselves on the issues pertaining to their happiness. The other brother has to decide if he wants to split the inheritance with his brother and gain a brother. **"A brother offended is harder to be won than a strong city."** This was certainly the case with Esau and Jacob. So Esau **"despised his birthright"**, and I have the feeling he stewed with a quiet resentment for a long time. Esau was careless about something he should have valued, and it appears that his belly was his god. Let us beware that we do not value the pleasures of this world over the treasures of the next.

In Genesis 27, we find Isaac getting old and blind and "did not know the day of his death". However, he did end up living at least another 20 years. The following incident severely fractures the family, to everyone's loss. And I have to say that Esau is the only one of the four who was not at fault here. Isaac calls his older son, Esau, to go hunt some game and cook him a dinner such as he loves. This is to put him in the mood for pronouncing his blessing on him as his eldest son. Now what was old Isaac thinking? He is completely neglecting one son though they were the same age. He had no intention of blessing Jacob afterward. But why not bless both sons? Even the wording of the blessing could have been better worded to foster peace. The blessing he intended for Esau was worded, **"Nations shall bow down to you. Be master over your brethren, and let your mother's sons bow down to you."** Apparently, it did not even occur to him that his words would cause a bitter feud between his sons and among brother nations. Rebecca overhears the conversation and turns events to benefit her favorite son, but to disastrous effect. Surely she also carries a lot of guilt in this drama. She deceitfully dresses up Jacob to impersonate Esau. Then Rebecca and Jacob conspire together to bring Isaac the cooked dinner, after which Isaac blesses Jacob with the words that were intended for Esau. So Jacob is guilty as co-conspirator and deceiver. You can bet Isaac and Rebecca had hard words after Isaac figured out what happened. And Esau was so fiercely bitter that he plotted to kill his brother. Other than that, things were fine. There may have been more to Rebecca's motive than doing something for her favored son. Maybe she recognized that Esau's carnal, worldly ways made him less deserving that Jacob who valued the birthright and blessing. Maybe she also saw that Jacob had much more of a bent toward faith in God and righteousness. We find that later in Jacob's life, the eldest son is not always deserving of a blessing. His eldest son, Reuben became a moral disgrace.

So greatness in a man is not always found in the macho, manly types, although it's more expected. It also seems less likely that greatness would be found in the quiet, mild types at first.

JACOB'S VISION

Soon after, Isaac and Rebecca send Jacob away to her brother, Laban, several hundred miles away. So Jacob starts off on his journey. Thus Rebecca loses both sons within a couple of days. Rebecca expected Jacob to "stay with him a few days", but he is gone for 20 years and she dies before Jacob returns. And in a way,

Rebecca lost Esau at the same time because he was probably bitter for his mother's conspiring with Jacob. Sadly, all this deceit and manipulating was surely not necessary. God was perfectly willing to bless and give increase to Jacob rightly, the very thing Jacob and Rebecca worked to obtain wrongly. We will soon see that God is about to show favor toward Jacob that had nothing to do with his trickery.

On the first night of his journey to go see Uncle Laban, God appears to him in a dream. **"Then he dreamed, and behold, a ladder was set up on the earth, and its top reached to heaven; and there the angels of God were ascending and descending on it. And behold, the Lord stood above it and said, "I am the Lord God of Abraham your father and the God of Isaac; the land on which you lie I will give to you and your descendants. Also your descendants shall be as the dust of the earth; you shall spread abroad to the west and the east, to the north and the south; and in you and in your seed all the families of the earth shall be blessed. Behold I am with you and will keep you wherever you go, and will bring you back to this land; for I will not leave you until I have done what I have spoken to you."** (Genesis 28:12-15) What a wondrous scene Jacob beheld! It may have been in a dream, but what he saw portrayed reality. Jesus Himself said, **"Most assuredly, I say to you, hereafter you shall see heaven open, and the angels of God ascending and descending upon the Son of man."** Like the dreams and visions of Joseph and Ezekiel. A ladder to heaven with angels coming and going! We can be sure that there is most certainly such continuous interaction between heaven and earth. Our prayers are not just some kind of wishful thinking that soon disappears like steam from a pot. We learn from all over the Bible that our prayers dispatch angels and move the hand of God. **"The effectual fervent prayers of a righteous man avail much."**

This was a life-changing event for Jacob. He certainly believed in God from this time on. Notice the timing of this vision of God and the promise: Jacob is virtually running for his life; he (hopefully) feels terribly guilty for what he has done; he is alone for the first time in his life; he is traveling light and probably poor. He doesn't even have a pillow. He was accustomed to living comfortably under the care of his rich parents.

So God appears to him at what may have been the lowest point of Jacob's life. This seems to happen often. For He is near to those who are of a broken heart. Blessed are they that mourn, for they shall be comforted. And when Jesus in his darkest hour, agonized in Gethsemane, **"an angel appeared to Him from heaven, strengthening Him."** And when it's our turn to walk through the valley of the shadow of death, we need fear no evil, for He will be with us – especially so.

Jacob really needed the reassurance of God's words, **"Behold I am with you and will keep you wherever you go."** Why did God choose to be so kind to him? It doesn't seem to be for his virtue. But Jacob was showing early signs of faith. He desired the blessing. And God just simply chose him. He has every right to do so. He is sovereign and just. Even before Jacob was born, God chose him. He told Rebecca, **"Two nations are in your womb, two peoples shall be separated from your body; one people shall be stronger than the other, and the older shall serve the younger."** (Genesis 25:23) Before either boy did good or bad,

God chose or "elected" Jacob. Some may be thinking, "But that's not fair." However, God is not obligated to give every person an equal start or opportunity in life. He may choose to give much or little to any one of us. It's for us to decide how well we do with what we're given. Then God will judge us with perfect fairness. To whom much is given, much is expected. It's interesting to note that God revealed to Rebecca that He would put a special "election" on Jacob. It is possible that Isaac was not aware of this. That would explain why Rebecca favored Jacob and why Isaac favored his eldest son. But it did not justify Rebecca's deceit to bring God's promise to fulfillment, as if she would help God.

Notice Jacob's response to the vision. **"Jacob awoke from his sleep and said, "Surely the Lord is in this place, and I did not know it."** Then he builds an altar and pours oil on it. He names the place Bethel, "house of God" and makes a vow to give a tenth to the Lord. I have to wonder what Esau would have done if God had given him that vision. Maybe he would have said, "Wow, that was some dream! That was nice," and resumed his journey. This would be how the residents of Jerusalem responded to the announcement by the magi that the Messiah had arrived. It's as if they said, "Oh, well that's nice" and went about their business, without going to pay honor to the new- born King. God is not one to give his pearls to swine (the unappreciative). But God knew that Jacob would improve much on the vision he saw. How well do we take to heart the excellent preaching He sends our way, or rich truths He gives us from the Bible or a good Christian book or documentary? We would do well to be fertile ground for such excellent seeds. Maybe God would give us more.

9

In v. 17, we see that Jacob was afraid and said, **"How awesome is this place!"** A man is getting a good start when he begins to fear God. The fear of the Lord is the beginning of wisdom. Finally, we find a proper use of "awesome"! To me, only God is awesome.

We can see the beginnings of righteousness and Godliness in Jacob in v. 20, **"If God will be with me, and keep me in this way that I am going, and give me bread to eat and clothing to put on, so that I come back to my father's house in peace, then the Lord shall be my God."** It doesn't seem like making a bargain with God is a very good idea. But God is patient and doesn't chide with him for it. I have to wonder what Jacob would have done if he had ended up returning as poor as when he left. Would he have said, "Sorry, God. If this is the best you can do for me, I'll just keep shopping. No deal." Jacob is just a young fellow, just getting started in life. Still how much better it would have been if Jacob had bowed and worshipped the Lord at Bethel and said, "Surely you are God, and there is no other. Please be my companion wherever I will sojourn. Whatever shall be my lot in life, you shall surely be my God." I know, that's easy for me to say. I've had plenty time to think about it.

Now God already knew what He was going to do for Jacob twenty years later. A vast household of wives, children and servants as well large flocks of sheep, goats, camels, cattle and donkeys! If we assume that what he sent to his brother, Esau, was a tenth of his possessions, then he had something like 5,800 total animals! And Jacob made a deal that he would live for God, if he make it back home with food and clothes. How God must love to do exceeding abundantly above all that we ask or think!

10

JACOB IN HARAN

After several weeks of journeying on foot, Jacob arrives in Haran and gets off to a good start. This is like the trip taken by the prodigal (wasteful) son in Jesus's parable, who also went to a far country and wasted his possessions with prodigal living. He was like Jacob in that he had an older brother who stayed at home. The prodigal son left rich and came home poor; Jacob left home poor and came back rich. The prodigal son kept company with many ladies, with whom he had much pleasure without waiting. Jacob fell in love with one lady and waited for her for seven years. Both Jacob and the prodigal son tended flocks, though the prodigal son nearly starved to death feeding only pigs. Other than that job, we have no record of him working at all.

Jacob worked day and night for twenty years and had much to show for it. He worked wisely and became very smart in his business. **"Do you see a man diligent in his business? He shall stand before kings."** He was not only a good herdsman, he was a good businessman. He returned home with a high hand. The prodigal son returned home with only one thoroughly learned lesson: money does not make friends. When he came home, he had an angry brother. When Jacob came home, he had a reconciled brother. A lot can happen in Haran. Our sojourning can turn into prosperity or disaster. It's our choice. Jacob's kindness got him a wife, Rachel. His perseverance and hard work got him riches. And the grace of God got him a restored brother. Just in time.

11

JACOB AND RACHEL

Soon after arriving in Haran, he meets Rachel tending the family's sheep. He did her a very good service in rolling the stone from the well's mouth and watering her sheep. She would have had to wait much longer. He falls in love with her at first sight. And she probably fell in love with him too for his gallantry. And Jacob kissed her. (Genesis 29:11)

Jacob is welcomed into the family and begins working for the family. He works for a month without any mention of getting paid. What a contrast to some who will go and visit relatives, eat their food, occupy a room in the house, and get waited on for their entire stay. Sometimes for many days. A guest in such cases should do what he can to help around the house. One young couple visited her parents, my brother and his wife, for a few days. While the family was busy around town, the son in law jacked up the somewhat decrepit golf cart and cut out the badly rusted undercarriage framing and rebuilt it with new galvanized metal. He didn't care for sitting around the house. (I'm planning to invite him to come stay at my house.) Blessed are those who will help with the cooking, washing the dishes, raking the yard, weeding the garden or whatever appears to be needed. Every man should carry his share of the load, wherever he goes. Joseph carried his share of caring even while in prison. Let a man jump in and help at every opportunity. You never know what kind of blessing may come from charitable helping, even for no pay. If the person you help cannot or will not pay you, or never have the opportunity to repay you, God most certainly will.

I remember in the aftermath of Hurricane Katrina, during the massive storm recovery effort, I was with a crew working one street after another, doing a variety of manual labor, clearing debris and fallen trees from the streets and clearing the front yards of homes, and loading it all into trucks. As we were clearing our way past one house, I saw a couple of healthy looking young men sitting in the shade of a front porch idly watching us. I invited them to come help us.

They declined and said they weren't getting paid for it. I replied, "Don't you live here?" They said they did. I asked, "Don't you want to at least help out with your own house and your own street?" They repeated that they weren't getting paid for it. I was too out of breath to pursue it at the time, but it occurred to me later, that they would have a hard time getting hired with that attitude. What a contrast to the thousands of men (and women) who drove hundreds of miles to come and labor for the Katrina victims at their own expense, for weeks and in some cases for months at a time. Most of them took unpaid vacation and time off from their regular jobs to come help us out of our troubles. The guys on the porch did not know what they were missing. A golden opportunity passed them by.

Something we easily forget is that God is a great compensator. When a man works for no pay out of his own good will, God will surely compensate him in good measure, usually more sooner that later. **"With good will doing service, as to the Lord, and not to men, knowing that whatever good anyone does, he will receive the same from the Lord, whether he is slave or free."** (Eph. 6:7,8) When God repays a man, it seems that He often does so in-kind. That is, he will be rewarded in a way similar to what he did for the other person. So the man who pulls over and helps some damsel in distress with a flat tire, it is very possible that he will be spared from his own next regularly scheduled flat tire. Though he may never know it. Or the next three, if God so pleases. God operates with the principle of good measure. He repays us more than we did. Jesus taught us, **"Give and it will be given to you: good measure, pressed down, shaken together, and running over it will be put into your bosom. For with the same measure that you use, it will be measured back to you."** (Luke 6:38) But we should not stop and help just to get a nice reward. Rather, we should have it in our mind that we just want to help the lady. With good will.

This is all Jacob cared about: Rachel needed help with watering her sheep. It didn't matter that she was beautiful or from a wealthy family. He was a lot like his mother, Rebecca, when at another well, she offered to water a *caravan* of camels for Abraham's servant. She didn't have the slightest thought that the servant had plans to make her rich. Blessed are those angels among us who just love to do good for the enjoyment of it. So Jacob just enjoys doing good and being useful.

Jacob ends up staying with Uncle Laban for some time. In Genesis 29:15, Laban says, **"Because you are my relative, should you therefore serve me for nothing?"** Apparently Jacob had been staying busy with helping around the farm, probably working as diligently as any of the servants. What a contrast to the busy-body in Proverbs 27:17, **"Seldom set your foot in your neighbor's house, lest he become weary of you."**

Finally, Uncle Laban offers to put Jacob on the payroll. But Jacob declines and requests Rachel's hand in marriage for seven years of service. I have to wonder if Jacob later re-thought about that seven years. But time flew by for the lovers and the wedding day approached. A big wedding feast was put together, and finally Jacob gets married. He takes his lovely veiled bride home and they spend their first night together. The only problem was that he just spent the night sleeping with, not Rachel, but her older sister, Leah. But it was Uncle Laban's doing, with Leah only a willing co-conspirator. Sort of like when Jacob and his mother were co-conspirators in stealing Esau's blessing. So the trickster gets tricked. Sometimes we learn the hard way that we reap what we sow.

Naturally, Jacob is a little upset. But Uncle Laban has his answer already worked out. He explains to Jacob that their custom is that the elder daughter is supposed to marry first, before the younger. And not to worry: he would give Rachel to Jacob after a week was fulfilled for Leah. But of course, Jacob would have to work for Laban another 7 years. What a sneaking, conniving trickster! But no more than Jacob deserved. He had no choice but to agree. He must have been about as frustrated as Esau. But the sneaky conniving and plotting is not over. We have another round coming.

JACOB'S MARITAL BLISS

Now Jacob enters married life, with built in issues. Two wives at odds with each other over who has more rights to Jacob as husband. So Laban gets the ingenious idea to add two more women into the mix. He gives each of his daughters a personal handmaid. He gives Bilhah to Rachel as a maid; and Zilpah to Leah. Just think, if the names had been the other way around, with Zilpah and Bilhah being the wives, then we'd have all these ladies and girls around us named Zilpah and Bilhah, instead of Rachel and Leah. Thank God for His little mercies!

In the rest of Genesis 29 and in Genesis 30, we have the baby-making sweepstakes. The two sisters compete to have the most children. But Rachel isn't having any children. So in desperation, she gives her handmaid, Bilhah to Jacob so that she could bear children "for Rachel". Sure enough, Bilhah has two sons, which Rachel counts as her own, sort of.

Not to be outdone, Leah also gives Jacob her handmaid, Zilpah, who also begins bearing children, which adds to Leah's score. I don't know how Jacob got any sleep. And we think we've got marriage problems? I wonder if Jacob was ever glad that Laban didn't have 6 daughters. This was not a friendly rivalry among a loving family. It was nasty. Fighting over the husband, fighting over the children. Remember, this is the family through which the Messiah would come. Here it looks more like it gets derailed. Now we can see why God planned for marriage to be one man and one wife. What a deeply satisfying relationship this can be! I cannot imagine anything being more fulfilling. (With the possible exception of a fully-dressed cheeseburger.) Besides the usual affection and romance of a marriage, the man finds great satisfaction in protecting and providing for his wife. Which God also planned. And the woman is comforted by the security of her husband and taking care of him. And both relish being loved. Every effort should be made to preserve the peace and happiness and love of the marriage. That effort sometimes requires self-denial, letting the other have their way, or working as long as it takes to provide for the family. Jacob did this very well.

Noticed he stays with all four wives, never divorcing or sending away any of them, as Grandfather Abraham sent away Hagar. Even if Jacob had decided to divorce a couple of them, he'd still be married. He did not shirk or try to lighten his heavy load of responsibility. He probably figured, **"God's grace is sufficient for me."** When some folks give up their severely handicapped children or relatives to professional care facilities, they have declined to bear the cross that God had carefully designed for them. And they are probably forfeiting some of the greatest blessings God had planned for them. **"No temptation (or trial) has overtaken you except as is common to man; but God is faithful who will not allow you to be tempted beyond what you are able...to bear."** (I Corinthians 10:13)

According to <u>caregiveraction.org.statistic</u>s, 65 million people in the United States "provide care for a chronically ill, disabled or aged family member... providing care for their loved one." *Caregiving in the U.S." (November 2009)[4]* That's about a quarter of the adults in the U.S. Yes it may be difficult caring for your loved one, but it is not more than you can bear and it is still common among men.

JACOB'S WORK ETHIC

Consider these elements of Jacob's strong work ethic. In Genesis 31:38-41, we get the details:

a. **He provided special care to the pregnant animals of Laban's flock,** so that none of them miscarried. I know almost nothing about being a shepherd, but it looks like this was above and beyond the call of duty. This would be like an employee staying late after work (on his own time) to repair broken down equipment for his boss. It would have been a lot easier to call in the breakdown and go home for the night.

b. **He did not eat the rams of Laban's flock.** There were probably shepherds who considered that to be a fringe benefit. And no need for the boss to hear about it. One sheep in a flock of a few hundred would not be noticed. There are employees today who enjoy "fringe benefits" of their company. You know, little things that the boss wouldn't mind, and does not need to know about it. Like using the copier for personal documents, or using the company vehicles for personal errands or trips. Other employees fill their pockets or tool bags or purses with hardware or tools that would never be missed. Other employees know how to alter computer records and skim off the profits for their personal use. But not Jacob. He was shrewd enough that he could have padded his own pockets with profits that did not belong to him, but he never did. Why not? He feared God. So should we.

c. **If one of Laban's flock was lost due to theft or being killed by another animal, Laban billed Jacob for the loss.** This is pretty hard treatment by an employer and relative. Especially considering Laban was wealthy and Jacob was poor and feeding a lot of mouths. In spite of all this, Jacob's work and care was making Laban a lot of money.

d. **He stayed with the flocks in all types of weather, protecting them.** He didn't overuse his sick leave or paid time off. He is like a man who voluntarily

18

works overtime for no pay to protect equipment endangered by the elements. It would be even more commendable if he did so without even telling the boss. "Let another man praise you and not your own mouth."

e. **He endure personal hardships** such as spending cold, wet, sleepless nights with the flocks or scorching hot days. I imagine that if it started raining on a cold night, most shepherds would shut up the flock in a sheepfold and head home for the night.

All this and still he was cheated out of his pay by Laban changing the agreement they had. Jacob's pay was to be given any speckled and spotted sheep that were born. (A small minority of the sheep.) But when the flock started producing a lot of speckled and spotted lambs, then Laban would change Jacob's pay being given streak-colored lambs. Laban changed it like this ten times, trying to get more lambs for himself. Yet God saw the dishonesty of Laban and turned it against him. So, for example, when Laban changed Jacob's pay to streak-colored lambs, then the flock started bearing streak-colored.

There are a lot of people who practice crooked dealings trying to get more money. For the love of money is still the root of all sorts of evil. Yet God is able to confound the schemes of the wicked and turn it against them. **"He takes the wise in their craftiness."** Contractors will overcharge for a service, or charge more hours than were actually worked, or claim to have done more work than was actually performed. But God keeps close accounts and requires it of them sooner or later. In this same story, we learn that God also sees exactly how much the innocent party is cheated. And

19

He knows how to make it up to them. So there's no need for revenge. And no need to sue for losses. Let God do his job.

In a dramatic example of this, a near neighbor of mine once hired a contractor to build a deck onto his house. He paid a sum of money to get the materials purchased and the work started. Exactly three posts were installed and the contractor disappeared with the money. My neighbor was a single man raising a small child. After it sat for months, I asked my neighbor about it and he explained what happened. I presented the case to the men's fellowship at my church, and it was unanimously agreed that we would complete the porch and provide the materials at our expense. The sizeable porch was built over 4 Saturdays. He was very grateful. Not long afterwards, my neighbor told me that he had recently heard from the contractor. He had broken both legs.

JACOB'S PARENTING

When Jacob started getting his own flocks, he decided it would be a good idea to separate his flock from Laban's flock. (Even though they were already easily distinguished by colors.) So he puts his teenage sons in charge of the family flock and stations them at a distance of three days journey. Children being away from the monitoring and supervision of the parents is almost always a bad idea. **"The rod and rebuke give wisdom, but a child left to himself brings shame to his mother."** (Proverbs 29:15) Especially true for teens. Some fathers may be thinking, "But my kids don't want to hear anything I have to say." That's proof

20

that they need it. Shame on kids who disrespect the words of their parents! This is particularly angering to God. **"My son, hear the instruction of your father, and do not forsake the law of your mother; for they will be a graceful ornament on your head, and chains about your neck."** (Proverbs 1:8,9) By the way, those "chains" at the end are jewelry, not prisoner chains. As for the cocky teenagers who roll their eyes when their parents are speaking to them, the Bible has a verse for them. **"The eye that mocks his father, and scorns obedience to his mother, the ravens of the valley will pick it out, and the young eagles will eat it."** Some may be wondering whether God is serious about that. You don't want to find out.

It's understandable that Jacob already had his hands full with work and financial responsibilities, but neglecting his children's character should not be an option. How did it work out for Jacob's family? It wasn't long before Jacob's ten older sons got a poisonous jealousy over little Joseph's dreams. They could not speak peaceably to him. I'm an older brother with eight younger siblings. Nothing could have broken my love for my little brothers and sisters. Some got better grades than I did. Others excelled in sports far past me. I would express how proud I was of them, like Dad and Mom did. But I had the good influence of my mother and father. And like Jacob, my Dad had a lot of mouths to feed. Twelve, not counting pets. My Dad or Mom would immediately snuff out any ill treatment or behavior of one of their children toward another. Both my Dad and Mom used the rod and reproof to give us all wisdom.

But where was Jacob? At a distance of three days journey. With no texting. Jacob was out of touch with his older boys. But he was very close to Joseph, his youngest child, at the time. And the son of his beloved wife, Rachel. I can just picture Jacob, Rachel and their son Joseph living in a separate tent as a family unit.

Joseph got some very good fathering in his early years. Lots of father-son talks. Probably family prayer time. He surely taught Joseph much about the God of Abraham and Isaac. We see evidence that Joseph was taught a lot of good principles like abstinence, honesty, caring, integrity. A kid does not get that from the internet or TV or other kids.

In Genesis 37:1, young Joseph is working with some of his older brothers and sees some of their bad behavior. We are told, **"Joseph brought a bad report of them to his father."** We are left to guess what the older brothers, now young men, were doing. Sadly, we go a long period of time without seeing Jacob having meaningful, constructive interaction with the older sons.

JACOB AND LABAN

It happens commonly that relationships start off pleasant and agreeable and end up sour and disgruntled. This is what happened with Laban and Jacob. Even though he was a son-in-law twice over and a good employee, Laban began to have bad will toward Jacob. It appears that Laban was mostly jealous of Jacob's success. We can be sure that a lot of bad will came out of Laban changing Jacob's wage ten times, trying to cheat him of his fair earnings. But Jacob also had way of manipulating the flocks so they would bear more colored sheep for him and less for Laban. Once again, Jacob sought by questionable means to increase his wealth. Laban and his sons picked up on that and were increasingly sullen toward Jacob and his sons. Surely there was no need for Jacob to stoop to such tactics. God could easily have blessed him and multiplied him just fine without it. Just as God could have blessed Jacob plentifully without having to trick his own brother out of his birthright. And let's not point the finger too much at Jacob. To this day, a lot of us try to get wrongly what God was already planning to give us rightly.

In Genesis 31:20, Jacob and his family secretly pack up and begin traveling back to Canaan. They sneak away three days before Laban finds out about it. Then Laban and probably a large contingency of men, make hot pursuit after Jacob and the family. Laban was so angry that God had to intervene and warn him in a dream, **"Be careful that you speak to Jacob neither good nor bad."** Our God knows how to watch over his beloved ones. **"He permitted no one to do them wrong; saying, do not touch my anointed ones and do my prophets no harm."** Let us keep our own hands from avenging ourselves when we serve such a mighty God.

I realize God told Jacob it's time to pack up and come home, but I don't believe God approved of his leaving without having a "good-by" get together. Jacob shouldn't just sneak away without giving Laban and the rest of the family a chance to say good-by to the two daughters, two hand maids and eleven grandchildren. Was Jacob worried about reprisals from Laban? He should have trusted in God and do the right thing. He could have rested in the fact that God had just *told him* to go back to Canaan.

Laban and company catch Jacob and company in 7

days. After God's rebuke to Laban in Genesis 31:24, we can be sure he chose his words carefully. When they met, he expressed his indignation at Jacob's secret, unannounced departure and says, **"Now you have done foolishly in so doing."** I have to agree with him. Like many of us, he was very good at pointing out the faults of others. Like two children shouting at each other in a schoolyard, these men declared their own good and the other's faults. Imagine what a difference it would have made if instead they had calmly confessed their own faults and pointed out the good the other had done. "Laban, I have to apologize to you for leaving so abruptly. I don't know what I was thinking. You were kind enough to take me in when I had nowhere to go and give me a job all these years. And I can't thank you enough for trusting me with your two daughters. You have treated me like family and I have not shown you much gratitude. I hope you can forgive me for all my wrong." Laban may have replied, "I'm also sorry for being so hot-headed about you leaving. I guess I can't blame you for leaving. I have to admit, I haven't been fair to you either. Why don't we make a nice big dinner and have a proper going away party for you all." Could you imagine Rachel and Leah exchanging glances at this interchange? What's wrong with them? What conniving are they up to now? Well it's too late for them to change the bad will between them. But it's not too late for us. What troubled relationship is there in our life that needs a dose of Proverbs 15:1? **"A soft answer turns away wrath, but a harsh word stirs up anger."** I have to admit, the "soft answer" goes counter-grain to most of us, but God's grace is sufficient for us. He can help us handle the situation calmly. The rewards would be great.

At least they all had a nice going away dinner. Men tend to solve a lot of their problems with eating. The next morning Jacob and his family got a nice sending off. Everyone kissed each other good-by and went home. Jacob the rascal barely escapes paying the consequences of his sins and deceit.

JACOB WRESTLES WITH GOD

After a long season of wrestling with men, he now tries his hand at wrestling with God. We don't realize it, but we all wrestle with God. In our consciences and in our decisions. **"For the flesh lusts against the Spirit and the Spirit against the flesh."** (Galatians 5:16) The Holy Spirit continually tries to restrain us against our worldly lusts. If you want to know what would happen if the Holy Spirit ceased to restrain us, read Revelation 13 and following.

Jacob barely gets past Laban when he begins to approach Esau's country. He probably gets the sensation of being between a rock and a hard place. But he plows on, relying on the word of God, **"Now arise, get out of this land, and return to the land of your family."** Where God directs, He protects. Even when the heavy consequences we are facing are the result of our own sins, he preserves us. **"I am your shield and your exceedingly great reward."** Now Jacob faces the most serious problem of his life: Esau's anger. With this dread in his heart, we see God giving him some comfort.

So Jacob went on his way, and the angels of God met him. When Jacob saw them, he said, **"This is**

God's camp." When you are facing your greatest fears, you can reasonably expect God's greatest grace. But don't mistake this: the angels were not for Jacob's protection; they were for his reassurance. God's word was his protection. And ours. We should believe on His promises. To do that, we have to know them.

As Jacob came close to where Esau lived, he sends messengers to greet him. They were to say to him, **"Thus your servant Jacob says, 'I have dwelt with Laban and stayed there until now. I have oxen, donkeys, flocks, and male and female servants; and I have sent to tell my lord, that I may find favor in your sight."** This was civil enough and very humble on Jacob's part. The servants were instructed to address him as lord over Jacob. He refers to himself as Esau's servant. He seeks to find favor in Esau's sight. This very gracious message would have worked well for just about anybody but Jacob. But Esau was highly suspicious of Jacob and wondered what kind of motive he had for all that sweet talk. Esau was not going to be fooled. He picked up the old bitterness right where it left off twenty years ago. So he rounds up a 400 man posse to go say "hello" to his brother. When Jacob's messengers return with that news, he schedules an emergency prayer meeting. Meanwhile he prepares for the worst.

In Genesis 32:9, he makes this magnificent prayer of faith:

> **O God of my father Abraham and God of my father Isaac, the Lord who said to me, "Return to your country and to your family, and I will deal well with you":**
> **I am not worthy of the least of all the mercies and of all the truth which you have shown your servant; for I crossed over this Jordan with my**

staff, and now I have become two companies. Deliver me from the hand of my brother, from the hand of Esau; for I fear him, lest he come and attack me and the mother and the children. For you said, "Surely I will treat you well, and make your descendants as the sand of the sea, which cannot be numbered for multitude."

Jacob did not read this prayer as if he had written it all down ahead of time. He prayed all this from his heart with a sense of urgency. First let's notice that he addresses his prayer to God. Not to any of the false, invented gods of his time, but to the real God, the God of Abraham and Isaac. He could have added "to the God who met with me at Bethel". He prayed to God alone; not to God and someone else; not to God by some other name.

"The Lord who said to me" He is building a proper view of God in his mind. We might do it this way, "O God, the only God, Almighty God; You created the heavens and the earth and you created me. You who know my inward-most thoughts and judge with all righteousness." Or if you're pressed for time, as when Peter was sinking in the waves, keep it short: "Lord, help!" I think we lose something when we tritely jump right into our prayers with, "Lord please help me do a good job today." We have so much opportunity to worship and exalt our God.

"O God, you parted the Red Sea and allowed Israel to pass over, but kept back Pharaoh and his army. You are the same God who raised up the little daughter of Jairus from the dead. Surely it is a small thing to help my sick little boy to recover. Thank you for your many mercies."

"The Lord who said to me, 'Return to your country

and to your family, and I will deal well with you." Of course, Jacob is quoting the very words which God had spoken to him. Quoting the word of God in our prayers can be highly effective.

"Lord, did you not say that we should seek first the kingdom of God and your righteousness and all these other things will be added to us? Well please notice: my wife and children and I attend church faithfully, we pray together to you, we put You above all else in our life. You know that I have been laid off for a month now and finances are scarce. Please give us this day our daily bread and enough to get by. Please don't let Your children, who are known to be Christians, end up asking for help from others. Show Yourself to be our Father, who are in heaven. Hallowed be Your name."

In v. 9, Jacob presents to God a conditional promise, as in the sample prayer above. Now in v. 10, Jacob displays such a genuine humility as we have not seen to this point in his life. This "gun-point" praying works pretty well. Next time you're under the gun, try praying. The idea is like telling God, "I did my part, now please do Your part." In v. 10, Jacob just prays exactly the way he feels. This is not canned or pre-meditated. He has no ulterior motive to pretend like he's humble. **"I am not worthy of the least of all the mercies** (I have to agree) **and of all the truth which you have shown your servant; for I crossed over this Jordan with my staff, and now I have become two companies."** He feels so humble and undeserving. Jesus was highly pleased with another man who prayed similarly, **"Lord, I am not worthy that you should come under my roof. But only speak a word, and my servant will be healed."** So in the beginning of his prayer, he puts God in the high

28

place where He belongs, and now here, he puts himself in the very low place where he himself belongs.

In v. 11 and 12, he gets to the main point of his prayer. This sounds a little like the Lord's prayer, **"deliver us from evil."** I sometimes feel like I should add, "especially my own evil."

Deliver me from the hand of my brother, from the hand of Esau; for I fear him, lest he come and attack me and the mother and the children. For you said, "Surely I will treat you well, and make your descendants as the sand of the sea, which cannot be numbered for multitude."

I'm guessing that before Jacob finished speaking this request, it was already granted. This is like the prayer of Daniel, when he had been a while in effectual, fervent prayer for the restoration of Jerusalem. Gabriel appeared to him and stated, **"at the beginning of your supplications the command went out, and I have come to tell you, for you are greatly beloved."** In other words, Daniel's petition was granted way back in the beginning of his prayer. It just took Gabriel a while to get there. It's probable that Jacob's prayer was much longer than what we have recorded, as it was in Daniel's case.

It intrigues me that Jacob mentions all the mercies and all the truth God showed him. (v. 10) He seems to be well aware of the many times when God showed him mercy. I'm afraid we completely miss most of the mercies God sends us, just as it never dawned on the Israelites that their clothes and sandals never wore out in their forty years in the wilderness. Maybe the pastoral life of a shepherd gave him plenty of time to think and meditate. Jacob surely knew that his own father did likewise. It was probably in those times of meditation that God revealed special truth to Jacob. He had no preachers, no church to attend, no Bible or books to study. But he had a God and a Helper to reveal truth to him. How much more should we be seekers of truth and wisdom and knowledge of God, who have the same God, the same Helper and every conceivable tool to help us.

It is not surprising that soon after this prayer time, Jacob gets the inspiration of sending a series of gifts to Esau, each one separated by some space. Each gift is to be presented to Esau as he approaches, and the servants were to say, **"these belong to your servant Jacob. It is a present sent to my lord Esau; and behold he is behind us."** The several flocks totaled 580 assorted animals! After that, there were 3 more groups of young mothers and children, finally Jacob was last of all. This was not at all cowardly of Jacob. Rather it was to allow as much time as possible for it all to impact Esau favorably. That would be enough to soften any man's heart. It would also remove any remaining suspicion in Esau's mind that Jacob was coming to claim his birthright of the majority of the inheritance from Isaac.

With Esau a day away, Jacob divides up all his flocks and families into the proper order and after nightfall, he sends everyone over the Jordan and remains alone on the east side. He and God have some unfinished business. He would have to settle this alone. What follows is a perfect picture of a man's salvation. It is sort of like his Gethsemane, which Jesus had to face alone. Jesus went a little farther.

For both Jesus and Jacob, it is the most important hours of their life. Without Jesus's victory in Gethsemane, there would have been no Calvary. It's interesting that Jesus's victory, consisted of his full surrender to the Father's will. But His victory was bringing his flesh and soul into total subjection to the Father's will. "Not my will, but yours be done." This was an agonizing process for him. It took three hours to settle the matter. But Jesus was not so much anxious about the humiliation, beatings and taunting of the Sanhedrin and their guards. Yes, it was a painful grief that his closest friends abandoned Him and fled. Yes, the terrible 39 stripes would be excruciating. All this so weakened him physically, that He could not even carry His own cross. A guy from Africa, named Simon, was made to carry it for Him. This man was the only person to help Him all that day. He knew He would also face the most horrible form of execution men could think of: crucifixion. To impale a human being in both hands and feet and let him hang by those nails until he either bled to death or asphyxiated was so cruel that even the most hardened of men must have turned away their faces from seeing it. But remember, all of this was long ago foreordained for the offering of God's Lamb. I suppose that even the method and degree of pain were carefully prescribed so as to be completely sufficient to cover the sins of all mankind. **Behold the Lamb of God, Who takes away the sin of the world."** If Jesus had accepted a sip of the wine and myrrh that was offered to him, maybe the price He paid would not have extended as far as to us today. But

Jesus paid it all, all to Him I owe,
Sin had left a crimson stain,

He washed it white as snow.

But even the horror of crucifixion was not the worst of what Jesus anticipated. John tells us that God's lamb would take away the sin of the world. But Jesus was also previewed by the scapegoat, in that all the sins of Israel

31

were imputed to be upon the scapegoat. **"The goat shall bear on itself all their iniquities to an uninhabited land."** Peter confirms this, **"Who Himself bore our sins in His own body on the tree, that we having died to sins, might live for righteousness – by whose stripes you were healed."** (I Peter 2:24) Unlike the scapegoat, Jesus *willingly* received all the collective sins of man and felt the weight of this black hole in His heart for the six hours He hung on the cross. If you can believe it, even this wasn't the worst of what Jesus dreaded! The worst one was the only one He "complained" about. He cried on the cross, **"My God, My God, why have you forsaken Me?"** Not only could the Father hardly bear the sight of his suffering Son, He could not bear the sight of all that sin. It actually made Jesus look hideous in the Father's sight. So the Father turns His back on His Son – His beloved Son and Friend from ages past. Many a man could endure a great deal of suffering or injury to protect his wife or child. But what man could endure his wife and children turning their back on him and abandoning him?

When Israel complained to God and Moses in the wilderness, God justly sent fiery serpents among the people and many died. So they cried out to Moses, "We're really sorry. Please take away the serpents." Instead of taking away the serpents, God had Moses set up a brass serpent high on a pole. Instructions were that if anyone was snake-bitten, they were to simply look at the serpent and they would be healed. Jesus referred to this incident as being a preview of His own death in being lifted up. I always wondered why God didn't have Moses put a lamb on the pole, since it symbolized the coming Lamb of God. Then one day it hit me: we look up to Jesus on the cross as our Lamb offering, but

God looks down to Jesus as if bitten by that old serpent, the devil. Bearing the curse of all our sins on that cross, even wearing a crown of cursed thorns, cursed for our sakes, being hung on a "tree", *He came to make His blessings flow far as the curse is found."* But He who humbled Himself has now been highly exalted and given a name above every name!

Please pardon the interlude of attention to our Savior and King. But Jacob is very much a prototype of the life of Jesus. Jacob, like Jesus, left his father to go to a faraway place. Then he returned bringing many souls with him, to the Promised Land. The day of Jacob's departure, he encounters the ladder that reached to heaven. When he returned and re-crossed Jordan, he met the Father face to face. He labors to gain himself a bride, two actually. Jesus labored on our behalf to purchase our redemption, as did Jacob in a sense. He had two households, sort of, just as Jesus also received a household of Jews and a household of Gentiles.

But back to Jacob. We read in Genesis 32:24, **"Then Jacob was left alone; and a Man wrestled with him until the breaking of day." The record says "man"** only because it was the appearance of a man. We have a double confirmation that it is actually God, coming in the likeness of a man. This is one of those several "theophany" appearances of the Old Testament. But this wrestling match is a portrayal of something much deeper. The physical wrestlings were like the many years and many circumstances in which Jacob's will was in conflict with God's will. Much of what Jacob did was wrong and selfish. And through it all, God through the Holy Spirit, had strivings with Jacob's conscience. Jacob was shrewd. He did not steal outright, but he plotted to get what he wanted, while thinking he was barely within the bounds of honesty. The problem was, he stayed barely within the lines that *he* drew. The Holy Spirit worked to convict him that God's boundaries were much stricter. **"All the ways of a man are clean in his own eyes."**

All his life, there was a contest of wills between God and Jacob. Just like us. God does not push or force His will on us. He leaves us to be free moral agents. He gently reasons with us. As he gently "wrestled" with Jacob. I suppose something happened in Jacob that was similar to what happened to Jesus, who also "wrestled" all night, when he finally acquiesced with, **"Not my will, but yours be done."** Jacob wrestled all night with the safety of his family in view; Jesus wrestled all night with our safety in view. A sort of veil seems to cover much of what transpired that night, but in the end, I think Jacob surrendered his will to God also. This is a fine picture of man's salvation. Our surrendering of our will and lives to Jesus Christ. It is choosing to live for His kingdom and His righteousness instead of our kingdom and our own righteousness.

In demonstration of his might and sovereignty, God touches Jacob's hip (after hours of wrestling) and puts his hip out of joint. Jacob ended up limping. We need not push things that far with God. We should surrender to Him who loves us, early in the fray. In Genesis 32:26, Jacob amazingly persists even after he clearly loses. He grabs hold tightly to his opponent and refuses to let go. I can picture God with a faint, amused smile when He says to Jacob, **"Let me go, for the day breaks."** Jacob has some nerve when he replies, **"I will not let you go unless you bless me!"** So God gives him this blessing, **"Your name shall no longer be called Jacob (Supplanter), but Israel** (One who struggles with God)."

But Jacob isn't through yet. In v. 29, Jacob asks, **"Tell me your name, I pray."** Meanwhile the day is getting lighter and lighter. God must have sighed and looked at His watch. He wouldn't give His name, but He does bless Jacob. Somewhere in all this interchange, if we could see blessings, we would probably see this little blessing fly across the river heading for Esau. Let's picture the blessing as resting un-noticed in Esau, until it melts in his heart at seeing all of Jacob's caravan, wives and children. I know that part is not in the Bible, but it sounds nice.

"Blessed is the man who endures temptation (trials, struggles), for when he has been approved (tried), he will receive the crown of life which the Lord has promised to them that love Him." As with Jacob. In his trial, Jacob endured the struggle and received his life in a sense, when it was very much in question. May God grant you like victories.

This event is the culmination of a lifetime of dealing with God. It's the Old Testament equivalent of our becoming Christians, born again. We can see a sharp change of character after this time.

JACOB AND ESAU

In Genesis 33:1, Jacob sees Esau coming with 400 men. But this time, we don't read that Jacob feared. (As in Genesis 32:7) Jacob lines up his caravan as previously planned. As each group of the caravan meets Esau, we can well imagine that he is more and more touched. It may be that no one had ever given him such gifts before. And when he saw the sweet young children and wives, he got to thinking, "these are my nephews and sisters."

I'd have to guess his eyes are beginning to well up with tears. Then last, and all by himself, vulnerable and with no bodyguards or weapons, here comes Jacob, bowing down repeatedly.

Finally Esau is overcome with love for his twin brother. But we know how he got to be so tenderhearted. We imagined it flew across the river. All the wives and children came and bowed to Esau. He must have felt like a king.

"The king's heart is in the hand of the Lord, like the rivers of water; He turns it wherever He wishes." (Proverbs 21:1) Like a puddle of water on a kitchen counter that follows your finger wherever it traces. God can change a man's heart so easily, especially when we pray.

The brothers hug and they both wept. No mention is made of being sorry for past offenses. Nor was there any need. This is not the same Jacob who got in a shouting match with Uncle Laban. This is born-again Jacob, the new creation. Old things are passed away, all things are become new. The same internal overhaul is available to all applicants. They will run smoother, won't burn up as much gas, no more blowing smoke. All cleaned up. You get the idea.

At first, Esau declined to accept all the caravan of animals Jacob sent to give him. After all, he was far richer than Jacob. After Jacob persistently urged him, Esau finally accepts the gift. All 580 of them.

Back in Genesis 28:22, Jacob promised God that if he came back that way in peace, with food and clothing, he would give God a tenth of his possessions. I have to wonder if Jacob pondered his promise to God and thought, "Ok, God most certainly kept His side of the deal, but how do I go about giving Him my tenth?"

There was no temple or tabernacle where he could bring the offering. There was no priest or Levite to give it to. If grandfather Abraham had been still alive, Jacob would have probably called him on the phone to see if he had an address for Melchizedek. So he's scratching his head over this. Maybe he figures that his own father and grandfather were as close as he could come to finding a man of God to give his tithe to. Maybe he figures Esau was next in line and he could give it to him. Then I could see it hitting him that when he gave the tithe to Esau, it would also double as a peace offering. However the idea came to him, it worked out beautifully. He was giving his tithe to Esau, honoring him as his superior. As far as we know, neither brother ever again mentioned the birthright or the blessing. They were both so exceedingly rich, that why would they care? Esau had 3 wives who bore him 5 sons and some daughters. His descendants also became 12 tribes, as Jacob's family. To all outward appearances, they were about as equal as they could get. You could not tell which one got the birthright or the biggest blessing. But there was one major difference between them: Jacob had God. He had become a believer.

JACOB AND JOSEPH

Both Jacob and Isaac were highly favored sons. Both were almost lost as young men. Isaac as a boy was nearly offered up as a sacrifice by Abraham; Jacob, the favored son is gone from his parents for decades (as good as dead). Joseph nearly dies at the hand of jealous brothers. He is lost from his father, Jacob, for 15 years.

His mother was long deceased. This is a family of some long enduring heartaches. All these heart-wrenching times worked some hidden virtue in each one. Both the father and the lost or nearly lost child.

In a woman's case, she bears her child in her womb for nine months, sometimes with much sickness, usually with a lot of cramping and discomfort, and always with the unimaginable agony of the labor of child birth. Surely all this suffering also works a great deal of good in the woman. Different hidden virtues form, including a very strong bond of love for the child. The mother lives for the child; her life is bound up in the child. And as the apostle says, **"She shall be saved in childbearing."** That is to say, that when a woman bears a child and enters into motherhood, it has a powerful sanctifying effect on her. It conditions her admirably for receiving the gift of salvation, since she is living out much of what comes to us in the new creation.

Our point here is that men also can be endued with exceptional qualities through a different kind of hardship. What Jacob endures through the seeming death of his most beloved son, Joseph, was not just an unfortunate derailing of his life. It was ordained by God. **"This thing is from Me."** There shall no strange (foreign) thing happen to us. (I Peter 4:12) Jacob is a fine man now. No more scheming. No more greed.

He is humble. But like Job, whom God was proud of, God is not finished working on him. **"He who has begun a good work in you will complete it until the day of Jesus Christ."** A man's good behavior and life of faith does not exempt him from God's continuing to work in him. When we see God continuing to work in us, we should rejoice and be glad **to press toward the**

mark for the high calling of God in Christ Jesus.

In Genesis 37, the attention of Scripture begins to shift from Jacob to Joseph. Remember that except for baby Benjamin, Joseph was the only son of the only wife Jacob was in love with, Rachel. But she was now recently deceased. So Jacob has a special attachment for Joseph. They almost certainly lived in the same tent and the other three wives had their tents. So there was some separation between Jacob and his older boys. Maybe he figured this was acceptable since Grandpa Abraham sent away Aunt Hagar and Uncle Ishmael. At least he still lived close to his other three wives and their families. But in verse 3, we read that **"Israel (Jacob) loved Joseph more than all his children."** Jacob would say, "What's wrong with that?"
His own father Isaac clearly loved Esau more and Rebecca, his mother loved him more. So favoritism is natural, right? Yes, but so is sin. But we must resist it and do better than that.

Far from resisting it, Jacob made it worse. He made him a tunic of many colors. But he did nothing special for the others. What was he thinking? Didn't he remember all the harm favoritism did in the family when he was growing up? If our parents were not perfect, at least we can learn from their mistakes instead of repeating them. It doesn't have to be the case that if a man is very good at some things, that he can be lousy at others. Jacob was excellent in business and a man of God. But he doesn't have to be so poor a father. Samuel was an excellent judge and prophet, but he did poorly at raising his sons. David was unsurpassed as a military leader, outstanding as a Psalm writer and a wise ruler and man of God. But his failure to be a good parent resulted in death and disaster among his children.

39

At this point in Jacob's life, being a good father was by far the most important issue in his life. Bad parenting is a common failure today for a lot of men. "I'll be a good provider; let the wife take care of the kids." Men who think like this are grossly negligent of their God-given responsibility and sadly miss out on the greatest joy and satisfaction of their life. According to God's word, the raising of the children falls squarely on the father's shoulders. **"And you, fathers, do not provoke your children to wrath, but bring them up in the nurture and admonition of the Lord."** (Ephesians 6:4) Granted the wife is well equipped to be a good nurturer, but the man should be a nurturer as well. And fathers are usually experts at admonition, but the wife can have admonishing skills as well. Both parents should do both. And all should be done patiently and in love. We cannot neglect a responsibility because it is distasteful to us. If we do our job as parents, we will be heroes to our children.

Jacob being so short-sighted and being so partial to Joseph is incomprehensible. Couldn't he perceive the hatred of the brothers toward Joseph? I like what some fathers do: they have special one-on-one time with each of their children. Like a father – daughter dinner date. Or taking his son to the hardware store with him. Even if it's just a father son talk together on the back porch or in the office. They love having Daddy all to themselves for an hour. These are great opportunities to instill good qualities in the children. Maybe this can offset the damage caused by Hollywood or the internet.

As if he is completely clue-less, Jacob sends Joseph out to report on the brothers. By now, Joseph was known as a tattler and a dreamer. Too bad Jacob didn't caution Joseph to keep his dreams confidential instead of telling all his brothers. "Hey fella's, guess what? I had a dream last night where all you guys bowed down to me." "Well that's nice, Joseph. I'm happy for you." How did he think the brothers would take it? I fault Jacob for not stopping the problem before it got worse. The disastrous outcome is seen in Genesis 37:18, "Now when they saw him afar off, even before he came near them, they conspired against him to kill him." What good are all his flocks and his business and possessions if his son is killed and by his own brothers. Here is a case where a man reaps what he did not sow. If he had sowed good nurturing and parental equity, this would not have happened. You probably know the story: at the last second, the brothers decide not to kill Joseph, but to fake his death and sell him as a slave to some Ishmaelites heading for Egypt. So they tore his multi-colored tunic and bloodied it and presented it to their father. So they killed the tunic instead of Joseph. It also half killed Jacob, so that his sins of neglect found him out.

It seems like most of the great men of the Bible had their one besetting sin that was their downfall. Samson had his Delilah, Solomon had his 700 wives, Peter denied Jesus, Moses struck the rock twice, Paul and Barnabas had their feud. And now Jacob joins the list. We can thank God that He sometimes takes the shambles we make of our lives and turns it into something beautiful. We can see this in the way the story ends in the life of Joseph. So there's always hope.

Jacob is a fine picture of a man becoming born again, to the saving of his soul. In Genesis 35:1, God directs Jacob, **"Arise, go up to Bethel and dwell there and make there an altar."** So Jacob cleans house. He gets rid of all the foreign gods that were among

41

his family and servants. They washed themselves and changed their clothes. Jacob's worship improved. Then he built an altar, poured a drink offering on it, poured oil on it and offered sacrifices on it, as if to say, "I don't want to forget this." Jacob was a different man after his "salvation" at the ford of Jabbok. He had a diminished love of possessions, there was no more trickery and deceit, he humbled himself before Esau and was reconciled with him. It was here that God changed his name to Israel, at least in usage. A new name for a new man. Let us go and do likewise.

JOSEPH

It was a sweet love affair. Complete with knight in shining armor. Well…make that dusty robes. But Jacob, Joseph's father, was just as valiant toward Rachel at first sight. Just arriving in Haran after a month's journey, he sees his future wife as she is waiting with her flock of sheep at the community well. He watered her flock of sheep over everyone else's objection. Then he kissed her and came to tears over meeting this lovely young woman whom he would marry. Practically love at first sight. They got married 7 years later, not exactly a whirlwind romance. Then their wedding was spoiled when Jacob was tricked by Rachel's father into marrying her older sister first. A week later, he finally marries Rachel, the love of his life. Soon his two wives give him their two handmaids, whom he also "marries". So now he is "married" to four ladies who grew up in the same household. We see that Joseph learned a lot from all this, since he later married only one wife.

Let's consider that Jacob and Rachel courted each other for seven years, probably talking about their future and having children. Being Godly believers, it's a safe assumption they prayed much about their coming children. Blessed are those children who enter this world, much anticipated, lovingly welcomed and much prayed for. Such was Joseph. And Samuel. And John. And Samson. And Isaac. This sounds like a hall of fame. May God grant that your children be added to the list of great men. But it's up to you. For several years after they married, Rachel was unable to have a child. In the same period of time, her sister Leah had four children. This only heightened her anxiety and yearning for a child. It likely also intensified her praying, as when Hannah was taunted by Peninah. So now it's something like eleven or twelve years that Rachel pours out her soul before God for a baby. "What manner of child will this be?" As Elisabeth's neighbors wondered in regard to John.

Finally we read in Genesis 30:22, "Then God remembered Rachel, and God listened to her and opened her womb." Better than all the fertility drugs in the world is the prayer of faith made to God from a humble and sincere soul. So this child of faith, Joseph, enters this world in a home of much love and care. Now even though they were all one big family, each of the four wives lived in a separate tent. Most of the time, Jacob and Rachel lived in their own tent and there Joseph grew up. As with the child Jesus, we're not told much about Joseph's early childhood. But we can be sure he grew up with daily family prayers and worship. As the years progressed, the other ten sons of Jacob (and a number of employees) began doing more and more of the shepherding and managing of the family business. Correspondingly, Jacob likely spent more and more time at home. His heart's desire was to spend time with Joseph teaching him, building good manners in him and cultivating faith and every virtue in him. Every good parent knows the feeling. Jacob himself was surely raised that way, with both Isaac and Rebecca contributing to his character development. This surely influenced him in rearing his own son. Sadly, he did not seem to have the same interest in his other children.

Let's watch and see if there is a difference in the way Joseph turns out and the way his brothers and sister turn out.

Joseph grew up with twelve other siblings, all of them problem children. And only one of them was a girl.

- Reuben, the eldest, was an adulterer.
- Simeon and Levi brutally avenged their sister's being sexually assaulted.
- Judah had relations with a woman of ill repute.
- Joseph was a bit of a boaster and a tattler.
- None of them are very wise.
- All the brothers and Jacob completely overlook Joseph's spiritual gifts.
- The majority of the brothers plotted to kill Joseph.
- Jacob himself needs a Remedial Parenting course.

Other than these faults, they are a wonderful family.

We first hear of Joseph as a seventeen year old lad in Genesis 37. This is where the focus of the Bible shifts from Jacob to Joseph. Verse 2 tells us that he was tending sheep with his older brothers, and that **"Joseph brought a bad report of them to his father."** It seems that they did not share the same values and qualities as Joseph. Maybe their language was bad. Maybe they talked about sinful, shameful things. Out of the abundance of the heart, the mouth speaks. Some would say, "Well boys will be boys." This is usually said to excuse behavior that ought to be rebuked. We can figure how they got to be of poor behavior: **"The child left to himself will bring shame to his mother."** (Proverbs 29:15) Marbles tend to roll downhill, and so does a child's character. If you're wondering if that's a Bible verse, No, but it ought to be.

45

No mention is made in the passage of any comment Jacob made on Joseph's report. But he should have had the wisdom to tell Joseph not to speak badly of others. And he should have been fore-sighted enough to realize the resentment that Joseph's words could lead to. Joseph's report should have been a wakeup call as to his sons' bad character and he should have acted to correct it. A little bit of good fathering could have precluded Simeon and Levi's slaughtering the men of Shechem. And it could have kept Dinah from hanging around with a bad crowd. Instead of correcting Joseph's tendency to tattle on his brothers, he actually sends him again to check on his brothers and come back with the report. (Genesis 37:14)

To Jacob's credit, verse 3 tells us that **"Israel (Jacob) loved Joseph."** He couldn't help but love the son he prayed for over 12 years. Then he poured his heart into nurturing Godly qualities in his son; he spent quality time with his son; he cherished his son and (I hope) gave his boy a hug when he went to bed every night. When that much care and love is invested into someone, we can't help but love them. He also made him a coat of many colors. But he did no such thing for the other 10 boys. It's one thing when a father has to be away from his family a lot and is not able to spend good time with his son (or daughter), but when he's right there and snubs one child in favor of another child, it can be very damaging emotionally. Step children need just as much love and affirmation as the natural child. **"He who pampers his servant** (or step child) **from childhood will have him as a son in the end."** It is a wonder to me that nothing is said about whether Rachel or Joseph or the other three wives commented about the mounting jealousy or tried to make amends. But the damage continued to escalate until it became all but irreparable.

"But when his brothers saw that their father loved him more than all his brothers, they hated him and could not speak peaceably to him." (37:4) Didn't Jacob remember how his own brother was bitter against him as a result of favoritism, and how that fractured his whole family? "A brother offended is harder to be won than a strong city." But Jacob seems to do what most of us do: he ignored the problem and hoped it would go away. Jacob would later pay dearly for this neglect.

Something else needs to be said here: although it is not the brothers' fault that they were neglected, it is still their responsibility to become the man they should be. Any one of them could have decided to love their little brother and been kind to him in spite of the circumstances. Nobody else's actions can force us to be a bad person. No matter how bad of a crowd we may be surrounded with, we are still master of our own destiny and our soul.

In Genesis 37:5, the brothers' jealousy and resentment go from bad to worse. "Now Joseph had a dream, and he told it to his brothers; and they hated him even more." This may be expecting too much of a naïve young seventeen year old, but if he had given any thought to sharing his dream with them, he might have kept it quiet. But too often it is the case that "a fool utters all his mind", and not very often that "a wise man keeps it in till afterwards." (Proverbs 29:11 KJV) Mary was more discreet about such sensitive information: "But Mary kept all these things and pondered them in her heart." Some of us take longer than others to learn this. Part of why Joseph may have been eager to share his dream is that it was somewhat self-serving. God help us to not be like the man, who

47

in every story he tells, he is the hero. Remember in Joseph's dream the brothers' sheaves of wheat bowed down to his sheave of wheat. So naturally the brothers hated him even more. Joseph had to be able to read that in their faces. That should have completely shut down his words. But incredibly, he also tells them about his second dream, which was even more self-serving. **"Look, I have dreamed another dream. And this time, the sun, the moon, and the eleven stars bowed down to me."** (Genesis 37:9) "Well that's nice, little brother. It must have been a sweet dream." We would expect that kind of response from a Godly family. But in verse 11, we're told that the brothers now envied him, along with their hating him. We will see how jealousy unharnessed can turn into an insane rage. Remember Cain. But Jacob **"kept the matter in mind."** He had learned earlier in life that God can speak through dreams.

The brothers go back to work tending their flocks, while Joseph remained at home. At seventeen years old, it seems that Joseph spent more time at home than helping with the family business. If he had worked more often with his brothers, it might have raised their respect for him and cooled their resentment. Jacob may have been overly protective of Joseph as he later was with Benjamin. It is no new thing that some parents coddle their children excessively and hamper their development into adulthood. At a young age, Mary traveled a long way through hill country to spend three months taking care of Aunt Elisabeth, who was in her sixth month. That's character building. David was about the same age as Joseph when his father, Jesse, sent him to bring food to his older brothers, who were with the army. Of course he didn't get much respect either.

In Genesis 37:13, Jacob sends Joseph on a trip to check on his brothers. I do like Joseph's response to his father **"Here I am."** No complaint. No debate. This is rather like Isaiah's, "Here am I, Lord. Send me." There was no "Aw, Dad, do I have to?" Or "Can't somebody else go?" Or "Am I going to get paid?" Here is another one whose only desire was to do the will of him who sent him and to finish his work. God has big plans for such a young man. If you have teenage children in your house, feel free to copy this page and tape it to the refrigerator.

While searching for his brothers, they easily spot him a long way off, with his multi-colored robe and conspired to kill him. This is not unlike another despised and rejected One against whom **"the people plot a vain thing and ...take counsel together against...his anointed."** (Psalm 2:1,2) He is not the only lad who was nearly put to death as a type of Christ. He probably heard the story of his own grandfather, Isaac, on Mt. Moriah.

In Genesis 37:18 we see that this family is self-destructing: **"Now when they saw him afar off...they conspired against him to kill him."** In verse 20, the brothers take counsel together and plot a vain thing. But they were not plotting against Joseph only, they were unwittingly plotting against God, against His purposes and against His anointed. They plot to make it look like a wild beast killed Joseph. So they take his colored robe from him and put him in a pit, saying, "We shall see what will become of his dreams!" They were right about that. After doing their cruel deed, **"they sat down to eat a meal"**, as did the king and Haman. But Reuben, the eldest brother, planned to secretly save Joseph and bring him back home.

It is surely a providence of God that about that time, a caravan of Midianite traders come by. The brothers agree that it would be better to sell Joseph than to kill him. So they do so, betraying their own brother for 20 pieces of silver. Meanwhile Reuben, who was not in on this, goes back to the pit and finds Joseph is missing. He was very upset. You probably remember that the brothers dipped Joseph's robe in blood and made it look like a wild animal killed him. So they bring the coat back to their father, Jacob, and show it to him. He concludes that Joseph has been killed. He is so distraught that he tears his clothes, puts on sackcloth and **"mourned for his son many days."** Verse 35 tells how hard it was on him, **"And all his sons and daughters arose to comfort him; but he refused to be comforted, and he said, 'For I shall go down into the grave to my son in mourning.' Thus his father wept for him."** By now I imagine the nine brothers who did this deceit felt very bad about it. They hadn't thought about how hard it would be on their Dad and on all the rest of their family, including Reuben. If we would think about the consequences of our actions ahead of time, we would spare a lot of misery. Oh sure, revenge is sweet, but it leaves a long term bitter aftertaste. Now they have to hold that deathly secret in their own hearts for many years, never being able to tell anyone. The family camp must have been like a funeral parlor for months. It was all very depressing. And even worse, the nine brothers had to bear a very black burden in their hearts. I think they terribly regretted what they had done. But they were sort of trapped and could not undo it. This is the deadly price of sin: the ripples of its consequences spread much farther and cut deeper into others' hearts than they had ever imagined. And they caused a great deal of pain for their family. Guilt tormented their own consciences worse than anything they had ever experienced. It robbed them of sleep at night; it haunted them in their waking hours; and there was no relent even years later. No more does the revenge feel sweet. Maybe they want to throw away the pieces of silver, as Judas did. After fifteen years, when they stood before Joseph's throne, they were still terribly burdened about what they had done.

If the misery of their guilt equaled the pain and anguish of everyone they hurt, it would be just. Those of us who have done wrong to others and have never received full retribution for our sins, need never be in the crowd who cry out for justice. Who can tell the far-reaching consequences of our sins? For the wages of sin is death, and beyond. But to the glory of God's grace, He is willing to forgive. **"Though our sins be like scarlet, They shall be as white as snow; Though they are red like crimson, They shall be as wool."** (Isaiah 1:18) **If we confess our sins, He is faithful and just to forgive us our sins and to cleanse us from all unrighteousness.** (I John 1:9) By the shedding of the blood of Jesus, all our sins may be washed away. All that remains for us to do is confess them directly to God, who alone has power to forgive.

JOSEPH IN EGYPT

Meanwhile Joseph is brought to Egypt and is sold to Potiphar, an officer of Pharaoh and captain of the guard. Genesis 39:2 tells us that **"the Lord was with Joseph, and he was a successful man."** Maybe as much as the Lord was with Joseph, the Lord was also departed from the guilty brothers. Who can say? If God were to punish them, it would also injure the innocent members of the family. And who knows whether some or all of them later confessed and repented of their cruelty to Joseph. What we do know is that they suffered heavy losses in the great famine years later.

"And his master saw that the Lord was with him and that the Lord made all he did to prosper in his hand." (Genesis 39:3) What a fine testimony Joseph must have had. First, he identified himself as a believer in God. Second, all the cultivating and courtesies taught to him by his father shined clearly. His integrity and good work ethic were without question. So captain Potiphar gives Joseph more and more responsibility. And **"the Lord blessed the Egyptian's house for Joseph's sake." (v. 5) A similar thing happened to the house of Obed-Edom. "The ark of the Lord remained in the house of Obed-Edom the Gittite three months. And the Lord blessed Obed-Edom and all his household."**
(II Samuel 6:11) Believers in God today are like Joseph and the ark, since we are the temple of the Holy Spirit. If we live a Godly, blameless life, we can be a similar blessing wherever we go. And an employer who has a Christian working for them should put a great value on them, since God will bless him on their behalf. Potiphar eventually turned over everything he had to Joseph.

FALSELY ACCUSED

But trouble was brewing in Potiphar's house. His wife found Joseph attractive and propositioned him. Joseph being a principled man flatly refused. He did not consider whether she was attractive or not. He did not give any thought to what the chances were of getting caught. He just knew it was wrong and refused her. He patiently explains that it would be a wrong to her husband and a sin against God. Like most men of principle, his decision was made long before the temptation arrived. "If it is wrong, I will not do it. I cannot afford to sin against God." Very likely he learned this from his father. But Ms Potiphar was very willful and persistent. In Genesis 39:10, Joseph does what he can to avoid this temptation, **"Day by day... he did not heed her, to lie with her or to be with her."** Even though they lived in the same house, he tried to avoid her. **"Do not enter into the path of the wicked, and do not walk in the way of evil. Avoid it, do not travel on it, turn away from it and pass on."** (Proverbs 4:14,15) That is, stay away from the vicinity of evil. Evil is like a magnet: the farther you are from it, the less is the force of its pull. Being out of sight of it also helps. Or changing the channel. Sometimes my work requires me to drive along the beach highway. At times it looks like a Miss America bikini contest. You'll be happy to know that at those times, I choose a different route. Well, most of the time.

Something else impresses me about Joseph. During the time that Ms Potiphar was after him, he never mentioned it to Potiphar. I feel sure he thought of it, but he did not want to speak ill of his wife, even to protect his own reputation. Nor did he take action against her after he rose to being prime minister of Egypt. Nor against his brothers later. He was one of those who fully forgave those who trespassed against him. More of us should try that.

Well Ms Potiphar is not giving up. She waits for the house to be empty and grabs him, propositioning him again. Without a word, Joseph fled from the house, leaving his garment in her hand. Now here's a good strategy to fight temptation: run for your life. Realizing it was a lost cause, she decides to get even with him instead. She tells the men of the house and later her husband that Joseph came in to the house and attacked her, holding his garment as evidence. Potiphar believes his wife without questioning her. Neither did he question Joseph. **"The first one to plead his cause seems right, but his neighbor comes and examines him."** (Proverbs 18:17) Even if Joseph had testified later, he would be at a disadvantage. I have to wonder if Potiphar had an inkling of whether his wife may have been at fault. Joseph might not have been the only one she flirted with.

THE PRISON YEARS

Without any further examination, Joseph is put in prison. This had to be terribly disheartening to him. Being near to Pharaoh's house, Joseph is placed in the royal prison. No bail. No trial. No visitors. No idea how long he would be there. Joseph was dejected, but God must have been smiling, "Just as I had planned."
So much of the seeming setbacks of life are actually meticulously planned providences of God. Generally, we don't hear God telling us, **"This thing is from Me."** Even when we make of wreck of our lives, and have hurt so many people, and have sinned greatly against the Lord and our life is a hopeless disaster, God sometimes smiles and says, "Now it's time for My plan." (I Kings

12:24) Our job is to simply trust and move on. Was life moving along smoothly for you, well-employed, useful in your church, happy marriage, and abruptly you find out you have Crohn's disease or stage 3 cancer. "What happened, God? I thought You were watching over me. How did you let this satanic attack happen?" **"This thing is from Me."**

What do you mean it's from You? I thought You were the One who makes all things work together for good for those who love You." **"That's exactly what I'm doing."** "But God, I don't understand."

"You will."

So will Joseph. In the meantime it looks bad to him. But all that really counts is what it says in v. 21, **"But the Lord was with Joseph."** The safest place in the world is in God's hands. In troublesome times, let us say as David did, **"My times are in your hand."** Jonah was in a whale's mouth, but he was also in God's hand. God's care trumps all trouble. I know that's easy for me to say, I'm not the one in jail. When we walk through the valley of the shadow of death, let us say, **"I will fear no evil, for You are with me."** Notice the verse also says that the Lord gave him favor with the jailer. This is like what God did for Daniel in captivity, **"Now God had brought Daniel into the favor and goodwill of the chief of the eunuchs."** God seems to be nearer to us in our low times. He gives more grace when the burdens grow greater.

Always eager to do good, Joseph accepts responsibilities from the jailer. We don't know what he did, but it may have been something like organizing work crews, managing the kitchen, or other planned activities. But we do know that whatever work was going on in the prison, it soon came under Joseph's supervision. And everything he had oversight of prospered. God worked through Joseph's natural leadership skills and He made it to prosper.

He may have been in prison several years by the beginning of chapter 40. We find that Pharaoh got angry with his chief butler and chief baker and put them in prison. Joseph was promptly put in charge of them. Verse 4 elaborates that **"he served them"**. We would halfway expect to hear that they served Joseph, since he was the one in charge. But Joseph, the leader, the boss, served them. He took care of them, inquired of their well-being, what they needed, how they felt, maybe inquired of their spiritual condition. But Jesus defines true leadership, **"You know that the rulers of the Gentiles lord it over them...yet it shall not be so among you; but whoever desires to become great among you, let him be your servant...just as the Son of man did not come to be served, but to serve..."** (Matthew 20:25-28) Joseph's father, Jacob, lived by that principle and he successfully passed it on to Joseph. What qualities are you passing on?

Time continued to pass by for Joseph. His prison term went on and on. No reprieve in sight. Maybe he prayed in the quiet of the night, **"How long, O Lord? It seems as if you have forgotten me. How long will you hide your face from me? How long shall I take counsel in my soul, having sorrow in my heart daily?"** Unknown to Joseph, God watches Joseph closely as he prays. He can count every tear; He remembers every word; he feels every emotion. Let's imagine Joseph cries himself to sleep again. Let's also imagine God's face shaping into a gentle smile. "Thinks are progressing perfectly", He ponders. We don't realize it when it's happening, but at times God seasons us and adds sweet and sour spices into the recipe of our life. He is a master at shaping the character and soul of a person. It seems that some of us are special projects for Him. He stirs us more, puts us in the blender or the meat grinder, but does not do so to others. He turns up the heat in the oven higher and leaves us in the furnace longer than others. We don't see any grand plan He may have for us; we're just feeling the heat and we cry out, "Please turn down the heat and take away all this trouble!" For **"eyes have not seen, nor ears heard,** (neither has it) **entered into the heart of man the things that God has prepared for them that love Him."** (I Corinthians 2:9 KJV)

You might be thinking, "Why doesn't God just tell us what He's doing?" Beats me. You ask Him.

One night, the baker and the butler both have a scary dream, amazingly in the same night. They didn't know what to think about it, but they were both depressed. Joseph noticed. So in Genesis 40:7, he asks them, **"Why do you look so sad today?"** It is not a common quality, but ever so priceless that a person is caring enough to notice when someone else is down or distressed. Such a blessed soul puts their own interests and worries aside and asks about the other person's troubles. **"Look not every man on his own** (interests)**, but also on the** (interests) **of others."** The world needs more people like that. And it's my understanding that there are a lot of job openings. The butler and baker each tell their dream and state that they don't know how to interpret it. It's interesting that they could tell that their dreams were specially prophetic. Joseph hears the butler's dream and immediately gives the interpretation: the Pharaoh would restore him to his job in three days. He clearly has a spiritual gift for interpreting dreams.

But when the baker tells his dream, Joseph tells him he would be executed in three days. Contrary to popular opinion, the butler did not do it, the baker did. Well at least he cheered up one of them.

Joseph realized that the butler would soon be back in the presence of Pharaoh. So he asked him to put in a good word for Joseph to get him released from prison. But the butler just plain forgot. Joseph may have wondered if God forgot him too. At this point, he had been working for Potiphar and in prison for a combined eleven years. He's 28 years old. Life is passing him by. Two more years go by. Then in the middle of the night, something happens in the palace that would affect Joseph the rest of his life. And it would affect the lives of over three million people.

JOSEPH AND PHARAOH

In Genesis 41, Pharaoh, king of Egypt, has a dream. Seven cows come up out of the river plump and healthy. And as if that wasn't eerie enough, 7 more cows come up out of the river, lean and gaunt, which ate up the seven plump cows. We're not told what he ate the night before. He goes back to sleep and has another bad dream. Seven healthy heads of grain come up on one stalk. Then seven thin heads come up after them, which are blighted and sickly. Then the seven thin heads ate up the seven healthy heads. When Pharaoh woke up in the morning, he was troubled, like the butler and baker were after their dreams. Like them, Pharaoh got the sense that the dreams were not normal, but had some significance. It was so serious to him that he called for his wise men and magicians, but none of them could interpret the dreams. This was similar to the dilemma that faced emperors Nebuchadnezzar and Belshazzar.

The chief butler, standing nearby suddenly remembers his own prophetic dream and says to Pharaoh, **"I remember my faults this day."** Then he tells Pharaoh about the two dreams from two years ago and the Hebrew who correctly interpreted their dreams. So Pharaoh sends for Joseph out of the dungeon. So he cleans up and comes before Pharaoh. It was like God checked and sees that the biscuits are perfect and ready to take out of the oven.

Pharaoh presents his problem to Joseph, **"I have had a dream, and there is no one who can interpret it. But I have heard it said of you that you can understand a dream, to interpret it."** Genesis 41:15) Joseph answers admirably, **"It is not in me; God will give Pharaoh an answer of peace."** This is similar to Daniel's reply when King Nebuchadnezzar asked if he could tell and interpret his dream. **"There is a God in heaven who reveals secrets and He has made known to (you) what will be in the latter days."** Both immediately give credit and honor to God. Now Pharaoh tells his dreams to Joseph. We notice that dreams have come to Joseph in pairs. Two of his own dreams as a child; two dreams in the prison and now two dreams of Pharaoh. This is similar to the other Joseph, Mary's husband. He had two dreams regarding the birth of Jesus and three dreams regarding their fleeing to Egypt and returning home.

Joseph replies, **"The dreams of Pharaoh are one; God has shown Pharaoh what He is about to do."** Throughout Joseph's explanation, interpretation and recommendations, he takes no credit for himself nor even mentions himself. This is a man of polished humility. When Joseph told his own dreams years ago, it was very self-serving. But now he is a different man, shaped and fashioned by his heavenly Father. The words of that great old hymn, *How Firm a Foundation*, could apply to Joseph:

"When through fiery trials thy pathway shall lie,
My grace, all sufficient, shall be thy supply;
The flame shall not hurt thee; I only design
Thy dross to consume, and thy gold to refine."

Immediately upon hearing Pharaoh's dreams, he understands it's meaning and gives a recommended course of action. His words sound like someone reporting the results of a week's worth of congressional study and planning. He gives the impression of being an extremely wise man, with his goodness shining through his detailed interpretation and advice. You would think he'd been a senator for the last few years rather than a prisoner. Behold what God can do with a man completely surrendered to Him! Consider how much Pharaoh is caught up with admiration of Joseph, having known him for about fifteen minutes! **"So the advice was good in the eyes of Pharaoh and in the eyes of all his servants. And Pharaoh said to his servants, 'Can we find such a one as this, a man in whom is the Spirit of God?' Then Pharaoh said to Joseph, 'Inasmuch as God has shown you all this, there is no one as wise and discerning as you. You shall be over my house, and all my people shall be ruled according to your word; only in regard to the throne will I be greater than you.'"** (Genesis 41:37-40) It seems a little hasty to hand over the entire country to a young man in fifteen minutes! Remember king Herod, who was ready to give half his kingdom to a dancing girl? Or

Emperor Belshazzar who made Daniel the third ruler of the Babylonian Empire for interpreting four words on the wall?

In v. 41, Pharaoh says to Joseph, **"See, I have set you over all the land of Egypt."** After Joseph gets up off the floor, Pharaoh gives him his signet ring, clothes him with fine linen and puts a gold chain around his neck. Daniel was also given a gold chain around his neck, but his gifts lasted only a few hours. Pharaoh again clarifies to Joseph, **"I am Pharaoh, and without your consent no man may lift his hand or foot in all the land of Egypt."** He is underscoring his determination to put Joseph in complete command. Pharaoh also gives him a wife and his second best chariot, no doubt with power steering and air-conditioning.

In verse 46, we see Joseph touring all the land of Egypt, likely learning all he could about his new responsibilities, but also enjoying the scenery. Joseph is now 30 years old. He was a prototype of another Savior who began His life's work at 30 years old.

Joseph continues to desire to do a good job and care for people. He had been groomed to be a good manager in Potiphar's house, and while in jail, to take good care of people. Surely God is now admiring his finished product: Joseph. Who could have guessed what God was up to during all those thirteen years? Maybe He said of Joseph, "Very good", as he said of Adam's day. Or maybe He said something like what He said of Job, **"Have you considered my servant Job?"** But for the only begotten Son, He said, **"This is My beloved Son, in whom I am well pleased."** Are you a work in progress? May I recommend that you patiently submit to your Master's hand? Who knows what God has in store for you?

JOSEPH'S REIGN

The seven years of plenty predicted in Pharaoh's dream began, with the ground bringing forth abundantly, as predicted. It is reported that Joseph gathered up all the food and laid up in every city the food of the fields around that city. One fifth of the total produce, that is. But the crops were so successful, nobody complained about a 20 % tax. Consider the magnitude of this task. The population of Egypt about that time was approximately 3 million and Egypt is roughly one and a half times bigger than the state of Texas and four times the size of the United Kingdom today. Without belaboring the point, Joseph had a very big job to take on. He had to have an army of accountants, land surveyors and carpenters to build massive barns. Then they had to find a way to keep grain and other foods for several years. Without canning.

But he and his army got the job done. **"He laid up in every city the food of the fields which surrounded them. Joseph gathered very much grain, as the sand of the sea, until he stopped counting, for it was immeasurable."** (Genesis 41:48, 49)

In the midst of all this labor and responsibility, Joseph and Asenath, his wife, have two baby boys. I love what this father says about having a baby boy. **"God has made me forget all my toil and all my father's house."** The joy of having a baby outweighed all the labor and heartache of his life. May God give you such a heart to love your children more than your relatives and more than your successful career. And may God turn the hearts of our fathers to their children.

Then the years of prosperity ended. Very likely, everyone in Egypt knew what came next. The famine was worldwide. At least the inhabited world, the middle east. At the end of chapter 41, we find all the surrounding nations going to Egypt to buy food. "All countries came to Joseph in Egypt to buy grain." So Joseph was a savior for all the world, like Somebody else we know.

JOSEPH MEETS HIS BROTHERS

In Chapter 42, we find that the famine was severe for Jacob, his family and his herds. With all the grass dying, it would be particularly bad for the animals. In the extremity they found themselves in, Jacob sends his sons to Egypt to buy grain. We could almost expect that God would have warned Jacob of the impending famine. After all, He reveals his secrets to his servants the prophets. God did reveal another "worldwide" famine to Agabus, a prophet in the church at Antioch in Acts 11:28. As a result, the church sent relief funds to the believers in Judea, an agricultural region. But although God did not reveal it to Jacob, he did obtain relief through Joseph. In the same way, nations today that have plenty ought to provide for those who have little. That would work better for our peace than singing "God Bless America". If the United States were regular suppliers for hunger relief in heavily Muslim Sudan and Somalia, Muslim terrorists might think differently about targeting Americans. And maybe Somali pirates might discontinue attacking American shipping. Whether or not, God would be pleased, and what could be more important? **"And if you give yourself (or your goods) to the hungry and satisfy the desire of the afflicted, then your light will rise in darkness and your gloom** will become like midday." (Isaiah 58:10) This also works at the individual level.

What better person could there be than Joseph to see to the selling of grain to starving nations? Being a believer, along with his Godly upbringing, he was predisposed to be compassionate to the starving poor all around him. Let's be glad it wasn't Nabal, the churl, in power.

"So Joseph's ten brothers went down to buy grain in Egypt." (Genesis 42:3) Jacob kept Benjamin, his youngest son, at home, now being an older teenager. So the brothers went and got in line to buy grain. Like everybody else, they bowed down to prime minister Joseph, who instantly recognizes them. But they didn't realize who he was. He probably looked very different at 32 than he did at 17, also being dressed and groomed like an Egyptian prince. Even his tone of voice was different, since he spoke to them roughly. Then Joseph remembered his dreams of his brothers bowing down to him. He realizes that his brothers were there to get food for all their family and servants. Even at the first, he wants to give them food for their households. However, he plans to test their character first. At his last sight of them, their character was very bad. So he puts them through an inquisition, questioning them roughly and acting suspicious of them. He accuses them of being spies, though he knew they were not. I'm sure he is enjoying watching them sweat. Probably the most fun he had all day. He ends up threatening to imprison them until the youngest brother Benjamin is brought. He does put them in prison for three days, but releases them to bring food back to their families. He says to them through an interpreter, **"Do this and live, for I fear God: if you are honest men, let one of your**

brothers be confined to your prison house; but you go and carry grain for the famine of your houses. And bring your youngest brother to me; so your words will be verified, and you shall not die." And they did so. Then they said one to another (without realizing that Joseph understood them), **"We are truly guilty concerning our brother, for we saw the anguish of his soul when he pleaded with us, and we would not hear; therefore this distress is come upon us."** And Reuben answered them, saying, 'Did I not speak to you saying, "Do not sin against the boy", and you would not listen? Therefore behold, his blood is now required of us.' " Joseph is deeply touched that not only did they remember what they had done to him, but that they felt terribly guilty for it. This had been weighing on them for 15 years. Joseph had to hide himself while he wept. He didn't weep just because he had missed his brothers so much, but possibly because they had repented. This is the very thing that most touches the heart of God, when a man comes to be sorry for his sins. **"The Lord is near to those who are of a broken heart, and saves such as be of a contrite spirit."**

Now Joseph locks up Simeon and sends the brothers back home. He tells the brothers not to come back without the younger brother to prove they were telling the truth. Then he secretly instructs his servants to restore each of the brothers' money into their sacks of grain and to give them provisions for the journey home. This probably included extra containers of water, feed for their donkeys and other necessities. Maybe he did like kindnesses for other poorer folks coming for food. For he surely had the heart of God, who gives good measure, pressed down, shaken together, running over. This reminds me of the little lad whose mother had him deliver two fresh baked apple pies to Aunt May down the road. When he arrived, Aunt May exclaimed, "Well I can't wait to thank your mother for this pie!" The boy replied, "If you don't mind, would you thank her for two?" Like the brothers, he had something to eat on the road.

On the way home, one brother discovers his money is in his sack. When they discovered that all of their money was returned to them, **"Their hearts failed them and they were afraid, saying one to another, 'What is this that God has done to us?' "** They were probably worried that they were being framed for theft. However, this was nothing but a kindness to them from Joseph. But their long-standing guilt kept them fearful of when God was going to punish them for what they had done to Joseph. It is a good deterrent against sin to fear getting caught and fearing the law, but even better is the fear of having to remember what we did for the rest of our life. It's easier to forget the wrongs done to us, than it is to forget the wrongs we have done to others.

Later, when the grain they brought ran out, they explain to Jacob their need to bring young Benjamin with them to get more grain in Egypt. Jacob vehemently objects. Then Reuben the eldest brother, says, **"Kill my two sons if I do not bring him back to you; put (Benjamin) in my hands and I will bring him back to you."** The situation is getting desperate. Heated words were exchanged. Finally and reluctantly, Jacob agrees to let his beloved Benjamin go.

So all the brothers, with Benjamin, return to Egypt, bringing some of the best of the fruits and spices of their land. They also bring double the money to return the money that was put in their sacks. I don't count this as being honest on their part, because they figured that if it had been a setup the first time, there would be a record of it against them. It would be more commendable if they had returned it even if there was no chance of anyone knowing about it. I remember a deacon of a Baptist church nearby told of finding a roll of bills amounting to $400 lying in the parking lot of a store. He brought it to the store manager, who later returned it to the owner. He didn't wait around for a reward and it was not advertised in the local paper. That would be honesty. The New York Times reported that on July 10, 2019, an armored truck door came open and spilled $175,000 along a stretch of an Atlanta freeway. About a dozen car drivers stopped to grab up some of the loose cash. Only one gentleman returned what he had picked up.

Upon arrival in Egypt, they again stand before Joseph. He has them all brought to his personal home for dinner. Now when the brothers see this, they were afraid and said, **"it is because of the money, which was returned in our sacks the first time, that we are brought in, so that he may make a case against us and seize us, to take us as slaves with our donkeys."** The usual reaction would be, "Wow! We're being invited over for dinner!" But again we see that a guilty conscience is hindering a lot of happiness.

When the brothers presented the problem of their money being in their sacks on their last visit and that they brought it back to return it, the steward replied, **"Peace be with you, do not be afraid. Your God and the God of your fathers has given you treasure in your sacks; I had your money."** These patriarchs ought to be ashamed of themselves that this Gentile is displaying more faith than they are. This is also testimony to Joseph

67

sharing his faith with his coworkers and winning them to God. We do not read that the brothers had at any time prayed to God about anything. But I have the feeling that the current circumstances are changing that. When Joseph gets home from work and dinner starts, things warmed up nicely for the brothers. A nice big dinner does wonders to cheer up a group of hungry men. Joseph meets his nearly grown up little brother, Benjamin, who is his only full brother. He gets so emotional that he has to leave the room. Joseph had a little fun with his brothers again by seating them according to their age. This was particularly astonishing to them when we consider that ten of them were born within about 6 years. And they were all in their thirties and forties. No doubt he enjoyed watching their mystified expressions. Again it was probably the most fun he had all day. In Genesis 43:34, we read that Joseph personally served dinner to the brothers. This is reminiscent of Jesus washing the feet of his disciples and serving to them the Lord's supper.

As the brothers departed the next morning, Joseph again shows his brotherly love toward them. He directs his steward to fill their sacks with as much food as they could carry and to put all their money in their sacks again. Then he tests his brothers one last time. He directs his steward to put his personal drinking cup into Benjamin's sack, making it look like he had stolen it. It appears that Joseph wanted to see if his brothers would treat Benjamin any better than they treated him years ago. Would they give up Benjamin to being falsely accused and kept in Egypt or would they try their best to bring him safely back to his father?

One of my father's old friends told me this story at my Dad's memorial service. When my Dad was about

20 and his younger brother was about 13, his brother sneaked the family car out for a joy ride, being sure that he knew very well how to drive. The drive went fine until he smacked into another car. He was entirely in the wrong. The police were notified of the accident and were on the way. The younger brother was nearly in shock. Someone told my Dad about it and he jumped in his own car and hurried to the scene. He got out of his car, leaving the door open and the engine running. He walked over to the other car and pulls open the driver's door. He grabs his little brother's hand and pulls him out, telling him, "Get in my car and get out of here." Which he did. Then my Dad sat in the driver's seat of the damaged car, closed the door and waited for the police. This nicely portrays the doctrine of substitution. Jesus Christ died for our sins, the just for the unjust, that he might bring us to God. He substituted Himself for us on the cross. This is what Judah did, one of Joseph's brothers. When Benjamin was "caught" with the stolen cup, they all went back and stood before Joseph to plead their case.

Judah offers to take Benjamin's place and become a slave to Joseph. When Joseph sees that the brothers cared greatly about Benjamin, he realizes that they are not the same hateful men they once were. Joseph is so moved emotionally, that he breaks down in tears in their presence and reveals himself to them. "I am Joseph," he says to their utter shock. This is a fascinating picture of sinners who repent and confess before a savior, who then reveals himself to them. Not long after that, they come to live in a sort of promised land, where Joseph promises to provide for them throughout the famine years. Have you confessed your sins to our Savior?

Has He revealed Himself to you and showed you how he loves you? You can have as happy an ending as this story.

In chapter 45, Joseph explains everything to his brothers who were **"dismayed at his presence"**. The first thing he says to them is to ease the guilt which they have been carrying for years. **"Do not therefore be grieved or angry with yourselves because you sold me here; for God sent me here before you to preserve life. For these two years the famine has been in the land, and there are still five years in which there will be neither plowing nor harvesting. And God sent me before you to preserve a posterity for you in the earth, and to save your lives by a great deliverance. So it was not you who sent me here, but God; and He has made me a father to Pharaoh...and a ruler throughout all the land of Egypt."** Then he kisses all his brothers and weeps. His brothers finally relax.

Notice Joseph does not characterize their selling him into Egypt as sinful, but as a providence of God. A lesser man would have made much of their evil, using colorful language to degrade them for their disgrace. When Jesus forgave the woman caught in the very act of adultery, he does not even mention the word. He simply says, **"Neither do I condemn you, go and sin no more."** Love surely covers the multitude of sins. Accusers tend to amplify the sin, make much of it and mention it often. "This sinful, shameful woman was caught in the very act of adultery, violating the seventh commandment, sinning terribly against her poor husband, bringing a curse upon our land in committing this lewd, horrid sin!" They would have been glad to publish it in the nearest tabloid. **"With what judgment you judge, you will be judged."** Those of us who make

70

regular contributions to the sins of the world, should be lenient in judging others. Lord, help my words to be gracious and tender today, for tomorrow I might have to eat them.

Joseph mercifully changes the subject before they have a chance to respond. It's as if he said, "Oh, forget it, fellas." I can picture Joseph excitedly saying, **"Hurry and go up to my father, and say to him, 'Thus says your son Joseph: "God has made me Lord of all Egypt; come down to me, do not tarry. You shall dwell in the land of Goshen, and you shall be near to me, you and your children, and your children's children, your flocks and your herds, and all that you have. There I will provide for you, lest you and your household, and all that you have, come to poverty; for there are still five years of famine." ' "**

JOSEPH AND JESUS COMPARED

This is a remarkable preview of the coming Savior. Notice:
1. *Both Joseph and Jesus were betrayed into the hands of the Gentiles.*
2. *Joseph was sold for 20 pieces of silver, while Jesus was betrayed for 30 pieces of silver.* A lordly sum for either of these men. Some of us have betrayed our Savior for less.
3. *Both were betrayed by their kin.* **"The brothers conspired against him to kill him."** Jesus was betrayed by his own kin when they drove him out of Nazareth, and by his friend, when Judas betrayed Him to the high priests, and when the

71

Jews betrayed him to the Romans. So both were "wounded" in the house of their friends.

4. *Joseph and Jesus left their father to go to a far country for a long season and received a kingdom.*

5. *Both Joseph and Jesus were sent by God to save lives.* **God sent me before you to save your lives by a great deliverance."** (Genesis 45:7) **Jesus "has come to seek and to save that which was lost."**

6. **"All countries came to Joseph in Egypt to buy grain."** So Joseph was a savior for all the world, like Somebody else we know.

7. *Both began their life's work at 30 years old.*

8. At our Savior's invitation, we follow Him to our future home, a promised land. Goshen and heaven were promised to those who follow their Savior.

9. *Both "Saviors" invite their household for the same reason:* **"you shall be near to me."** Jesus wants us to be near to Him, even abiding in Him.

10. *As Joseph provided for his household, so our Savior plans to provide for us.* (Genesis 45:11) My God shall supply all your needs according to His riches in glory. Not just our bare subsistence, but according to His riches.

11. *As the brothers were to tell of Joseph's glory to the family still in the land of famine, so while we are in our land of famine, we are to tell of all our Savior's glory.* (v. 45:13)

12. *Like Pharaoh, our heavenly Father calls us to receive of the best of the land/heaven and to not be concerned about our worldly goods.* (v. 45:18, 20) **"Sell what you have and give alms;**

**provide yourselves money bags which do not
grow old, a treasure in the heavens that does
not fail."** (Luke 12:33)

13. *God provides us treasure not only at our eternal
destination, but for our journey on the way,* as
Pharaoh did, **"he gave them provisions for the
journey."** (45:21)

14. *And we see our Savior's will for us in our journey,*
"See to it that you do not quarrel on the way."
(Genesis 45:24 Evangelical Heritage Version)
We have sure fallen short of this.

15. **When we tell others of what is in store for us
in the land of promise, it sounds so good that
it is hard to believe. "And Jacob's heart stood
still, because he did not believe them."** It was
the same way when the queen of Sheba heard of
Solomon and his greatness. She said, **"I did not
believe the words until I came and saw with
my own eyes; and indeed the half was not told
me."** (I Kings 10:7) **"Eye has not seen, nor ear
heard, nor (has it) entered into the heart of
man the things which God has prepared for
those who love Him."** (I Corinthians 2:9)

16. *The key truth of all Christendom is that Jesus
rose from the dead.* It was likewise for Jacob
when his sons returned from Egypt. The first
thing they told him was, **"Joseph is still alive."**
In Genesis 45:27, we read, **"But when they told
him (Jacob) all the words which Joseph had said to
them, and when he saw the carts which Joseph had
sent to carry him, the spirit of Jacob their father
revived."** Compare this with the reaction of the queen
of Sheba when she saw the wisdom of Solomon, the
house he had built, the food on his table…his waiters

73

and their apparel and his entryway by which he went up to the house of the Lord. It is said, **"There was no more spirit in her."** Both Jacob and the queen of Sheba were at first slow of heart to believe, but when the truth began to dawn on them, it overcame them. It brought Jacob up from his trough of despondency to belief, and brought the queen of Sheba down from her high ground of skepticism to belief. The question remains: how must God bring you to believe in His truth? Must the mountain be brought low, as Saul; or the valley raised up, as the adulterous woman; the crooked way made straight (as with Zaccheus), or the rough places be made smooth (as with the Philippian jailer)? *Then* **"the glory of the Lord shall be revealed, and all flesh shall see it together; for the mouth of the Lord has spoken."** (Isaiah 40:5)

JACOB AND FAMILY GO TO EGYPT

Chapter 45 concludes with **"Then Israel said, 'It is enough. Joseph my son is still alive. I will go and see him before I die.'"** Thus may we say: "It is enough that Jesus my Savior is alive. I will go and see Him *when* I die."

When Jacob and his household move to Egypt, it is reflective of another Holy Family going to Egypt, fleeing from king Herod. Jacob traveled to Egypt, aided by gifts from a king, Pharaoh. Joseph, Mary and Jesus traveled to Egypt, probably helped by the kingly gifts of the magi.

In chapter 46, we see this journey to Egypt, which is a picture of the Christian's pilgrimage through this life enroute to meet our Savior. On their way, we see them

74

tarrying at Beersheba to offer sacrifices to God and communing with Him. This is the only event of the trip mentioned. And this is the premier duty of the Christian in his pilgrimage: the sacrifices of our prayers and communing with our God. Notice God's word to those who embark on this pilgrimage, **"I will go down with you to Egypt."** (v. 4) We have the blessed assurance that our God is with us, our Emmanuel. When the people of Israel traversed through the wilderness, they were assured of God's presence with the pillar of fire. Today we have the equally assuring presence of God by His Holy Spirit in us.

What happens to those who stay in Canaan, who do not set their hearts on following the Savior? **"Now there was no bread in all the land; for the famine was very severe...and the land of Canaan languished because of the famine."** Very few made their way to their promised land of Goshen, only the household of Jacob. Seventy souls. So it is today: few shall find the way. (Matthew 7:14) But we have a Savior who so loves the world and He is not willing that any would perish. After living in this world and loving us so much, and teaching us His way to eternal life, He gave His life as a one time offering for all sin in dying on the cross for us. He was both the sacrificial lamb who shed His blood to atone for our sins, and He was the scapegoat who willingly accepted all our guilt and carried our sins far away. What more could He do for us? He also gave us His precious Holy Spirit to seal and preserve us through all of life's hazards. When He departed from this world, He made only one request of us: bring His message of salvation to our starving, languishing world, our Canaan. That is God's plan for the world receiving the gospel. But we seem to be falling terribly short. You may be wondering if there is a Plan B. There is no Plan B. It's us or nothing. "But I don't like that plan." Me either. But we don't get a vote. We just have a job – the only thing He asked us to do.

SAMSON

1. Again the children of Israel did evil in the sight of the Lord, and the Lord delivered them into the hand of the Philistines for forty years.
2. Now there was a certain man from Zorah, of the family of the Danites, whose name was Manoah; and his wife was barren and had no children.
3. And the Angel of the Lord appeared to the woman and said to her, "Indeed now, you are barren and have borne no children, but you shall conceive and bear a son.
4. Now therefore, please be careful not to drink wine or similar drink, and not to eat anything unclean.
5. For behold, you shall conceive and bear a son. And no razor shall come upon his head, for the child shall be a Nazirite to God from the womb; and he shall begin to deliver Israel out of the hand of the Philistines."

v. 24 So the woman bore a son and called his name Samson; and the child grew, and the Lord
blessed him.
(Judges 13:1-5, 24)

SAMSON'S BEGINNINGS

Samson's story begins at an ebb tide in Israel's history. In verse one above, we see that Israel had been under the heavy-handed tyranny of the Philistines for 40 years, their longest period of subjection in the book of Judges. They had been subdued to virtual slavery by various surrounding nations for periods of 7 years, 18 years, 20 years, 7 years, 18 years and now 40 years. Israel had gotten into the cycle of serving God for a time, neglecting God in turning to idols, then being subdued again by another nation. God continued to chasten the children of Israel as a father would his own child. Now they are in the longest cycle of God's judgment to date: 40 years. The last time they had done this, the children of Israel cried out to the Lord to save them from the Ammonites, "We have sinned against you, because we have both forsaken our God and served the Baals." The Lord chides with them to the effect that He had already saved them repeatedly from various nations, and yet they kept turning back to other gods. So He says, "I will deliver you no more. Go and cry out to the gods which you have chosen; let them deliver you in your time of distress." I guess God was getting tired of the repeating cycle. So in a wise move, He makes Israel think He's giving up on them. So now Israel's really getting worried. They do some serious repenting and God finally relents and raises up another judge to save them: Jephthah. Well they behave for a while and then again go back to idolatry. It must have been exasperating to God to see this kind of stubbornness in His people. So this time, He let's the punishment period go for 40 years, seemingly turning a deaf ear to Israel's latest round of "I'm really sorry this time." But after this long period of silence, God gives a mighty Savior to His people. There is another long period of silence in Scripture: from the last prophet of the Old Testament to the commencing of the New Testament was roughly 400 years, possibly the longest in Bible times. After this long period of "silence", God gives us another mighty Savior.

In Judges 13:2, we see a good Israelite couple, who could not have a baby. No doubt, they prayed long for a child just as Abraham and Sarah, Jacob and Rachel, Elkanah and Hannah, and the parents of John the Baptist, Zacharias and Elisabeth. Each of these waited and prayed long for a child. For 3 of the 4, an angel announced that they would have a child. All four babies turned out to be great men. This is not surprising since each child may have been prayed for more than any other child of their generation. At least that's my guess. So we can have high expectations of the baby of Manoah and his wife. Great men commonly have great beginnings. An angel comes twice to announce the coming of their child and to give directions for how to raise him. We get an insight into the character of this couple when they insist on preparing a nice dinner for the angel, whom they thought at first was a man. Just as Abraham and Sarah did. Some may entertain angels unawares to this day.

Manoah and his wife name their baby Samson. They knew they had a very special child. Surely they followed the angel's instructions to keep their child holy and set apart for God. As the boy grew older, God gives His sign of approval to the way he was being brought up, when we see that **"the Lord blessed him."**

In Judges 13:25, we see the culmination of a good upbringing, **"And the Spirit of the Lord began to move him at times in the camp of Dan."** (KJV) Men (and women) called to the ministry know how this feels. He felt the moving of God in his heart, as Samuel heard God's voice in his ears. Maybe Samson observed the local Philistine garrison raiding a neighbor's crops. When the owners rushed over to angrily object, they were beaten and shoved aside. I can picture the Holy Spirit whispering into Samson's heart, "Son of man, do you see these things?" Young Samson's heart must have boiled with anger, but what could a kid do? Little by little, he probably got an increasing burden for the sufferings of his people, the tribe of Dan.

Now what about Dan? They were the most backslidden tribe of Israel. They neglected to defeat the Canaanites in their lot of land given to them by Joshua. So they got pushed around by the Canaanites and were driven out of the land they were supposed to inhabit. That's why we see them in Judges 18:1, looking for someplace else to settle, **"In those days there was no king in Israel. And in those days the tribe of the Danites was seeking an inheritance for itself to dwell in; for until that day their inheritance among the tribes of Israel had not fallen to them."** Later we find that Dan finally found some free land in the northern-most extreme of Israel, past everybody else. Thus the expression **"all the children of Israel came out from Dan to Beersheba"**. (From the far north to the far south.) Not only was Dan getting robbed by Philistines and getting pushed around by Canaanites and the settled tribes of Israelites, they had also succumbed to a bad case of idolatry. Read how bad off they were in Judges 18. The people of Dan were also bullies and thieves. Dan did not look anything like children of Israel. This was Samson's people. It had to hurt him to see how bad they were. Surely it vexed his righteous soul from day to day. God can use a man like that.

SAMSON FALLS IN LOVE

In Judges 14:1, Samson falls in love with a woman from Timnah, which was at the border of Israel and the Philistines. But she was a Philistine. Timnah was a town where the lines between Israel and the Philistines were blurred. Israel was the people of God, who were given the holy law of Moses. The Philistines were idolators and warmongers. God had commanded His people to remain separate from the heathen nations around them. He wanted to protect His people from their ungodly influence. The only problem was that some of the Philistine girls were cute. It's amazing how much sin can be overlooked if the person is good looking. Well Samson found a cute one. He should never have met her. Being a separated man of God, he had no business hanging around the edges of ungodliness. Timnah was not the place to meet a virtuous woman. That was the equivalent of a young man hanging around bars and clubs. **"Blessed is the man who walks not in the counsel of the ungodly, nor stands in the way of sinners."** This was the objection of Samson's parents. **"Is there no woman among the daughters of your brethren, or among all my people, that you must go and get a wife from the uncircumcised Philistines?"**

Are there no women in church who interest you? Samson's first mistake was being in the wrong crowd. Now he makes his second mistake. Instead of respecting his father's advice, he ignores it. **"Hear, my children, the instruction of a father...for I give you good doctrine: do not forsake my law. Hear, my son, and receive my sayings, and the years of your life will be many."** (Proverbs 4:1, 10) Sadly, Samson dies as a middle aged man. Samson's reply to his father was, **"Get her for me, for she pleases me well."** He does not even discuss the matter with his father. He just flatly states his demand. I get the impression he was accustomed to getting his way. God is not very patient with this kind of selfwilled disrespect of parents.

The parents give in and go with Samson to meet the young lady and her family. On the way, Samson is attacked by a lion. Although he was alone and unarmed, he kills the lion and tears it into pieces. As far as we know, this is the first time he realized his great power. There is another lion after Samson, a roaring lion, seeking whom he may devour. When this lion comes, Samson better be armored with righteousness.

Samson surely was aware of the Spirit of the Lord coming mightily upon him. It is not stated in Scripture, but it is my opinion that Samson did not look much different from ordinary men. I don't think he had a massive chest and bulging biceps. The only times he performed super-human feats is when "the Spirit of the Lord came mightily upon him." Remember when the Philistines came to Delilah to ask her to **"entice him and find out where his great strength lies"**? It was a mystery to them. If he had looked like a super strong body builder, it would have been no mystery. If he had looked like the Hulk, I doubt the lion would have bothered with him. So his greatest strength was the power of God working in him. So it is with us: our greatest strength is when we appropriate by faith the power of the Holy Spirit. Our greatest wisdom is when we are filled the Spirit. Greater is He that is in us than he that is in the world. When we seek to be filled with the Spirit, we can accomplish much more than when we operate in the flesh. People who are endowed with exceptional physical strength or a brilliant mind are not as inclined to seek the Lord's strength. **"For you see your calling, brethren, that not many wise according to the flesh, not many mighty, not many noble, are called."** (I Corinthians 1:26) But those of us who have modest ability or strength have more need to rely on our God. As Paul wrote, **"And He said to me, 'My grace is sufficient for you, for My strength is made perfect in weakness.' Therefore most gladly I will rather boast in my infirmities, that the power of Christ may rest upon me... For when I am weak, then I am strong."** (I Corinthians 12:9,10)

TONY

I'll never forget my friend, Tony. The Lord taught me several lessons the night I met him forty-nine years ago. I was a new believer at the time. Being eager to grow as a Christian, I attended a Billy Graham Crusade in San Diego Stadium. I was in awe at the sight of 50,000 believers in the same place, listening to the 5,000 voice choir, and hearing the eloquence of Billy Graham. I was so fired up for God!

I remember praying, "I would do anything for you right now, God. Just challenge me." The next instant, Billy

Graham was saying, "…and I challenge you, I challenge to come down here by the hundreds and commit your life to God. Come and receive Christ as your Savior." A kind of shiver went through my mind as I realized that it had to be God responding to my prayer. As Mr. Graham continued repeating the invitation, I watched as hundreds of people got up out of the bleachers and started heading down to the stage area. Well I did the same. I was met by some very nice Christians who talked with me about my salvation. It was later in the evening, so the Christians took me to dinner with them. I got an extra hour of quality discipling – and a free dinner. They also gave me a brand new Bible as I headed for home.

On the way, I stopped at a gas station about 10 pm. As I pulled in, a very old and very big car caught my attention. It looked like it must have served in a tank battalion in World War II. It was a strange feeling, as if the car was tugging at my attention. It was parked at a gas pump near me. After I paid for my gas, I walked back toward my car, passing near the old car out of curiosity. It was occupied by an older black couple. The gentleman was standing outside the car door, apparently counting some change in his hand. He looked up and glanced at me walking by. He stammered as if he was trying to talk to me. But his face really caught my attention. He was frowning with the struggle of trying to communicate with me. He also had heavy wrinkles on his forehead, almost a deformity, that gave him a perpetual scowl. I subconsciously judged him, thinking, "He's probably a criminal." It took him several tries to get out every word he tried to speak to me. I could not tell what he was saying. Finally, he extended his hand with the change toward me and then pointed to the gas pump. Oh, he needs help getting gas! I asked him if that's what he wanted. He nodded without looking me in the face. He might have been thinking, "Thank you, God, for sending me this genius." He handed me the 95 cents in his hand and I went back inside to get him some gas. I don't think he realized it, but he ended up with $5.95 worth of gas. I remember being quite puffed up at what a nice Christian man I was, helping this deformed criminal. As I passed around the front of his car, I saw something on his front dash that made me choke with shame: a large, very worn Bible. Not just a Bible, but a very worn Bible. Not on the back seat buried under clothes or magazines, but on the front dash, as if recently used. It totally changed my opinion of him. This was a Godly old saint in need of some help.

He made sounds and gestures as if he was thanking me. His stutter was the worst I have ever heard. I wondered, "How does this guy function? He couldn't even get gas without help." I "conversed" with him some more trying to see if he needed any more help. I noticed that his car tag showed him to be several states from home. So I asked if he needed help with directions. He nodded. We were in a dense area of San Diego. It would have been easy to get lost. I pulled out my city map and showed him where we were. After much laborious communication, we established where he was trying to go. It was 3 or 4 miles away along a route that was a little complicated. At 10:30 at night, I got a good picture in my mind of the route we needed to follow and led the way in my car. Again I got that puffed up feeling of self-righteousness. I led slowly and waited at the turns to make sure he saw me. Things progressed smoothly for the first mile, traffic being light. Then I made a wrong turn, realizing it a couple of seconds too late. Coincidentally, Tony just happened to miss my turn and we got separated. I headed off quickly to catch him and resume my station in the lead. I beeped my horn to let him know I was back. Then we got back on the correct track and continued. I thought of how lucky Tony was that I was helping him. After about another mile or so, I made another wrong turn! It was so exasperating, not to mention humiliating. If you can believe it, Tony lost me on that turn as well. He just kept going straight, not realizing he missed my turn. The only two times Tony missed my turns was when I happened to go the wrong way. **"For as many as are led by the Spirit of God, these are the sons of God."** After that, I just followed him and he never missed a turn all the way to his destination! (Where he had never been before.) I was dumfounded. It was a night full of amazements. But the best was yet to come. I would never have remembered Tony, except for what happened next.

As we pulled into the modest looking facility, the parking lot was empty. I walked over to Tony's car. He rolled down the window, as his wife got out of the car carrying bags into the building. In a rich, deep voice Tony asked me, "What did you do earlier tonight, young man?" He spoke in a smooth, eloquent manner in perfect, unbroken English without the slightest stutter! I was so shocked at the transformation in the man, that I didn't know what to say. Even his composure and strong eye contact were not the same man. There is no doubt in my mind now that the power of God came upon the man. I finally stammered my reply, "I went to hear what a man of God had to say." Then I explained that I went to the Billy Graham crusade. At that point,

Tony launched into an hour long session of preaching, that to this day is about the richest I have ever heard. I remember thinking several times how much he sounded like Billy Graham. But to me, he was better than Billy Graham. He was authoritative without trying to be, quoting Scripture and convicting me at times and exhorting me at times. All the while, I was fascinated at the transformation in the man. I couldn't help waiting to see if he stuttered again. I don't think he did throughout the rest of our talk. I was spell-bound, soaking up the Word of God, like the hungry new believer that I was. I did not know at the time that what I was hearing is called "anointed preaching", a spiritual gift at work. I had never even heard of spiritual gifts. He did not speak in tongues. I was just amazed how well he spoke in English. Maybe God gave me my own private revival, since I missed most of Billy Graham's message. I wish I could remember all the words he spoke to me.

God taught me several lessons that night. First, never judge a man by his appearance. Second, be a humble servant, not a proud one. Third, when the Spirit of God comes on a man, the change can be astonishing. Four, God sometimes compensates a man who is weak in one area with greatness in another. Tony's appearance and severe speech impediment were difficult liabilities, but God compensated him with an unbelievable spiritual gift. Sometimes I look in the mirror and think, "Maybe there's hope for me yet." For Tony, though he was weak, yet he was strong. I was very glad to have met a spiritual version of Samson. The Spirit of the Lord can come upon anyone and do marvelous things with them. Especially for those who acknowledge their weakness. Paradoxically, those who are well educated and intelligent are commonly lacking in the power of God, especially if they rely on their credentials. Others who are athletic marvels or good-looking or wealthy often seem to have less aptitude for and interest in spiritual things. But there are exceptions. **"Blessed are the poor in spirit, for theirs is the kingdom of heaven."** So the poor are blessed in spirit. But even they must appropriate God's gifts by faith.

SAMSON'S FAILED WEDDING

Sometime later Samson returns with his parents to marry the girl of Timnah.

At the pre-wedding reception, Samson proposes a riddle to the thirty Philistine men who were invited. They could not figure it out, so they go to Samson's fiancé, threatening to kill her if she does not tell them the riddle. She cries and nags Samson until he tells her. In turn, she tells the guys and Samson has to pay up to the guys. So he goes to the neighboring city of Ashkelon, where the Spirit of the Lord comes mightily upon him for the second time and he kills thirty Philistines and gives their clothes to the thirty guys. Not much of a wedding party. So Samson gets mad and goes back home, and the bride is given to another man. When Samson finds out about it, he gets mad again and burns up their crops. In retaliation, the Philistines kill the woman and her father.

SAMSON'S STRENGTH

With hostilities escalating, Samson attacks the Philistines **"hip and thigh with a great slaughter."** All by himself. A one man army.

Samson is probably the strongest man that ever lived. There was never another like him. He was God's gift to Israel at an opportune time. None of David's mighty men could have attained to him. David himself would have been no match for him physically. Samson could have beaten Goliath to death with his bare hands. But only if the Spirit of the Lord came mightily upon him.

The Philistines are fixated and determined to kill this menace to their country. They invade Judah with an army to capture Samson. When the Philistines explain that they want to arrest Samson, three thousand men of Judah go to arrest Samson. They tie him up with ropes and deliver him to the Philistine army. "Thank you for your service, Samson." When the Philistines shouted against him, **"the Spirit of the Lord came mightily upon him; and the ropes that were on his arms became like flax that is burned with fire, and his bonds broke loose from his hands. He found a fresh jawbone of a donkey, reached out his hand and took it, and killed a thousand men with it."** (Judges 15:15, 16) Impossible, you say? Well I believe it. Humanly speaking, it would be impossible. But with God, all things are possible. This was the most impressive victory of his life. Verse 18 records that Samson was very thirst and cried out to God and He gave him water. This previews another Savior, who at his greatest victory, said "I thirst." Obviously God was working on his behalf. Remember, the ropes sort of melted off his arms. That was a supernatural occurrence. Likewise, Samson was supernaturally empowered.

Don't forget about Shamgar who killed 600 Philistines with an ox goad. (Judges 3:31) And then there's Adino, the Ezrite, who killed 800 men at one time. These were all hand to hand combat. This is nothing to boast about. I'd rather honor doctors who could say they have saved the lives of 800 or 1000 people. Now that's a hero. But Samson's feats are recorded in God's book, the Bible.

In Judges 16:1, we see another disappointing chapter in Samson's life. **"Now Samson went to Gaza."** (Meaning "the strong place"). Bad enough. **"And saw a harlot there."** Even worse. **"And went in to her."** Disaster. This is worse than his affair with the woman of Timnah. He barely escapes getting killed this time. With Philistine guards waiting for him at the gate, he waits till midnight and then rips up the two posts of the city gates, and carries the posts, the two doors and the bar all to Hebron in Judea. Thirty seven miles! Astonishing, but true. This is a preview of another man (a greater than Samson) who would capture the gates of another strong place: Hell. There would be another man who would carry another heavy wooden burden to another place in Judea called Calvary.

SAMSON AND DELILAH

In Judges 16:4, Samson courts yet another Philistine woman named Delilah. I wonder if his father's advice ever echoed in his conscience, "Is there no woman among the daughters of your brethren?" But Samson must fill up the measure of his sins, that God's judgement must come. He really tries the longsuffering of God. I suppose it is always with reluctance that God brings down the hammer of His judgement. Especially against His own people, the Jews – or the Christians. But with

90

some, God's patience seems to only encourage the disobedient in their sins. **"Because sentence against an evil work is not executed speedily, therefore the heart of the sons of men is fully set in them to do evil."** (Ecclesiastes 8:11) We sometimes think we are exempt from judgement because we do a lot of good. As in Nathaniel Hawthorne's *The Scarlet Letter*. But let us remember that "to the Jew first" came the law and to the Jew first comes the judgement. For judgement must begin at the house of God.

One thing really bugs me: for 20 years during all this time, Samson is a judge of Israel. He settles land disputes, punishes evil-doers and interprets God's law. Yet he is living a disgraceful, immoral life. That he was a judge is mentioned in Judges 16:31, the last verse in the saga of Samson, almost as if the writer was ashamed to mention it.

Samson just comes brashly into the land of the Philistines to see Delilah, making no apparent attempt to conceal his identity. Surely he is widely known or renowned in all their land. Public enemy number one. Today there would be WANTED posters in every city and village. "Anyone able to give information leading to his arrest will be given free burial services." The Philistines are immediately aware of his presence. The five lords of the Philistines secretly offer to pay Delilah a combined 5500 pieces of silver if she would find out the secret of his great strength. The love of money certainly works its evil in this case. Without hesitation, she betrays her lover and reveals his secret to the Philistine lords. Samson may have been a judge of Israel, but he sure did foolishly with Delilah. And he's not the only man who did foolishly with an immoral woman and it cost him dearly. Just a normal amount of wisdom would have forewarned a man when a woman says, **"Please tell me where your great strength lies, and with what you may be bound to afflict you."** Delilah tries this three times and Samson still does not take warning. **"Surely in vain the net is spread in the sight of any bird."** (Proverbs 1:17)Then he finally tells her his secret. It's like Samson has lost his mind. **"Harlotry, wine and new wine take away the understanding."** Hosea 4:11 NASB) It is well known that alcohol can significantly degrade a man's thinking. But it's not as well known that harlotry and fornication can do the same thing. Samson is exhibit A. He also seems to have the sense of being invincible. Nobody and no situation can beat him. **"The complacency of fools will destroy them."** (Proverbs 1:32) But he is brought to ruin by the very woman he loves. All his hair is cut off while he is sleeping. The Philistines come after him again. He wakes up as before and tries to fight them off. **"But he did not know that the Lord had departed from him."** (Judges 16:20) It is a terrible judgement from God when He leaves us to the consequences of our ways.

Samson has lost his great strength and is captured. His eyes are also put out. If he will not see the error of his ways, it is just that his eyes are taken away. If he will use his eyes to lust after foreign women, it is just that his eyes are taken away. It may not seem like it, but what happened to Samson is a mercy of God. He deserved the death penalty. It is strange that the Philistines did not put him to death immediately.

Testimony to God's mercy is that **"the hair of his head began to grow again after it had been shaven."** Although he forsook God, yet God did not abandon him. Still Samson remained a slave to his enemies the rest of his life. **"They bound him with bronze fetters, and he became a grinder in the prison."** Month after month, Samson paid the wages of sin. He might very well have died in such a dreary state, except for two things that happened.

First the Philistines celebrated their capture of Samson by gathering **"together to offer a great sacrifice to Dagon their god, and to rejoice. And they said: "Our god has delivered into our hands Samson our enemy!"** They praised their god; for they said: **"Our god has delivered into our hands our enemy, the destroyer of our land, and the one who multiplied our dead."** (Judges 16:24) At another big drinking party, Emperor Belshazzar and his guests drank from the sacred vessels that were stolen from Jerusalem. Then they praised their own hand-made idols, counting them to be greater than the God of Israel. Both parties ended in a very great disaster. Notice in the verses above that nearly the same expression is quoted in back to back verses. I take it these words are getting serious attention from God. This is a flagrant violation of the first and second commandments. Few sins stir the anger and jealousy of God like idolatry. They declare that their god, Dagon, delivered Samson into their hands, insinuating that their god is greater than the God of Israel. Whereas the truth is, God delivered Samson into their hands, for his own good. The second thing that happened is that his months of captivity worked humility in him and probably a sincere repentance. For only the second time in the record of Samson, he prays.

Several thousand attend the celebration of Samson's capture at the temple of Dagon. During the party Samson is called for to provide entertainment. They place him sort of center stage. He may have seen the place before and knew about the two center pillars supporting the massive roof structure. Three thousand people watched Samson from the roof, with probably several thousand more on the main floor. With help from a lad, he gets his hands on the two pillars. I'm guessing he whispers to the lad to get out of the building – fast.

At this point Samson makes what I believe to be a sincere and humble prayer. **"O Lord God, remember me, I pray! Strengthen me, I pray, just this once, O God, that I may with one blow take vengeance on the Philistines for my two eyes."** Twice he says, **"O God"** and **"O Lord God"**. I sense a pleading, imploring tone in this. Here is a man who presents his urgent plea to His mighty God. He says, **"Strengthen me, I pray."** Strengthen me, please. Strengthen me, I beg. He acknowledges his own weakness and God's power by his plea. This is the cry of a man who has been sincerely humbled.. He has had probably months to ponder his ways, his arrogance, his disrespect of his parents, his immorality, his refusal to obey the Holy Spirit in his conscience. "Samson, don't go there." "Stay away from this lady. She is not a believer." Maybe he thought about the fact that he was a Nazirite to God from the womb. "Oh God, I have terribly disgraced your calling on my life. I am not worthy of the least of all your mercies." He may have even regretted and repented of the slaughtering of the thirty men just to get their clothes. Or the vengeful burning down the Philistines' crops. Oh sure, God was probably using Samson as His hammer of retribution on the Philistines for their many years of cruelty toward the people of Israel. But that doesn't justify Samson's fornication, harlotry or vengeful behavior. Yes, God was glorified

94

in his mighty exploits. But how much more might God have been glorified if Samson had lived righteously and performed great victories in proper warfare in defending his nation? David did so to a great degree. The man after God's own heart.

So it seems that Samson prayed with all his might. Then we read in 16:29, **"And Samson took hold of the two middle pillars which supported the temple, and he braced himself against them, one on his right and the other on his left. Then Samson said, "Let me die with the Philistines!" And he pushed with all his might, and the temple fell on the lords and all the people who were in it. So the dead that he killed at his death were more than he had killed in his life."**

SAMSON COMPARED TO JESUS

1. *Both were heaven-announced "miracle" births.*
2. *Both were announced by angels to be saviors of their people.*
3. *Jesus was "subject" to his parents; Samson disobeyed his.*
4. *Both dwelt among sinners. Jesus was "the friend of sinners".* He associated with them because God calls sinners to repentance. Samson associated with sinners for lustful purposes.
5. *Both died among sinners. At his death, Samson said, "Let me die with the Philistines."* Jesus "was numbered with the transgressors".
6. *Jesus died between two sinners;* Samson died between two pillars. Samson reached out to two *pillars; Jesus reached out to one sinner.*
7. *Samson suffered for his own sins; Jesus suffered for our sins.* "The just for the unjust."

8. Samson single-handedly slew 1000 men at one time; Jesus once single-handedly cast out 2000 demons.
9. Samson became weak when he got into sin; Jesus became weak when He took on "the likeness of sinful flesh."
10. As both men neared the end of their lives, their hands were bound by their enemies. Samson easily broke free from the bonds. Jesus also could have done so. But He did not, because He had already determined to go to the cross willingly.
11. Both were mocked and abused by their enemies just before their deaths. "Call for Samson that he may perform for us...and he performed for them." "And when they had mocked Him, they took the purple off Him...and led Him out to crucify him."
12. Both Samson and Jesus took for themselves a Gentile bride.
13. Samson's victories was in killing others. Jesus's victories was in giving life to others.
14. Both crippled the power of the enemy. The Philistines said, "Our god has delivered into our hands our enemy, the destroyer of our land and the one who multiplied our dead." Of Jesus is it said, "Through death He might destroy him who had the power of death, that is, the devil". For the accuser of our brethren is cast down." "Jesus Christ ...has abolished death." Through Him, death has no more sting and the grave has no more victory. "I am He that lives and was dead and behold I am alive forevermore, Amen, and I have the keys of hell and of death."
15. Both accomplished a greater victory at death than all the victories of their life combined.

When Samson collapsed the temple of Dagon, he killed more enemy Philistines than in all his life.

LOOK AGAIN AT CALVARY!

See the invisible Philistines, principalities, powers, rulers of the darkness of this world jeering and mocking at their victim: Jesus. See the ravenous dogs surrounding Him and the bulls of Bashan encircling Him, shouting against this greater than Samson! They did not know their murderous plot would backfire on them disastrously! "For had they known, they would not have crucified the Lord of glory."

But Jesus, like Samson, bowed Himself with all his might, "only this once", "once for all", and broke all the power of hell. He broke the two central pillars of hell's grip on mankind: SIN and DEATH. "O death, where is your sting? O, grave, where is your victory?"

When Jesus died at Calvary, it looked like He was defeated, but it was actually His greatest victory. His death on the cross was a greater victory than:
- All the sick folk He had healed,
- All the miracles He performed,
- All the demons He had cast out,
- All the dead he had raised,
- All the souls He had saved through his preaching,
COMBINED!
His death and resurrection avails for the salvation of millions of "whosoever believes" for ages to come! And His blood will never lose its power!

MORDECAI

The book of Esther could easily have been named the book of Mordecai. He was a truly great man. If he was in this discussion of who the book should be named after, I imagine he would have just smiled quietly and insisted that it be named after her. He had no interest in fame or recognition. All through this charming Bible book, Mordecai occupies himself with nothing but attending to the needs of people around him.

CHAPTER ONE

The record of these events begins with Emperor Ahasuerus, who ruled from India to Ethiopia, putting on a world class party, lasting 6 months. The whole point of the party is given in Esther 1:4, **"He showed the riches of his glorious kingdom and the splendor of his excellent majesty for many days."** This was treading dangerous ground. For he that exalts himself shall be humbled. And the last time a world emperor so exalted himself, he was terribly humbled for seven years. And that was after Daniel had warned him a year previously. Yet we read of Emperor Nebuchadnezzar, **"The king spoke, saying, 'Is this not great Babylon, that I have built for a royal dwelling by my mighty power and for the honor of my majesty?' "** (Daniel 4:30) In the very next verse, he loses his mind and is deposed to live with the beasts of the field for seven years. Then there was Emperor Belshazzar, who also put on a big party, which stopped abruptly when a hand wrote on the wall his imminent doom. Emperors really ought to read their history.

A sad consequence of this party was that King Ahasuerus sort of divorced his lovely wife, Queen Vashti. He had sent for her to come into the party so that her beauty could be displayed to the guests. But she knew that there was a lot of drinking going on and she refused to be made a spectacle. I don't blame her. King Ahasuerus ends up banishing her. Soon after, he decides to start dating. Beautiful young virgins were brought to the king from all over the provinces.

CHAPTER TWO

Meanwhile Mordecai, a good Jew, lives right in the capital city, Shushan. His family had been captured as slaves and taken from Jerusalem. So he was of a lowly lineage, probably coming from a line of servants. He did have one thing going for him: he was a Jew. He believed in God. In general, all the Jews that were deported from Jerusalem in the first group were quality, good people. According to Jeremiah, they were the good figs in the vision God showed him. In Jeremiah 24:5-7, God tells Jeremiah the prophet, **"Like these good figs, so will I acknowledge those who are carried away captive from Judah, whom I have sent out of this place for their own good, into the land of the Chaldeans...I will give them a heart to know Me, that I am the Lord; and they shall be My people, and I will be their God, for they shall return to Me with their whole heart."** So this was the group Mordecai was a part of, not just a Jew by nationality, but he was a Jew indeed.

The first thing we learn about Mordecai is found in Esther 2:7, where we see that he adopted a young relative who was orphaned. He didn't just take her in to be a servant or a tax deduction. She didn't come with a social security check or any kind of inheritance. We're not told that he had a wife or other children. He was a single man, living alone and probably set in his ways. But he was willing to completely change his life and take on the expense and responsibility of raising a child. The Bible says **"he took her as his own daughter."** A loaded expression. He became for her what she needed: father and mother. As a good Jew, whom the Lord had put it in his heart to return to God with his whole heart, he no doubt raised up Esther to also love the Lord her God with all her heart and soul, as he did. He surely taught her all the righteous law of God, to love her neighbor as herself, to honor her father and mother and her husband some day, to speak the truth to her neighbor, to be honest in all her dealings, to give a tenth of all her increase to the Lord, to dress modestly, to be kind to the poor and to children. He would have instilled in her every imaginable quality and virtue. There is every indication that he lived for this one child. As Jacob was toward Benjamin, his life was bound up in her life. We can safely assume he was wise about it. He wouldn't have pampered her and spoiled her and bought her every little thing she wanted. He would have taught her to avoid such coveting. I have no doubt he required her to participate in household chores such as cleaning, laundry, cooking, etc. It is no kindness to a child to wait on them, serve them and do everything for them and require no labor or difficult task of them. Why should they be deprived of so much excellent training and building of good character? If he was wise, he even taught her to wait on him, as much as it would go against his grain. And as she grew older, he probably tasked her with preparing their meals and to take care of shopping. As she would do each of these tasks, I picture him commending her and telling her she was doing so well and that he was so proud of her. She would have beamed with happiness and lived to hear his kind, loving words. Even when she was trying to learn how to cook, and probably was not very successful at first, she would bring him a bowl of something she made to see if he liked it. As many fathers know, this is a situation where lying is perfectly acceptable. "Esther, this tastes wonderful!", as he struggled to swallow it.

Some may accuse me of making up a fairy-tale picture of Esther's upbringing, that couldn't possibly be real. But I beg to differ. The above description is actually the normal way of raising a child. This is just doing the basics. And every step child should be treated as our own child.

"The young woman was lovely and beautiful." Some may think I'm a little too fanciful, but I'm convinced that much of what made Esther so beautiful was all the deep treasury of her virtues shining outwardly, thanks to Mordecai. This kind of beauty is so much better than a woman who obsesses over herself in front of a mirror hours every day, with makeup and hairstyling. This can breed a lot of selfcenteredness. Gentlemen, this would not be a good time to say "Amen!", if there are women present.

Meanwhile, the royal wife hunt sweepstakes is underway in Shushan. Lovely ladies from all over are being brought in for King Ahasuerus to look over. The only quality he required was good looks. A lot of men date by the same standards. However, more spiritual-minded men live by better values than that. Out of all the gorgeous babes available, they choose the most virtuous one. Well what is the proper way to date? Very simple. Let God choose your wife for you. Consider Adam: God chose his wife for him and she was the most beautiful woman in the world. In actuality, when God does the choosing, regardless of her initial appearance, she will become beautiful in your eyes, because God lets you begin to see her the way He does. The search for a proper, good wife becomes a lot easier when we stop looking for the perfect woman and start working on being the perfect man. Well happy hunting to you single guys. Even if you're as shallow as Ahasuerus, God might lead an Esther right to you. Let's hope you are more deserving of her than Ahasuerus.

It must have looked like a Miss America pageant under way. All the contestants were gathered into the king's palace and put through a twelve month beautification program. Like they needed it! Can you imagine what this did to the ladies' personalities? They were already pampered and spoiled for being so beautiful and everybody doting on them. They already adored themselves, at least in some cases. What they needed was twelve months of character training. I can think of the perfect guy to do the training. If any of you readers decide to enter your daughter into a beauty pageant, please write me and let me know. I'd like to spend some time fasting and praying for the poor girl.

The selection procedure was that when each lady's turn came up, she was allowed to have anything she wanted before going in to visit Ahasuerus. This was feeding the monster of selfishness already in the beautiful ladies.

So picture the woman visiting the king for dinner and a romantic evening. Maybe she had practiced looking sexy or coy. She probably had heavy makeup and was dressed to spotlight her sexy body with fancy, expensive clothes. Just like dating today. Maybe sitting at dinner, she would put on an air of arrogance toward the butlers and servants, as it she expected the best of everything. Surely this would make her appealing to the king. The king endured this act every night with a different woman for maybe months. There's no telling how many women he had dated and rendered them no longer eligible to marry someone. They would be the king's concubine for life, even though he would not recognize most of them later or even remember their name. He'd be doing well to remember their name the next morning. But in Esther 2:15, something very different happened. Esther's turn came up to meet the king. Now it was Esther's turn to request anything she wanted before going in to the king. But she requested nothing but what the custodian advised. She was accustomed to taking advice from an older man. After twelve months in the beautification program, we see the result, **"And Esther obtained favor in the sight of all who saw her."** The same thing happens in v. 17, when the king meets her, **"The king loved Esther more than all the other women, and she obtained grace and favor in his sight more than all the virgins."** Who knows how much all the good parenting affected her beauty and grace that evening? Train up a child in the way they should go, and when they are older, they will not depart from it. It's beautiful when a woman is truly modest. I wonder if she was the only lady who at dinner, thanked the butlers and waiters with a smile. This would have shocked Ahasuerus, but made him deeply appreciate her. Her modest dressing and modest amount of makeup would also make her more appealing. It would to me. Based on what the king saw of her in one night, he marries her. That is, he made her queen and put the crown on her head. He would find out as time went on that the lady whom he thought was the most beautiful just happened to also be the most virtuous. This story is not intended to be a model for our dating. We should plan to date someone a little longer than one night.

During all this time, Mordecai paced daily in front of the court of the women's quarters. At least 365 days. He continually enquired of Esther's welfare and what was happening to her. And she would have been glad to be in touch. At the time she was selected to go to the palace, he had wisely instructed her not to divulge that she was from a Jewish family. A God worshipper. He knew that a lot of people hated Jews. Sadly, like today. And Esther was unfailingly obedient to Mordecai, even in his absence. The Christian of today is also despised and rejected by many, as was our Savior. But for us, the mandate is to spread the gospel; to go and make disciples of all nations. But in Esther's case, her life could be in danger, as we'll soon see.

During the time Mordecai sat inside the king's gate (near the women's quarters), he quietly listened to the local gossip. It was probably the smoking area. He must have remained inconspicuous, maybe quietly sitting in the shadows, because he heard a lot of gossip that people would rather not have become public information. But he had been a familiar face there for a year, and may have been thought to be a palace employee. At one point two palace employees (gate keepers) got really mad at Ahasuerus and said how they'd like to get their hands on him, apparently intent on killing him. The matter came to Mordecai's ears. They had probably never read in Ecclesiastes, **"Do not curse the king, even in your thought…for a bird of the air may carry your voice…and may tell the matter."** In Esther 2:22, we see that Mordecai tells Queen Esther about the plot. Is he being a snitch or a tattler? Absolutely not. He's protecting the life of his king – and his son-in-law. We owe no loyalty to would-be assassins or other criminals. The matter was investigated and confirmed and the two conspirators were hanged. The whole matter was written in the king's chronicles. Mordecai was content to do this good, glad to save someone's life. As far as we know he never once boasted of it or sought any credit for it.

This is reminiscent of the time Joseph spent several years in prison. He had been caring for the imprisoned baker and butler of Pharaoh, and a number of other prisoners. He had a sort of prison ministry. When he rightly interpreted their dreams, the butler was restored to his old job working for Pharaoh. The baker was executed. Joseph never sought credit for all the good he did. But like Mordecai, he finally came to the attention of the king years later.

CHAPTER 3

Esther is now in her fifth year as queen. Amazingly, we find Mordecai is still sitting daily at the gate, where he can keep in touch with now Queen Esther. Too bad they didn't have texting in those days.

In verse 1, we are introduced to Haman, whom Ahasuerus sets in the highest office in his administration. We see that Ahasuerus was no more careful about selecting a prime minister than he was a wife. Apparently one of the perks is that everybody has to bow down to him. And so everybody at the palace gate is ordered to do so. This would have included Mordecai. A good Jew, like Mordecai, would know the first commandment, **"You shall have no other gods before Me...you shall not bow down to them nor serve them."** He faces a similar predicament as did Shadrach, Meshach and Abednego. Remember them? By order of Emperor Nebuchadnezzar in the previous empire, everybody was required to bow down and worship his giant golden statue. Failure to comply would result in being prosecuted to the maximum extent of the law: getting thrown into the furnace. Well, Mordecai also courageously refused to bend.

In verse 3, Mordecai was questioned about this, **"Why do you transgress the king's command?"** In Matthew 15:2, religious leaders similarly asked Jesus why His disciples transgressed the tradition of the elders by not washing their hands before they ate. His reply was, **"Why do you also transgress the commandment of God because of your tradition?"** Man's traditions or laws must not contradict the word of God. If it does, then it's time to say "we ought to obey God rather than man." But don't expect the authorities to back down and say, "You know what? You've got a good point. Just disregard my law." In verse 4, Mordecai finally explains to them that he cannot bow down because he is a Jew, probably quoting the first commandment. He knew that stating this would not be popular, but more important to him was not disappointing God.

When this was brought to Haman's attention and he saw that Mordecai still refused to bow to him, **"Haman was filled with wrath."** But his anger seethed into a boiling rage. It seems that every high ranking official or rich man in Bible days was mean, unreasonably hateful and grouchy. Of course, that doesn't apply today. Right? Maybe that's part of the job description. Nabal, the churl, was rich. So naturally, he was churlish. King Saul was a great guy until he became king. Then he got in the habit of spearing his friends. Maybe he could argue that he had good reason to be in bad mood: the girls cheered better for David than for him.

At about that time Haman morphs hideously into a likeness of Hitler. He sets his rage against all Jews everywhere. And he was in a position to do them a great deal of damage. What did not occur to Haman was that he was picking a fight against the Living God. He would find this to be a most terrible mistake. Verse 6 records for us, **"But he disdained to lay hands on Mordecai alone ... but he sought to destroy all the Jews who were throughout the whole kingdom."** It seemed to be the going thing in those days, that instead of just killing the guy who gets on your nerves, you kill everybody related to the guy or who even knew him. That had to be a headache because you had to take a poll and figure out who all those people were.

For some reason, Haman decides to cast lots to decide when to schedule the execution of the Jews. It is no doubt the providence of God that the lot gives him a date 12 months later. We will see that this worked against Haman and against his evil plot. **"The lot is cast into the lap, but its every decision is from the Lord."**

In Esther 3:8, Haman makes his case against the Jews to king Ahasuerus. He does not mention Mordecai or the Jewish people specifically. The only charge he could bring against them was **"Their laws are different from all other people's and they do not keep the king's laws."** Governments should be concerned whether their laws are in keeping with God's law. Not the other way around. There are people who read the writings of the various world religions. I don't. But I am told that the Bible is far above the others in wisdom, goodness, beauty and in the power to change men's lives. Not surprising, considering its Author. I really doubt Haman did much research on the subject. I suspect he knew little more than the fact that the Jews' Scriptures do not allow bowing down to any other than God. Haman suggests that the empire of Ahasuerus would be better off without Jews. He is proposing genocide against the Jewish race!

In verse 9, Haman seems to think he has a weak case, so he offers to pay for the executions. He offers to pay 10,000 talents of silver out of his own riches, which is the equivalent of $161 million dollars today. In verse 10, king Ahasuerus does the inexplicable: without any further questioning or discussion, he gives Haman his authorization to slaughter the Jews. What a gross dereliction of duty to his subjects! One of the most evil men of all time meets one of the most irresponsible men of all time.

News of this is about to make shock waves throughout the empire. This would be worse news than to hear that the Greek empire is attacking from the west. Haman sends letters to every province of the empire giving instructions to prepare to execute every Jew and plunder all their property on the date given. They would

108

have several months to get ready. The terrible decree was also proclaimed all over Shushan, the capital. Jews everywhere are terrified. But we read at the end of chapter 3, **"So the king and Haman sat down to drink, but the city of Shushan was perplexed."** This was as black a contrast to the distress of his people as the legend of Nero playing music while Rome burned. Consider the fuming indignation of God Almighty toward Haman for all this! It is a fearful thing to fall into the hands of an angry God. Stay tuned.

CHAPTER 4

When Mordecai hears the news, he cries out with a loud bitter cry. He tears his clothes and puts on sackcloth and ashes. The sackcloth and ashes were religious expressions of mourning before God, usually accompanied with fasting. As the decree spread around the empire, Jews everywhere also began mourning and fasting. And many of them put on sackcloth and ashes and prayed. Esther finds out about the decree and hears that Mordecai is wearing sackcloth and ashes. She is terribly distressed, but cannot go out to visit with him, because no one could enter the palace in sackcloth and ashes. She sends him clothes, but he refuses them. Through a servant, Mordecai explains all the circumstances to her, sending a copy of the decree. After some interchange between them, Mordecai tells Esther to go in to the king, her husband, and plead on behalf of the Jews. But there's a problem. No one is allowed to just walk in to the king's court who has not been specifically invited. If a person just walks in uninvited, they are immediately brought out and executed. The only exception to that is if the king extends his golden scepter to them. That probably kept all the salesmen out. Complicating the problem is the fact that Esther had not been invited to see the king for a month now. They had been married five years by that time. And if Ahasuerus got tired of his wife, he had plenty of spares. So in Esther's mind it was very risky to try to get a hearing with the king. But Mordecai is not backing down. In v. 14, he speaks these immortal words, **"For if you remain completely silent at this time, relief and deliverance will arise for the Jews from another place, but you and your father's house will perish. Yet who knows whether you have come to the kingdom for such a time as this?"**

Esther agrees and lays this task on Mordecai, **"Go and gather all the Jews who are present in Shushan, and fast for me; neither eat nor drink for three days, night or day. My maids and I will fast likewise. And so will I go to the king, which is against the law; and if I perish, I perish."** (Esther 4:16) This would have been a gathering of possibly a thousand people. Mordecai complies. So a thousand or so people gather for fasting and prayer for three days. We can expect to see great things begin to happen. We should be doing the same thing. As William Carey would say, "We should expect great things from God and attempt great things for God." Carey and his words did a great deal to spark the modern missionary movement. In Acts 13, the church at Antioch ministered to the Lord and fasted and prayed. The result was the first time ever that a missionary team was launched forth to preach the gospel to the world. And Paul and Barnabas made history from there. May God raise you up to fast and pray and go forth to attempt great things for God. In what way or place are you in a unique position to make a great impact for the gospel?

THE QUEEN'S REQUEST

At the end of the three days of fasting, Esther dons her royal robes and went and stood in the king's court. She did not know whether she would live or die in the next five minutes. Esther 5:2 is a milestone answer to prayer. **"So it was when the king saw Queen Esther standing in the court, that she found favor in his sight, and the king held out to Esther the golden scepter that was in his hand. Then Esther went near and touched the top of the scepter."** If this had been televised, there would have been crowds of Jews cheering raucously around the world. And if that was not encouraging enough, listen to what the king says in the next verse, **"What do you wish, Queen Esther? It shall be given to you – up to half the kingdom."** She must have felt like crying with relief. Some day each of God's beloved saints will come to stand before Him. When we behold His holiness and majesty, we may be as fearful as Esther was here. And God will surely feel about like Ahasuerus felt, ready to reassure His child that it is their Father's good pleasure to give them the kingdom.

My personal conviction is that the effectual, fervent praying of thousands of believing Jews shaped Ahasuerus's feeling toward Esther. He could have been coolly indifferent toward his wife of 5 years. He could have thought he was about ready for a new one. But we know that even **"The king's heart is in the hand of the Lord, like the rivers of water; He turns**

111

it wherever He wishes." And God can do exceeding abundantly above all that we ask or think, according to the power that works in us. As the prayers of the saints fuel the judgments of the seven seals in Revelation, so the prayers of these saints will cause the release of one judgment after another against Haman.

Meanwhile, with things looking so hopeful right now, I wonder if she considered presenting her petition right then. Whether or not, she prudently stuck with her original plan. She probably wanted to strengthen her position as much as possible with the king before she faced Haman. So in verse 4, she humbly requests the honor of cooking dinner for him, along with Haman. It was as if she cared more for her husband's company than for half the kingdom.

So they came over for dinner, an absolute banquet! She knows what she's doing: feed the man. So Ahasuerus is first renewed in his love for her and now feels indebted to her. He's bursting with curiosity to know what her request is. But she coyly says please come over again tomorrow evening and then I'll tell you. After she feeds him the next night, he won't stand a chance. She's handling this man like a pro. Some of you guys know the feeling.

In Esther 5:9, Haman's heading out the palace gate, all proud of himself for being the only person invited to a private dinner with the king and queen. But his pleasure darkens, when he sees Mordecai continuing to refuse to bow to him. I love a man who stands his ground. Many a Christian man is persecuted for righteousness sake even in these days. According to the Master, he shall be exceedingly blessed.

In Esther 5:10 and following, Haman goes home and puts on a "ME" party. **"And he sent and called for his** friends and his wife Zeresh. **Then Haman told them of his great riches, the multitude of his children, everything in which the king had promoted him, and how he had advanced him above the officials and servants of the king.** (As if they didn't already know.) **Moreover Haman said, 'Besides Queen Esther invited no one but me to come in with the king to the banquet that she prepared; and tomorrow I am again invited by her along with the king."** Have you ever been to a "ME" party? Let me guess: they had good food. Because there would be no other reason to stay. Half the fun of having riches is being able to brag about it. But there are hazards. **"Pride goes before destruction and a haughty spirit before a fall."** There might not be a more apt illustration of this truth anywhere in the Bible than Haman.

But his pride and boasting is cut short when he remembers Mordecai at the gate refusing to bow to him. Then his wife and friends come up with this idea: (v.14) **"Let a gallows be made, fifty cubits high and in the morning suggest to the king that Mordecai be hanged on it; then go merrily with the king to the banquet."** "Great idea, Honey. I'll do just that!" And he got the gallows started.

THE FALL OF HAMAN

Esther chapter 6 begins with the first of several divine providences. This is no doubt the result of several hundred believing Jews praying, fasting and some wearing sackcloth and ashes for three days straight. They neither ate nor drank anything like food. (They may have drunk water.) Have you ever tried that? It's

113

rough. As for the sackcloth, not only is it uncomfortable, but it's very humiliating to wear it around. We should all keep a set hanging in our closet for emergencies.

In 6:1, we read that king Ahasuerus can't sleep. *Providence number one.* But **"He gives his beloved sleep".** Also **"the sleep of a laboring man is sweet... but the abundance of the rich will not permit him to sleep."** (Ecclesiastes 5:12) So the king gets someone to read from the court records, well known to put people to sleep. So as it was being read, the incident comes up where Mordecai saves the king's life by exposing the plot of the two eunuchs. *Providence number two.* The king was curious and asks, **"What honor or dignity has been bestowed on Mordecai for this?"** The answer was, **"Nothing has been done for him."**

V. 4 continues, **"So the king said, 'Who is in the court?' Now Haman had just entered the outer court of the king's palace to suggest that the king hang Mordecai on the gallows that he had prepared for him.** *(Providence number three.* Unmistakably God is at work.) **The king's servants said to him, 'Haman is there standing in the court.' And the king said, 'Let him come in.' So Haman came in, and the king asked him, 'What shall be done for the man whom the king delights to honor?' Now Haman thought in his heart, 'Whom would the king delight to honor more than me?'** Behold the twisted thinking of a vain man! **And Haman answered the king, 'For the man whom the king delights to honor, let a royal robe be brought which the king has worn, and a horse on which the king has ridden, which has a royal crest placed on its head. Then let this robe and horse be delivered to the hand of one of the king's most noble princes, that he may array the man whom the king**

114

delights to honor. Then parade him on horseback through the city square, and proclaim before him, 'Thus shall it be done to the man whom the king delights to honor.' "

"Then the king said to Haman, 'Hurry, take the robe and the horse, as you have suggested, and do so for Mordecai the Jew who sits within the king's gate! Leave nothing undone of all that you have spoken.' " Then a horrified Haman does everything exactly as he had just said. But the king had no idea how Haman felt about Mordecai. Rushing home afterwards, he plans a "WOE IS ME" party, but gets cut short by the king's eunuchs hastening him to the second Esther banquet.

In chapter seven, Esther's dinner commences, with the king and Haman attending. The king eagerly awaits hearing Esther's request. He repeats his willingness to give her half his kingdom, which was the mighty Medo-Persian Empire. This is like the time King Herod promised to give the daughter of Herodias up to half his kingdom for such a nice dance. I wouldn't be surprised to find out both kings were drinking at the time. Imagine Ahasuerus's surprise when Esther asks only for her life and the lives of her people. This must have jolted him into being sober.

Esther explains, **"For we have been sold, my people and I, to be killed and to be annihilated. Had we been sold to be male and female slaves, I would have held my tongue, although the enemy could never compensate the king's loss."** (7:4) She was saying that the death of the Jewish people would be a terrible loss to the king. No amount of money could pay for that loss. The king is now indignant. **"Who is he, and where is he, who would dare presume in his heart to do such a thing?"** (Mainly to kill his wife.)

115

She wisely declines to mention that the king had rashly given Haman permission for the executions. No doubt his temper is rising and the tone of his voice changes, almost matching the passion in Esther's voice and hardened expression.

The next words spoken were like a physical blow to Haman's heart. With fiery eyes and a finger knifing its aim at Haman's face, Esther unleashes her angry words, **"The adversary and enemy is this wicked Haman!"** It's a wonder he didn't die of heart failure on the spot. Now don't forget: Haman was rushed to the banquet in a shaken condition after being given a good scare from his wife and friends. They had said to him, **"If Mordecai, before you have begun to fall, is of Jewish descent, you will not prevail against him but will surely fall before him."** So Haman is made fearful before he even arrives at the banquet. *Providence number four.* If those words were a warning from God to Haman, it would be a very remarkable display of the greatness of His grace. If Haman had repented at that time of the pride, hatred and murder in his heart, God would have surely forgiven him. He would much rather make us a trophy of His grace than a testimony of His judgment.

V. 7 **"Then the king arose in his wrath from the banquet of wine and went into the palace garden."** This is a good move to help a man regain his composure when something really angers him. Sometimes anger is righteous, but venting it properly requires self-control. It usually works nicely if we give it a few minutes before responding.

Haman took this opportunity to plea bargain with Esther. Apparently, he got nowhere. He kneels down and leans toward her pleading his case. At the worst

116

possible moment, the king walks back inside and sees Haman leaning over his wife. *Providence number five.* Although it was not what the king thought it was, it sure looked like it. **"The king said, 'Will he also assault the queen while I am in the house?' As the word left the king's mouth, they covered Haman's face. Now Harbonah, one of the king's eunuchs, said to the king, 'Look! The gallows, 50 cubits high, which Haman made for Mordecai, who spoke good on the king's behalf, is standing at the house of Haman.' Then the king said, 'Hang him on it.' "** *Providence number six:* Just the right guy was standing by observing all this. Interestingly, Harbonah knew about the gallows, who had built it and who it was intended for. That was probably not public information, but he knew it and divulged it at a very opportune time. Haman was hanged immediately on his own gallows. **"He made a pit and dug it out, and has fallen into the ditch which he made."** (Psalm 7:15) God knows how to execute justice and there is no escaping Him. And His judgments, as well as his rewards, are usually remarkably fitting. The anguish on Haman's face must have closely matched the expressions on the faces of thousands of Jews when their death warrant was read to them. **"There was great mourning among the Jews, with fasting, weeping and wailing."** I couldn't help but notice that Haman died while fasting. Remember he was hurried out of his house after walking Mordecai's horse around the square, and likely missed breakfast. Then while he was at Esther's "banquet of wine", that is, before dinner was served, he is accused and arrested. Fitting enough, since all those terrified Jews fasted and prayed. When God judges, nothing is overlooked.

Providence/judgement number seven: the execution of Haman. This is very much like the seven seal judgments, most of which result in deaths. For the wages of sin is death. And Haman's death was a cursed death, since **"cursed is everyone who hangs on a tree"**. The very type of death Haman had planned for Mordecai. But in a sense, wicked Haman was justly substituted for righteous Mordecai. On another "tree", another One substituted His life to pay for the sins of all mankind, in this case, the Just dying for the unjust, that He might bring us to God. In both cases, the death of the substitute brought great joy to the world, especially to believers. The parallels continue:

- Jesus carried his cross; Haman built his. (the gallows).
- Both died on a "tree", a cursed death. Jesus bore the curse for us; Haman bore it for himself.
- The last meal of both men was the night before.
- Jesus was wrongly accused, and sentenced to death immediately; Haman was rightly accused and sentenced to death immediately.
- Jesus was the most righteous man on the face of the earth; Haman was arguably the most wicked.
- Jesus' death resulted in the salvation of many; Haman's death was the first step toward the saving of many lives.
- Haman, a very wealthy man, gave a great sum of money to subsidize the death of many; Jesus, who made himself poor for our sakes, shed his own priceless blood to save the lives of many.
- Haman had a great hatred and a driving desire to kill many; the driving force in Jesus was his love for the world and a desire to save the lives of many.

The Old Testament is rich with many types of Christ, but this one is an opposite type of Christ.

In 8:17 we read of one of the outcomes of Esther and Mordecai's reversal decree, **"And in every province and city, wherever the king's command and decree came ... many of the people of the land became Jews, because fear of the Jews fell upon them."** The reversal decree gave Jews the right to execute their enemies who had been planning to kill them. I can't help but imagine what might have happened if Mordecai and Esther had thought about their reversal decree. Suppose Esther had said to Mordecai, "Don't get me wrong, I'm glad we got rid of Haman. He was a murderous villain. But I don't feel right about killing thousands of others just because they don't like our people. What's everybody else going to think of us?" Mordecai may have replied, "They're probably going to hate us even more." Suppose they decided to send out a third decree which would dissolve the second decree, so that the Jews cancel their plans to execute their enemies. This would give a huge relief to their enemies after giving them a bad scare. What kind of effect would that have had on all the provinces? The Jews in effect, would be forgiving their enemies. Didn't Jesus teach us, **"But I say to you, love your enemies, bless those who curse you, do good to those who hate you, and pray for those who despitefully use you and persecute you."** (Matthew 5:44) Who knows whether that might have resulted in many more souls being turned to God. For the kindness of God leads to repentance. Maybe they would have changed the name of their new holiday from the Feast of Purim to the Feast of Forgiveness.

Meanwhile, in chapter 8, king Ahasuerus gives Mordecai his signet ring, an emblem of great authority.

119

Mordecai steps into this leadership role and thrives, growing toward greatness in leaps and bounds. In the last verse of the book of Esther, we see that **"Mordecai the Jew was second to king Ahasuerus."** This is like Joseph rising to power instantaneously and came to be second in command to Pharaoh. Or Daniel, who became the top minister under the emperors of two different empires. All Jews. Believers.

Mordecai didn't suddenly become great, he was greatness waiting to happen. It is our duty to be faithful in the little things and to wait on God to ripen the opportunity. It begins with growing deep, inner character and being conformed to Godly qualities, not just growing in fame and popularity or placing well in the polls. **"And do not be conformed to this world, but be transformed by the renewing of your mind, that you may prove what is that good and acceptable and perfect will of God."** (Romans 12:2)

This is somewhat paradoxical. For a man who pursues greatness is probably most unfit for it. Greatness is a man finding great usefulness in life. He is very helpful and beneficial to others, not just well known. Progress toward greatness begins when a man "crucifies" his selfish desires for power, riches or fame. The very things normally associated with greatness.

We did things a little differently with "MORDECAI" since we had two other men of interest in this story in Ahasuerus and Haman. I hope you got some valuable lessons from their lives as well as from Mordecai's. It's also my hope that if anybody has a genocide planned, that they would reconsider.

DAVID

It was a time of disillusionment. Samuel had been an ideal judge and an excellent leader for all Israel. But Samuel grew old and the people got tired of him. So Samuel set up his two sons as judges in his place. But they did poorly, taking bribes and perverting justice. It's hard to say what promotes crime more: poor law enforcement or a crooked or ineffective judicial system. Well now the people are further disillusioned with crooked judges. So the people said to Samuel, "Hey Samuel. Look, we really appreciate the fine job you've done for us over the years, but your sons just aren't cutting it." Or words to that effect. "Do you think you could get us a king? The judge thing just isn't working out. We would love to have a king. You know, kings always dress nice and wear lots of jewelry. It would be nice to have some kind of good looking, celebrity figure we could admire. As long as he's big on defense and easy on taxes, we'll all be fine with it." So God leads Samuel to "choice and handsome" Saul and he is presented to the people. So the people looked him over for a couple of minutes and instantly voted him king – before he said a single word, or presented his platform. Hey as long as he looks good, vote him in. Just like American politics.

It wasn't long before Saul's poor character began to show. Being king soon made him proud and disagreeable. He eventually degraded into a mean, bossy tyrant. Almost like getting married. The people again got disenchanted. In I Samuel 15:35, we read **"And the Lord regretted that He had made Saul king over Israel."** Even God decided it was time to remove the incumbent. Commonly a good idea. So Samuel is sent back to the drawing board to find another king. They should have had term limits. God, who searches the hearts of men, "finds" the next king. Now God didn't discover Saul and then later find that he wouldn't work out. He knew far in advance what Saul would become. But we make rash choices and later find out it was a mistake. Maybe God chose Saul to show Israel how good they had it when Samuel was judge and God was king. God's choice of Saul also presents a dull backdrop against which the next king would be brightly displayed. God giving the people Saul as king was also somewhat of a judgment on the poor values of the people for giving acclamation for Saul to become king. They begged and begged for a king. Finally God "gave them their request, but sent leanness into their souls." Let us pray that God won't give us the president that we deserve.

THE ANNOINTING OF DAVID

In I Samuel 16:1, we see that God honors His prophets above kings. Maybe we should. He again sends Samuel to appoint and anoint the next king of Israel. **"Now the Lord said to Samuel, 'How long will you mourn for Saul, seeing I have rejected him from reigning over Israel? Fill your horn with oil, and go; I am sending you to Jesse the Bethlehemite. For I have provided Myself a king among his sons.' "** I get the impression from the words **"I have provided Myself"** that God has already been at work shaping David to become a king.

Verse 2 reveals just how bad Saul had become. Power usually corrupts. **"And Samuel said, 'How can I go? If Saul hears it, he will kill me.'"**

Verse 4 shows why Samuel was such a successful prophet. **"So Samuel did what the Lord said."** When he arrived at Bethlehem, we see that Samuel was still highly respected as a prophet. **"And the elders of the town trembled at his coming, and said, 'Do you come peaceably?' And he said, 'Peaceably; I have come to sacrifice to the Lord. Sanctify yourselves, and come with me to the sacrifice.'"** So they have a big dinner and invite Jesse and all his sons. When they arrive, Samuel observes all the sons, wondering which one would be the king. He sees tall, well-built Eliab and figures that's the guy. The last king he anointed was tall and well-built. But the Lord said to Samuel, **"Do not look at his appearance or at his physical stature, because I have refused him. For the Lord does not see as man sees; for man looks at the outward appearance, but the Lord looks at the heart."** Sometimes there is great treasure hidden beneath an unlikely looking outward appearance. One by one seven of Jesse's sons pass by Samuel, but the Lord chose none of them. Finally the youngest son is called in, who was out tending sheep. When David comes in, the Lord affirms to Samuel, **"Arise, anoint him; for this is the one."** David is described as **"ruddy, with bright eyes, and good-looking."** Verse 13 states **that "Samuel took the horn of oil and anointed him in the midst of his brothers; and the Spirit of the Lord came upon David from that day forward."** But he didn't become king for another

15 years. Our presidents elect have to wait only three months.

There were a number of other residents of Bethlehem at the dinner with Jesse's family observing David's anointing. It is impressive that they kept the matter a secret all those years. If Saul would have killed Samuel for anointing David king, he would surely have put to death David, all his family and everyone at the dinner. Remember, on Doeg's word, Saul slaughtered 85 innocent priests and their entire home town for giving David some provisions. But all the men at that dinner kept the matter quiet – for 15 years.

In verse 14 we read that the Spirit of the Lord departed from Saul as much as the Spirit came upon David. Let us beware that we do not quench the same Holy Spirit who comes upon us as Who came upon David. How is the Spirit quenched? Well it happened to Saul as a result of his disobedience to God and Samuel. Maybe because of his abuse of the power of his office. Saul sought to honor himself rather than God and God's man. Maybe all of these. Even though Saul gave the appearance of repentance, he never did change his ways. In I Samuel 15:24, **"Saul said to Samuel, 'I have sinned, for I have transgressed against the commandment of the Lord...because I feared the people and obeyed their voice."** Thus the fear of man brings a snare. Notice Saul's confession consisted mostly of blaming others. I suspect he really didn't fear the people so much as wanting to keep all the good cattle. As Samuel observed, **"What then is this bleating of the sheep in my ears?"** So what it came down to is Saul chose worldly possessions over the presence of God in his life. We are sometimes presented with the same choice.

124

When the Spirit of the Lord departed from Saul, **"a distressing spirit from the Lord troubled him."** You may have seen this before: someone gets in a sour mood when they themselves did something wrong.

I've seen it too – in the mirror. But for Saul this was actually a mercy of God. If a man's conscience is troubling him, it is God moving him to repent. It is a terrible darkness when a man's conscience ceases to trouble him. Such is the case when God gives a man over to a reprobate mind. It is a cursed state when God's Spirit no longer strives with a man. It is then that all restraint and all hope is gone. The Holy Spirit continued to strive with Saul to the end, though it appears that it was to no avail.

THE RISE OF DAVID

It was getting to where Saul was depressed nearly all the time. It's interesting that Saul's servants recognized the problem even when Saul did not. This is usually the case. Saul was fixated on blaming Samuel for being unreasonable or blaming the others for keeping the forbidden cattle. If he had only done some soul-searching and admitted his own fault in the matter, it would surely have given him relief from his depression. But he had made only a half-hearted effort at repenting. He was just too proud to admit fault. So he addresses his depression in the usual way, fix the symptoms rather than the cause.

In I Samuel 16:16, it was his servants who came up with a solution, **"Let our master now command your servants...to seek out a man who is a skillful player on the harp. And it shall be that he will play it with** his hand when the distressing spirit from God is upon you, and you shall be well." Naturally Saul likes the idea of people doing something nice for him. Yet it usually works better for the depressed soul to do something nice for others. "And if you give yourself to the hungry, and satisfy the desire of the afflicted, then your light will rise in darkness, and your gloom will become like midday." (Isaiah 58:10 NASB)

V. 17 "So Saul said to his servants, 'Provide me now with a man who can play well, and bring him to me.' Then one of his servants answered and said, 'Look, I have seen a son of Jesse the Bethlehemite, who is skillful in playing, a mighty man of valor, a man of war, prudent in speech, and a handsome person; and the Lord is with him.' " Quite a resume. Of course we know that the closest any man comes to perfection is on his resume. Can you imagine how a recruitment letter to Jesse might have read? "The army needs another one of your sons. We understand that David's a good harp player."

Saul contacts Jesse asking him to send his son, David. Jesse being the good citizen he was, gives good measure back to his government. He sends with David a donkey loaded with bread and wine along with a tender young goat. It is not clear whether this was a gift to the king or payment for all the food he knew his teenage son would be eating.

"So David came and stood before him. And he (Saul) loved him greatly, and he became his armorbearer." (v. 21) Apparently the job interview went well and David is hired. How often it is that young believers find great favor with others. Consider:

- Esther being given into the care of Hegai, the custodian of the women in Ahasueras' palace,

126

"Now the young woman pleased him, and she obtained his favor." Not long after, she obtains favor with King Ahasueras, who **"loved her more than all the other women, and she obtained grace and favor in his sight."** (Esther 2:9 and 17)

- **"Now God had brought Daniel into the favor and goodwill of the chief of the eunuchs."** (Daniel 1:9)
- Joseph in the house of Potiphar, **"So Joseph found favor in his sight and served him."** (Genesis 39:4)
- Mary's favor with God was announced by Gabriel, **"Rejoice, highly favored one, the Lord is with you; blessed are you among women."** (Luke 1:28)

It's a pretty good chance that all four of these were teenagers. And God gave each of these favor with others because they already had faith in Him.

Chapter 16 concludes with David serving honorably before the king. **"And so it was, whenever the spirit from God was upon Saul, that David would take a harp and play it with his hand. Then Saul would become refreshed and well, and the distressing spirit would depart from him."**

DAVID AND GOLIATH

"Now the Philistines gathered their armies together to battle, and were gathered at Sochoh, which belongs to Judah." (I Samuel 17:1) They gathered their armies to attack Israel to retaliate against them for Jonathan's virtually single-handed attack. (See I Samuel 14)

However, the Philistines had been raiding Israel and stealing their crops and livestock for years, unopposed. Now the war-mongering Philistines are again attacking the Israelites, who are mostly farmers and shepherds. The two armies face off against each other in the Valley of Elah. Then an interesting thing happens: **"And a champion went out from the camp of the Philistines, named Goliath, from Gath, whose height was six cubits and a span."** This would make him somewhere around 9 ft. tall, a few inches taller than the tallest man on record. His armor weighed about 150 pounds. The poor guy probably had a hard time getting around. He had also been trained all his life to be a fighter. With all this going for him, he was not brave at all. For 40 days, he presented himself before the armies of Israel, challenging them to provide a man to fight with him. Of course he knew that there was nobody near his size. It was the equivalent of a man challenging any kid in the grade school to fight with him. His challenge was not even gentlemanly. He was defiant and insulting. **"I defy the armies of Israel this day."** His intimidating words had the desired effect, **"All the men of Israel, when they saw the man, fled from him and were dreadfully afraid."** (I Samuel 17:24) The deal was that if someone would fight with Goliath, whichever man lost, his country would agree to serve the winner's country. But when the Philistines lost, they did not keep to the terms of the agreement. Bully's are usually sore losers.

It was a long day for David. He rose early in the morning and like Joseph, he obeyed his father's instructions to go see how his brothers were doing. and to deliver another shipment of food to the men on the front lines. Even though David was a shepherd, he had a keen interest in the war and jumped at the opportunity to see the battle. While he was there, he saw the giant of Gath and heard his words. David was indignant that Goliath **"should defy the armies of the living God."** It was mentioned that the men of Israel's army were afraid, but it is not mentioned that David feared at any time. David's oldest brother hears David asking about Goliath's challenge and scolds him. **"Why did you come down here? ... I know your pride and the insolence of your heart, for you have come down to see the battle."** That had to be very deflating for David. He leaves Eliab and asks others about what reward there would be for the man who kills the giant. King Saul hears about David and calls for him. We have the conversation starting in verse 32. **"Then David said to Saul, "Let no man's heart fail because of him; your servant will go and fight with this Philistine."**

And Saul said to David, "You are not able to go against this Philistine to fight with him; for you are a youth, and he a man of war from his youth."

But David said to Saul, "Your servant used to keep his father's sheep, and when a lion or a bear came and took a lamb out of the flock, I went out after it and struck it, and delivered the lamb from its mouth; and when it arose against me, I caught it by its beard, and struck and killed it. Your servant has killed both lion and bear; and this uncircumcised Philistine will be like one of them, seeing he has defied the armies of the living God." Moreover David said, "The LORD, who delivered me from the paw of the lion and from the paw of the bear, He will deliver me from the hand of this Philistine."
And Saul said to David, "Go, and the LORD be with you!"

At first it may appear that David is being a little boastful, but when he gives such details of killing the lion and bear, it is more convincing that he actually did this. He emphatically repeats it: **"Your servant has killed both lion and bear."** Rather than boasting, it looks more like he's trying to persuade Saul to let him go after Goliath. I get the sense that he's not after any glory; rather he's trying to get rid of the loudmouth. He just can't stand by idly while God and Israel are being insulted. He assures Saul that God will be with him. David was already sure of it.

In verse 38, Saul very generously offers to let David use his own armor for the fight. Maybe Saul felt guilty that this teenager is going against Goliath instead of himself. After all, Saul was head and shoulders taller than anyone else in Israel. So David politely tries on the armor, even though it was probably about 5 sizes too big. He declined, explaining that he couldn't even walk with them.

In verse 40, David takes the weapons he was accustomed to, his shepherd's staff and his sling. Let every Christian fight the good fight using whatever comes to his hand. Let him not be intimidated at the size of the problem or the taunting of the adversary. Let your tools and weapons be what you know or do best. Let your confidence not be in your ability, but in the Lord of hosts. Let your goal be to serve others to the glory of God and not yourself. Has God gifted you with music? Or legal counseling? Do you have lawn care skills and equipment? Do you have home repair experience? Maybe you have computer problem solving skills. (If you do, please send me your phone number.) Do what you do best to the glory of God and for winning of souls. If someone cannot repay you, or if you decline payment, remember that **"you shall be repaid at the resurrection of the just."** And you can collect interest on it in the meantime.

As David approached Goliath, seemingly without fear, Goliath sees this young teenager, apparently unarmed and insults him. He curses David by his own gods, and declares that he will give David's carcass to the wild animals. Goliath is accustomed to intimidating men with his words. For the past 40 days, he has terrorized the armies of Israel with his words. They **"fled from him and were dreadfully afraid."** But David does not even flinch. It's not that David was fearless, he just completely trusts in God. If we may judge a man by the words of his mouth, we would have to conclude that Goliath was not very polite. But listen to these immortal words of David's response, **"You come to me with a sword, with a spear, and with a javelin. But I come to you in the name of the Lord of hosts, the God of the armies of Israel, whom you have defied. This day the Lord will deliver you into my hand, and I will strike you and take your head from you. And this day I will give the carcasses of the camp of the Philistines to the birds of the air and the wild beasts of the earth, that all the earth may know that there is a God in Israel. Then all this assembly shall know that the Lord does not save with sword and spear; for the battle is the Lord's and He will give you into our hands."** David wins this opening skirmish of words. He acts in the Lord's name and for a just cause – the defense of a righteous nation. In advance, David gives God credit for the victory, and wishes for God to be glorified. How I wish that every American soldier and sailor would advance into the battle with like divine assurance:

- That he is a believer and comes in the name of the Lord,
- That he is under God's protection,
- That the enemy will be delivered into his hands,
- That the battle is the Lord's,
- That God would be glorified.

May God make us worthy of these words of our own national anthem:

"Blest with victory and peace, may the heaven rescued land
Praise the power that hath made and preserved us a nation!
Then conquer we must, when our cause it is just,
And this be our motto - "In God is our trust."

As Goliath advanced toward David, we see that David ran forward to meet the enemy. The rest of Israel's army ran in retreat. Joan of Arc was 17 (about the same age as David when he killed Goliath) when she led 3,000 French knights in battle. On one occasion, she told a military general: "I will lead the way over the wall." The general replied, "Not a man will follow you." Joan replied, "I won't be looking back."
Another famous saying by Joan of Arc nicely suits David in this incident,

"Hope in God. If you have good hope and faith in Him, You shall be delivered from your enemies."

In I Samuel 17:49, we read, **"Then David put his hand in the bag and took out a stone; and he slung and struck the Philistine in his forehead, so that the stone sank into his forehead, and he fell on his face**

to the earth." When David cuts off his head, it was the Philistines' turn to run.

It was an exceptional shot since Goliath wore a helmet, and a coat of mail, his stone had to hit a very small target at his forehead. Whether God guided the rock or not, we're not told. But it was not a lucky shot. David had likely practiced with his sling until he was expert. Remember that the tribe of Benjamin had an elite group of 700 soldiers **"who could sling a stone at a hair's breadth and not miss."** They were as accurate as a sniper with a rifle. David would have been as good as them. Not only did David hit his "bull's eye", he slung it so hard that it sank into Goliath's very hard head. His stone would have been about half the size of a 50 caliber bullet and traveling at approximately 150 mph. If we are going to fight God's battles, let us sharpen our skills and be strong in the Lord.

David's courage and victory inspired others. Goliath had 4 other giant brothers as nasty as he was. There was Ishbibenob, Saph, Lahmi and another. All four fought against Israel and all four were defeated in one on one combat: one by Abishai, a cousin of David; one by a nephew of David; another by a guy from David's home town; and the fourth by another Israelite. **"The people who know their God shall be strong, and carry out great exploits."** Now it's your turn.

David became exceptionally strong and skilled in warfare when he joined the military. But the most remarkable thing about him is that **"the Lord preserved David wherever he went."** (I Chronicles 18:6) This is because David completely trusted God. He did not rely on his own remarkable skills. It could be said that he was also very courageous. But David's courage was inseparably intertwined with his faith in God. It was

David who wrote **"Whenever I am afraid, I will trust in You."** When we are afraid, we tend to either fixate on the threat or trust in our tennis shoes. When a toddler is afraid, he runs for Daddy. That's a better plan. When Peter began to sink in the waves, he got it right when cried out to Jesus, **"Lord, save me!"** This is the shortest prayer in the Bible. But then, he was a little pressed for time.

DAVID'S POPULARITY

King Saul is much impressed with David. Shortly after his defeat of Goliath, Saul sets David over some of the men of war. **"So David went out wherever Saul sent him, and (he) behaved wisely."** He quickly became admired by all the people. When the army of Israel returned from one of their victories, the women danced and sang **"Saul has slain his thousands, and David his ten thousands."** Sadly, Saul took this as a personal affront and became jealous of David. It's too bad Saul didn't take a fatherly pride in young David and smiled at all the attention he was getting. From that day on, Saul became incurably jealous of David and eyed him suspiciously. Consider who was hurt by Saul's bad attitude. It sure wasn't David, since he wasn't even aware of it. It was probably depressing to the men who had to be around Saul, but it surely hurt Saul more than anyone else. Jealousy isn't worth the trouble.

David was also well loved by Saul's son, Jonathan. They became best friends. This was one of those rare cases where someone loved their neighbor as themselves. Jonathan, a well-to-do son of King Saul gave this poor shepherd boy his own robe, his armor, sword, bow and belt. How much better David could now do, being well-equipped with good weapons. Let us all be on the lookout for men and women of high potential who could do so well in life if they could only get an education, or technical training in their area of specialty. One father of a 14 year old girl who loved to run and wanted to run the marathon one day, decided he would help her achieve her goal, whatever it takes. Since it was unsafe for her to go on long distance training runs by herself, he decided he would escort her whenever she went running. So he drove his car alongside of her hour after hour, day after day. The training paid off and one day she competed in a marathon and finished the entire 26 miles, without stopping. Did I mention that the father was a paraplegic?

King Saul's daughter, Michal, also was in love with David. (Along with probably a few hundred other young Israelite girls.) What a perfect match David would have been for the royal family: The son was his best friend, the daughter was in love with him, and he was one of Saul's top leaders in his army. It's too bad Saul was such a grouch.

The more popular David became, the more resentful Saul was. One day while Saul was having one of his bouts of depression, David was playing his harp to soothe him. Saul happened to be holding his spear, and the notion hit to pin David to the wall with it. But David escaped. Now Saul was afraid of David and stationed him somewhere else. But David continued to do wisely and became a very successful leader of a thousand man regiment. This made Saul even more afraid of him. Eventually we read, **"that David behaved more** wisely than all the servants of Saul, so that his name became highly esteemed." (I Samuel 18:30)

Eventually, Saul finds out that his daughter, Michal, is in love with David. So he plans to use Michal to be a snare to David. So he sends a servant to David and announces that "the king has delight in you, and all his servants love you. Now therefore become the king's son in law. ...and David said, 'Does it seem to you a light thing to be a king's son in law, seeing that I am poor and lightly esteemed?' " (I Samuel 18:22,23) This was a very humble reply. At the same time, it also showed respect toward Saul. Also implied is that David did not hold it against Saul when he tried to kill him earlier. What exceptional character for David! This was a great opportunity for Saul to make peace with David. Unfortunately, Saul sets a trap for David instead. He sends word to David that he will not require of David the customary dowry for the bride (since David had no money). He said he would accept one hundred foreskins of the Philistines instead, hoping that he would get killed. David and his men deliver two hundred instead.

DAVID'S WISDOM

Solomon is usually the first that comes to mind when we think of wise men in Israel. But David's wisdom is also highly praised in the scriptures. In I Samuel 18:15, it is written that "David behaved wisely in all his ways and the Lord was with him." Any man who has the Lord with him can hardly miss doing wisely. In verse 30, we read "that David behaved more wisely than all the servants of Saul, so that his name became highly esteemed." It seems that David's wisdom

136

related mostly to his skills in warfare. No doubt God was guiding his thoughts, his plans and his military strategies. Later God told him, **"I have been with you wherever you have gone, and have cut off all your enemies from before you."**

David's wisdom consisted largely of hearing from God and acting accordingly. This is nicely illustrated in the campaign of the Valley of Rephaim. (II Samuel 5:19-25) **"The Philistines also went and deployed themselves in the Valley of Rephaim.**

"So David inquired of the Lord, saying, 'Shall I go up against the Philistines? Will You deliver them into my hand?' And the Lord said to David, 'Go up, for I will doubtless deliver the Philistines into your hand.'

"So David went to Baal Perazim, and David defeated them there; and he said, 'The Lord has broken through my enemies before me, like a breakthrough of water.'

"And they left their images there, and David and his men carried them away.

"Then the Philistines went up once again and deployed themselves in the Valley of Rephaim.

"Therefore David inquired of the Lord, and He said, 'You shall not go up; circle around behind them, and come upon them in front of the mulberry trees.

"And it shall be when you hear the sound of marching in the tops of the mulberry trees, then you shall advance quickly. For then the Lord will go out before you to strike the camp of the Philistines.'

"And David did so, as the Lord commanded ; and he drove back the Philistines from Geba as far as Geber." It was God's directions, but it made David look wise.

In a similar incident, Joshua and his men received explicit directions from God in defeating and sacking

Jericho, a major Canaanite city. They obeyed God and had a flawless victory. When considering the next city in their conquests, Ai, Joshua did not seek the Lord's counsel. It was such a small city, Joshua and the people acted in their own wisdom and sent just a small force to go capture Ai. Nobody prayed about it. Maybe they figured, now that they have the hang of it, there's no need to pray every time. The result was that Joshua suffered his only defeat in five years and lost thirty-six good soldiers. Then they prayed and made their peace with God. The next morning, following God's instructions, they executed a brilliant strategy and easily captured Ai. **"In all your ways, acknowledge Him and He will direct your paths."**

DAVID'S HUMILITY

Normally humility and greatness are mutually exclusive. When a humble man becomes successful, he usually loses some of his humility. Or if a man isn't doing so great, it can help with his humility. Blessed in the man who can survive success without losing the grace of humility. What a pleasure it is to be in the company of a man of great success without hearing about it constantly! David could teach a class on the subject.

In I Chronicles 17, in about his eighth year as king, David talks with Nathan the prophet about wanting to build a house for the Lord.

Apparently God was deeply touched that David wanted to build a house for the Him. David's friend, Hiram, king of Tyre, had just built David a fine house of cedar. Meanwhile, David had erected a new tabernacle for the

138

Lord and the ark, close to his own house in the city of David, in Jerusalem. But it disturbed David that he lived in such a nice house, while the Lord "lived" under tent curtains.

Then the word of the Lord came to Nathan, in which God declares, **"I took you from…following the sheep, to be ruler over My people Israel. And I have been with you wherever you have gone, and have cut off all your enemies from before you, and have made you a name like the name of the great men who are on the earth…Also I will subdue all your enemies. Furthermore I tell you that the Lord will build you a house…that I will set up your seed after you…and I will establish his kingdom. He shall build Me a house, and I will establish his throne forever."** (I Chronicles 17:7,8,10- 12)

David is so overwhelmed at all these promises of God, that he **"went in and sat before the Lord; and he said, "Who am I, O Lord God? And what is my house, that You have brought me this far? And (You) have regarded me according to the rank of a man of high degree, O Lord God."** (v.16,17) This is a rare expression of deep humility. It is like when Peter fell down at Jesus' knees and said, **"Depart from me, for I am a sinful man, O Lord."** Most men are so much in the habit of exalting themselves, that even in their praying, they are boasting. **"God I thank you that I am not like other men – extortioners, unjust, adulterers, or even as this tax collector. I fast twice a week; I give tithes of all that I possess."**
We notice that this parable begins with, **"The Pharisee stood and prayed thus with himself."** It gives the impression that he was praying more to himself, rather than to God.

139

David seems to have forgotten all the great works he had done for the Lord's sake. From defending God's honor against Goliath, to risking his life in defending Israel against the Philistines, in refusing to avenge himself when Saul tried to kill him. Too many of us rehearse over and over our good deeds and victories. It would be better for our humility to remember our sins and failures instead. **"God resists the proud, but gives grace to the humble."** God's heart greatly warms toward David in this interchange. If David was not a man after God's heart before this conversation, he certainly would be after.

David never boasted or sought self-promotion. After David refused to kill Saul when he had the chance, even Saul said, **"I know indeed that you shall surely be king, and that the kingdom of Israel shall be established in your hand."** (I Samuel 24:20)

DAVID'S RIGHTEOUSNESS

A sterling example of David's righteousness is found in I Samuel 24. David and his men are fleeing for their lives from Saul. They had to really rough it, hiding in woods and caves. One day, while Saul and the army of Israel were hunting David, he happens to go rest in a cave where David is hiding. But David sneaks up on Saul and cuts off a corner of Saul's robe, amazingly, without Saul realizing it. David's men urge him to kill Saul while the golden opportunity presents itself. David declines, saying he would not stretch out his hand against the Lord's anointed. In spite of Saul trying to kill him twice, David does not characterize him as his enemy. David has the principle imbedded in him which Jesus would someday give us, **"But I say unto you, love your enemies, bless those who curse you, do good to those who hate you, and pray for those who spitefully use you and persecute you."** In verse 5, David even feels guilty about cutting off the corner of Saul's robe. Blessed is the man whose conscience won't let him get away with a thing.

In another incident, in chapter 25, David is barely kept from killing wicked "Nabal, the churl", as the King James version puts it. David and his men had done a considerable kindness to this wealthy man. (Not to mention having defended the people of Israel for several years, without pay.) Messengers were sent to Nabal's ranch, where they made a humble request for food. They were harshly rebuffed and insulted. David rounded up his troops and set out to go execute Nabal and all his males. This would have been acting like Saul. (Remember Saul had slaughtered 85 priests and everyone in the priest's city of Nob because one of them gave David some bread when he was hungry.)

So David and 400 armed and angry soldiers marched toward Nabal's ranch, intending to slaughter them. But an attractive lady stops them in their tracks and turns them around. Her name was Abigail, Nabal's wife. With excellent wisdom and tact, she persuades David not to go through with something he would regret for the rest of his life, like avenging himself. Abigail is certainly the heroine of this story, but it is to David's credit that he accepted the advice of good woman. A lot of us need to do likewise. Ten days later, Nabal died of a heart disorder. **"Beloved, never avenge yourselves, but leave it to the wrath of God, for it is written, 'Vengeance is mine, I will repay, says the Lord.' "** (ESV)

THE ZIKLAG INCIDENT

I Samuel 30:1-6

1. Now it happened, when David and his men came to Ziklag, on the third day, that the Amalekites had invaded the South and Ziklag, attacked Ziklag and burned it with fire,
2. And had taken captive the women and those who were there, from small to great; they did not kill anyone, but carried them away and went their way.
3. So David and his men came to the city, and there it was, burned with fire; and their wives, their sons, and their daughters had been taken captive.
4. Then David and the people who were with him lifted up their voices and wept, until they had no more power to weep.
5. And David's two wives, Ahinoam the Jezreelitess, and Abigail the widow of Nabal the Carmelite, had been taken captive.
6. Now David was greatly distressed, for the people spoke of stoning him, because the soul of all the people was grieved, every man for his sons and his daughters. But David strengthened himself in the LORD his God.

Ziklag was a town near the border of Israel and the land of the Philistines. David and his 600 men had moved there with their families to get away from Saul. For sixteen months, they had a happy, prosperous time, finally settling into a normal home life with their families. All the men had been gone for three days and came back to this terrible disaster.

David's life had been a roller coaster of ups and downs. Things had started off well for him. Samuel, the great prophet had anointed him king. (To become king someday.) There was the defeat of Goliath; his widespread fame and popularity; he had a good job and marriage; he had a promising future. But then things started taking a bad turn: instead of a good family, his wife was taken back by the king; instead of a good job, his boss tries to kill him; he goes from being popular to being an outcast; he goes from the kingdom to the cave; instead of a wealthy life, he comes to poverty and is a fugitive. Through all this ordeal, David never ceases to serve God and his country. He continues fighting the Philistine enemies. He never gives up his integrity. But fifteen years after Samuel anoints him to become king, the possibility seems as remote as ever. If that's not bad enough, the guy who is king is doing a poor job. The country is suffering from his poor leadership. The king was conceited; he had a nasty temper; he got in bad trouble with Samuel, twice he tried to kill David; he tampered with the occult and even God has rejected him. Other than that, he was fine.

David has been put through the meat grinder. And now, after so many years of faithful service and hard times, - Ziklag has burned! David has lost everything and his family is gone. His men hold David responsible and are about to stone him. When things could hardly get worse, when David was in desperate straits, notice what he does in the last words of the text, **"But David strengthened himself in the LORD his God."** When other men may get drunk, or rage against God, David says in effect, "At least I have you, God."

In verse 8, David **"inquired of the Lord"** before he decided on a course of action. I believe this entire incident is recorded in scripture to move us, the future readers, to do exactly what verse 8 says in our own time of crisis. To inquire of the Lord before we do anything else. **"For whatever things were written before were written for our learning, that we through the patience and comfort of the Scriptures might have hope."** (Romans 15:4) David suffered through this tragedy so that he might learn and so that we might learn.

Notice further in verse 8 that David had an idea of what he might do before he called on the Lord, "David inquired of the Lord, saying, **"Shall I pursue this troop? Shall I overtake them?"** But he would not act until he had word from the Lord. It was his understanding that he should pursue after them, but he trusted in the Lord with all his heart and leaned not unto his own understanding. In all his ways, he acknowledged God, that He would direct his paths. And God did. So David and his men pursued the invaders and ended up rescuing all their families and possessions. Not one person or item was missing. While they were pursuing, David's men by chance, came upon a sick man on the verge of dying. They revived the fellow with food and drink. Then the man gave intelligence where the invaders could be found.

This helped David catch them without delay. Maybe God directed their path to come across the sick man because David had inquired of the Lord. Who knows?

David's fortunes seem to be turning. He has his two wives back. He has recovered all his possessions and then some. He regains the support of his closest friends. (Like when Job's fortunes were reversed.)

Meanwhile on the same day, unknown to David, Saul and the armies of Israel are locked in battle with

144

the Philistines. Israel is beaten. Saul and his sons were killed. David's enemy is dead, and the throne of Israel is vacated. David becomes a national hero and is anointed king over Israel (again). (II Samuel 2:4) Notice: David never needed Ziklag again.

Notice also seven observations from the Ziklag incident:

1. *God knows the end at the beginning.*
   - David was anointed king as a boy, about fifteen years before it happened.
   - We don't have to know the end or the outcome. We just have to know the One who knows. We can look out the window of an airplane and worry that we have no idea where we are. All we have to know is that the pilot knows. And our Pilot can safely get us to our destination.
   - God had every detail of David's life pre-planned. And yours.

2. *Through it all, David never stopped serving God.*
David and his band of outcasts continued to defend their country against the invading Philistines. They rescued many towns from their raids.
David continued to do what he was able to do.
He didn't quit when his boss antagonized him.
He didn't quit when he lost his income.
He didn't quit when his first wife was taken away.
He didn't quit when he was rejected, became an outcast and a fugitive.
He didn't quit when he lived in a cave instead of a castle.
He didn't quit even when his closest friends turned on him.

He didn't quit even when Ziklag burned.

Have you had a Ziklag lately?

- Notice that Ziklags happen to God's childen. Like David.
- Ziklags happen even when you're faithful. *Especially* when you are faithful. To those who are especially pleasing to God. Consider God's servant Job.
- Ziklags happen to someone whom God has special plans for.
- A Ziklag will seem like nothing worse could happen to you. Even your friends may turn against you. You want to cry out, "My God, my God, why have you forsaken me?"

3. *At his lowest, darkest hour, David turns to God.*
Even when he walked through the valley of the shadow of death, David could cry out, **"Thou art with me."** It does not appear that anyone else in the passage turned to God. The time to decide that God is your rock, your anchor, is long before the crisis strikes. When a hurricane or tornado turns your home into a debris field, let your first response be, **"The Lord gives and the Lord takes away; blessed be the name of the Lord."** Let other men turn to liquor or the TV. But you have God.

> *Through this world of toils and snares,*
> *If I falter, Lord...who cares?*
> *Who with me my burden shares?*
> *None but Thee, dear Lord, none but Thee.*

> *Do you fear the gathering clouds of sorrow?*
> *Tell it to Jesus, tell it to Jesus!*

Are you anxious what shall be tomorrow?
Tell it to Jesus alone.

4. *Friends and foes were against him.*
In verse 6, **"the people spoke of stoning him."** Job's "friends" were miserable comforters and acted more like accusers. Joseph was betrayed by his own brothers, while Jesus was betrayed by a friend. **"Friend, why have you come?"** Jesus was wounded in the house of his friends. Don't expect any better for yourself.

5. *David was wrongly blamed, falsely accused.*
So was Jesus.
This was part of the package of trials God ordained for His chosen servant. David did not try to deflect the blame or defend himself. In the same way, he later allowed Shimei to continue to curse him. David put it this way, **"Let him alone and let him curse...it may be that the Lord will look on my affliction, and that the Lord will repay me with good for his cursing this day."** He would accept blame and shame, and wait for God to exonerate him. For he who humbles himself will be exalted. Jesus Himself did not put up any defense for Himself, so that Pilate marveled. There shall no "strange thing" happen to the child of God. No devilish malice can be unleashed against you; no foreign event can come upon you without God's express permission and design. God allows such things for a reason. They may mean it for evil, but God means it for good.

When through fiery trials thy pathway shall lie,
My grace all sufficient shall be thy supply;
The flame shall not hurt thee; I only design
The dross to consume, and thy gold to refine.

147

6. *Deep changes occur only in deep trials.*
Long-enduring qualities stem from long-lasting trials.
David's hardships were necessary. So are yours.
If you have more hardships, sufferings, setbacks and heartbreaks than others, **"rejoice and be exceedingly glad: for great is your reward in heaven."** (To quote well known expert.)
The whole Ziklag ordeal was God's will – or rather God's design.
God was grooming him for the kingdom.
I'm saying: Ziklag is necessary to the Christian.
Consider what the Holy Spirit says through Peter, **"Beloved, think it not strange concerning the fiery trial which is to try you, as though some strange (foreign) thing happened to you."** It is intricately designed and planned by God. Did you know that God never says "Oops" or "Oh, no! I left the oven on too long." (You can learn some great spiritual truths in this book.)
When Ziklag burns, disaster has struck close to home.
When Ziklag burns, it seems that God has forsaken you.
When Ziklag burns, it is trial by fire.
The wise man thanks God for Ziklag *before* the reason appears.

7. *David's most discouraging time occurred just before his greatest success.*
At the same time Ziklag was burning, God was already steering destiny for David to become king. The dark, excruciating hours of Gethsemane and crucifixion Friday immediately precede the glorious resurrection

Sunday. David could not possibly have understood all of what was happening. All he had to do was trust in the Lord with all his heart and lean not on his own understanding of events around him.

The message of Ziklag is simply: **Don't quit.** Especially when it seems like you have suffered irrecoverable loss; when you have been dealt a fatal blow; when an incurable illness has beset you. Don't quit, though your life seems to have come its darkest hour.

DON'T QUIT

When things go wrong as they sometimes will,
And the road you're trudging seems all uphill;
When the funds are low and the debts are high,
And you want to smile, but you have to sigh;
When care is pressing you down a bit,
Rest if you must, but don't you quit.

Life is strange with its twists and turns,
As every one of us sometimes learns;
And many a failure turns about,
When you might have won had you stuck it out.
So don't give up though the pace seems slow;
You might succeed with another blow.

Success is failure turned inside out,
The silver lining on clouds of doubt –
And (David), you never can tell how close you
are;
It may be near when it seems so far.
So (David), stick to the fight when you're hardest

hit –

It's when things seem worst that you must not quit.

(author unknown)

DAVID AS KING

When Saul died, it was the end of David's worst enemy. But against all expectations, David did not rejoice over his death, but rather mourned. **"Do not rejoice when your enemy falls, and do not let your heart be glad when he stumbles; lest the Lord see it and it displease Him."** Being a musician as well as a soldier, he also wrote a sort of memorial ballad honoring Saul and his son, Jonathan. (II Samuel 1:18) Apparently people were touched when David treated the deceased king with respect, though he didn't deserve it. **"Now all the people took note of it, and it pleased them, since whatever the king did pleased all the people."** (II Samuel 3:36) David became king at about 30 years old and he reigned over Judah seven and a half years in Hebron. Then he reigned over all Israel for thirty-three years in Jerusalem. He continued to lead the armies of Israel after becoming king. He was never defeated in battle. God himself explains why: **"I have been with you everywhere you have gone, and have cut off all your enemies from before you."** (II Samuel 7:9) David defeated his enemies on all sides. He was the only king of Israel who took possession of all the land that God had given to Israel, even as far as the Euphrates River.

(Deuteronomy 1:7) Another element of David's success was the remarkable men who rallied to David. The list of the thirty-seven great men found in II Samuel 23:8-39 includes men who would rival mighty Samson. Adino once slew 800 men single-handedly. Abishai, David's cousin once killed one of Goliath's brother and on another occasion killed 300 enemy soldiers. These thirty-seven men made quite a hall of fame. David army was very loyal to him, because he was loyal to them. He showed that he cared about them when he and his 600 men pursued after the Amalekites who had burned Ziklag. At one point when they came to a river, about 200 of his men were too exhausted to cross the river and continue the pursuit. They stayed behind with the supplies. The remaining 400 caught up with the Amalekites and defeated them. When they returned to the river, the victorious 400 refused to divide the spoil with the 200 who remained behind. Then David said they would not be excluded, but that all would share the spoils equally. That became a permanent law in Israel. Nobody in the military would deny the value of the supply ships and support battalions that deliver supplies and ammunition to the front lines. David certainly remembered delivering food to the armies of Israel as a teenager.

MEPHIBOSHETH

"Now David said, 'Is there still anyone who is left of the house of Saul, that I may show him kindness for Jonathan's sake?' " (II Samuel 9:1) Some time after David had been king, he remembers a promise he had made to his one time best friend, Jonathan. The promise was made 15-20 years earlier and Jonathan had been dead several years. In I Samuel 20:15, Jonathan says to David, **"You shall not cut off your kindness from my house forever, no, not when the Lord has cut off every one of the enemies of David…So Jonathan made a covenant with the house of David, saying, 'Let the Lord require it.'"** So Jonathan and David took an oath to be friends forever.

Now David wants to see if there is anything he can do to honor his promise to Jonathan. Apparently, he did know whether Jonathan had any survivors. So a search was made and Ziba was found, an old servant of Saul's family. He was brought to David and questioned. **"And Ziba said to the king, 'There is still a son of Jonathan who is lame on his feet.' So the king said to him, 'Where is he?' And Ziba said to the king, 'He is in the house of Machir the son of Ammiel, from Lo Debar.' Then king David send and brought him out of the house of Machir, the son of Ammiel, from Lo Debar. Now when Mephibosheth the son of Jonathan, the son of Saul, had come to David, he fell on his face and prostrated himself. Then David said, 'Mephibosheth?' And he answered, 'Here is your servant!' So David said to him, 'Do not fear, for I will surely show you kindness for Jonathan your father's sake, and will restore to you all the land of Saul your grandfather; and you shall eat bread at my table continually.' Then he bowed himself, and said, 'What is your servant, that you should look upon such a dead dog as I?'"** (II Samuel 9:4-8) Then David makes arrangements with Ziba and his 15 sons and 20 servants to farm all the land of Saul on behalf of Mephibosheth. So Mephibosheth becomes a major land holder and becomes like one of the king's sons all in one day. What an amazing turnaround for a young man who destitute and not able to do anything about it and living off the charity of a good citizen, Machir.

This man was wealthy and a supporter of David. He had to be surprised when David sends for Mephibosheth to come live in king David's house in Jerusalem. Years later, when David and many of his family and close friends were fleeing for their lives across the Jordan River to escape from Absalom, Machir met them with a caravan of food and relief. **"Cast your bread upon the waters, for it will come back to you after many days."**

This is a superb allegory of the salvation of man. In this incident, we are Mephibosheth and David represents God. David made the promise long before Mephibosheth was born, just as God promised a way for our salvation long ago. This was implied far back in Eden, when God shed blood to make coverings to clothe Adam and Eve. This was eventually fulfilled when Jesus, the Lamb of God shed His blood to cover over our sins.

Notice that David makes a decision to show kindness to someone he had never met. It did not matter whether the person was good or bad. By God's grace and His pre-determinate will, he chose to love us and to show His kindness to us before we did good or bad. In Mephibosheth's case, the decision to show kindness came before he was even born. It did not matter that Mephibosheth was from the family of his avowed enemy. In our case, we are of a race of sinners who have rebelled against God. Yet God loves us unconditionally. "And you, who were once alienated and enemies in your mind by wicked works, yet now He has reconciled." (Colossians 1:21) Notice at the end of this verse who initiates the reconciliation: "He", that is, God. Just as David chose to reconcile Mephibosheth to himself.

153

Mephibosheth was incapable of pursuing a relationship with David. He was unable to take even the first step, being a cripple. In the same way, we are spiritually crippled. **"But the natural man does not receive the things of the Spirit of God, for they are foolishness to him; nor can he know them, because they are spiritually discerned."** (I Corinthians 2:14)

Beside the fact that Mephibosheth was crippled, consider where he was: in Lo Debar, about 80 miles from Jerusalem. He was probably carried that far away to keep him safe from the new regime. It was common in those times for a new king to execute all the survivors of the old king. Also for someone to get from Lo Debar to Jerusalem, the royal city, they would have to cross the Jordan River and then climb 3800 ft. to get to Jerusalem. An impossibility for a cripple. It is an even greater impossibility for us to approach God. We have to cross over from the physical realm to the spiritual. Then our nature is so corrupt that we could not possibly approach His holy city or enter his holy light. We cannot get to heaven on our own strength or merit. God Himself will have to get us across that vast gulf to heaven.

Oh the love that drew salvation's plan,
Oh the grace that brought it down to man,
Oh the mighty gulf that God did span – at Calvary!

When Jesus was asked, **"Who then can be saved?"**, He replied, **"With men this is impossible; but with God all things are possible."**

Consider that David did not choose a healthy, valuable man. Neither does God choose us because we are so loveable, or talented or so good. We are foul, corrupt creatures who have made ourselves repugnant

154

by our sins. But God chooses us in spite of all our faults and our vile condition.

There was only one pet I adopted on purpose. (All the other ones adopted me, and wouldn't go away.) Years ago, when I lived in an apartment complex, there was medium size stray dog that roamed around the neighborhood. It was absolutely the ugliest dog I have ever seen. Angel had a very bad case of mange and fleas. All her fur had fallen off. She looked like she was walking around with no clothes on. She was terribly gaunt and looked like she would fall over if a wind came. She would hobble very slowly toward any people she saw, apparently hoping someone would feed her. Her frightful face looked like a ghostly specter, but had a sad, pleading expression. Children would flee from her screaming. Adults would angrily try to shoo her away. She would hobble away slowly, not able to go any faster. One day as I pondered her plight, I said a sort of prayer to God something like, "What do you think, God? How about if I adopt her and get her all fixed up? Let's see if we can make her a repair project." So I called a local veterinarian and asked for advice. He said to bring her in and he'd put her in his "dip" solution for treating mange and fleas.

So I wrapped her up in a big towel and delivered her to the veterinary clinic, where she stayed for three days. The doctor was optimistic and gave me advice on diet and care. I picked up Angel and brought her home. It was a long process getting her house-trained and feeding her raw eggs and different kinds of dog food. Gradually, she started gaining a little weight and gaining a little social confidence. I started walking her outside where she made friends with two other kindly pet dogs, who lived downstairs. Gradually her fur started to grow. It occurred to me that even after two months, that I still did not know what color she was or what kind of dog she was. Soon she was running and frolicking and yet never barked. She just made little friendly whining sounds. I don't speak "dog", but I think she was saying "Hi!" and "thank you" and "I like you" a lot. She turned out to be a stunningly beautiful, smaller golden retriever. Everybody loved her; several asked if they could have her. Life was a new beginning for Angel. You could say she was born again. Loving care brought out beauty and goodness in her that nobody knew was there. That's what God wants to do with us. But a man is not ready until he sees himself as a sinner: unclean and a spiritual cripple.

Notice Mephibosheth's response:
    1. He came to the king. He accepted the invitation.
    2. He worshiped.
    3. He trusted in David to be his Lord.

We, too, need to accept the invitation of the Son of David, bow in worship of Him and trust him as our personal Lord.

Notice the basis of God's grace toward us: The merit of Another. (For Jonathan, your father's sake.) In our case, all the grace and salvation of God comes to us by the merit of Jesus Christ. His righteousness is imputed to us, making us accepted in the Beloved. At the same time, our sins are imputed to *Him*. As the scripture has said, **"For He made Him who knew no sin to be sin for us, that we might become the righteousness of God in Him."** (II Corinthians 5:21) With a deal that good, it's hard to imagine how anyone could turn down God's offer of salvation.

In their first conversation, Mephibosheth is made rich at David's word. He gives all the possessions of former king Saul to Mephibosheth. (II Samuel 9:7) Mephibosheth is overwhelmed! At our first encounter with God, when we receive our salvation, we, too, are made rich beyond human comprehension. **"He has blessed us with every spiritual blessing in heavenly places."** (Ephesians 1:3) Eternal life and happiness and more! We see Mephibosheth's response to David's astonishing kindness, **"Then he bowed himself and said, 'What is your servant, that you should look upon such a dead dog as I?'"** This is how we will feel when we see all that God has done for us. **"Eye has not seen, nor ear heard, nor have entered into the heart of man the things that God has prepared for them that love Him."**

All the work needed on Mephibosheth's new possessions is done by others. (verses 9 and 10) In our case, all the work of our salvation is also done by Another. **"Being confident of this very thing, that He who has begun a good work in you will complete it until the day of Jesus Christ."** (Philippians 1:6) **"For we are his workmanship, created in Christ Jesus."** (Ephesians 2:10) We do not have to work for our salvation. We simply trust and rest in Jesus.

Mephibosheth dines continually at the king's table, as one of the king's sons. **"You shall eat bread at my table continually."** Likewise with us, who are **"raised up together, and made us sit together in the heavenly places in Christ Jesus."** (Ephesians 2:6) We are said to be adopted as children of God. The angels would wish to have what we will have!

This whole story of what happened to Mephibosheth could not have been scripted to better resemble what our heavenly King has planned for us. There is one distinction though: David never knew Mephibosheth before this. In our case, God knew each of us long before our birth. He also knew that we would make ourselves enemies to God by our sins, and yet He chose to show us all this kindness anyway. "And you who were once alienated and enemies in your mind by wicked works, yet now He has reconciled." (Colossians 1:21) God makes a point of displaying the greatness of His love for us. He loves not only the good people of this world, but also the sinners. He showed love for the thief who died next to Him on the cross. He prayed for the very people who crucified Him: "Father, forgive them." God saved Saul, who hunted down Christians to imprison and kill them. Let no man think that his sins are so great that God would not forgive him.

THE BATHSHEBA DISASTER

It makes you wonder if God said to Satan, "Have you considered my servant, David?" Of course He did not. But consider this: Both Job and David distinguished themselves in their generation for righteousness and prosperity. And God was surely as proud of David as He was of Job. David was remarkably courageous, almost blameless in righteousness and deeply trusted in God. David trusted in the Lord with all his heart and leaned not on his own understanding, not every once in a while (like us), but as a lifestyle. If an angel had ever appeared to David, he probably would have addressed him as, "O greatly beloved of God", as Gabriel did with Daniel. Or "O man after God's own heart." But if God *had* said that to Satan, he probably would have replied, "Does David fear God for nothing? Have you not made a hedge around him, and been with him everywhere he has gone, and cut off all his enemies before him and made him a great name?" God might have responded with, "Therefore you will be allowed to tempt him, but not above what he can bear." Once again, that conversation did *not* occur, but it sure seems that Satan targeted David with temptation. He actually did tempt David later, in the incident of the numbering of Israel. Although we don't hear anything about Satan in this case, I'm sure that if the crime scene had been investigated, Satan's fingerprints would have been found all over it.

"It happened in the spring of the year, at the time when kings go out to battle, that David sent Joab and all his servants with him, and all Israel; and they destroyed the people of Ammon and besieged Rabbah. But David remained at Jerusalem." (II Samuel 11:1)

Whether or not David was too old to be a soldier is not the issue here. He would surely have been the best general or battlefield commander, with his experience. The issue is that David declined to go to the front lines and stayed home for a leisurely life. That is what happened in verse 2. **"Then it happened one evening that David arose from his bed…"** The king of Israel and commander in chief of the armed forces is sleeping away the working hours of the day! Idleness will soon become the devil's workshop. All sorts of evil and loss come from undue idleness. **"Behold, this was the iniquity of your sister Sodom, pride, fulness of bread, and abundance of idleness was in her and in her daughters, neither did she strengthen the hand of**

159

the poor and needy." (Ezekiel 16:49) So abundance of idleness was a major contributor to the moral collapse of Sodom, renowned for its sexual perversions. David has set the stage for a moral collapse. The two men in this story, David and Uriah, will show the difference in the moral tendencies of an idle life and a hard life of service in the military.

Verse 2 continues, **"(David) walked on the roof of the king's house. And from the roof he saw a woman bathing..."** The verse should have ended right there. Once he saw the woman bathing, common decency and a desire for holiness should have made him turn and look away. But David allowed the lust of the eyes to prevail. We read next, **"and the woman was very beautiful to behold."** More deadly than the call of the sirens is the sight of a beautiful woman. Bathsheba should have been more careful to do her bathing in a private, enclosed area. Today we have a problem of epidemic proportions in America with indecent dress, particularly with our women. Surcly God does not intend a woman's sexual beauty to excite any man other than her husband. If a woman does so intentionally, she is as shameful as a seductress. Too much of ladies' apparel today is skin-tight and reveals every contour of even personal areas. For every man who is aroused by the sight, God would be just in holding the immodest woman partly to blame for whatever happens in the man's thought. **"But I say to you that whoever looks at a woman to lust for her has already committed adultery with her in his heart."** This is a much more serious sin than most people think. It would only be fair if the scantily dressed woman is also held guilty for the adultery she has caused. I wish every pastor would declare it is time for a revival of holiness in his church.

I also wish every leading lady of the church would say it's time to stop letting fashion dictate what our ladies will wear. May there be a revival in our churches like the one in Acts 19:18 and 19, **"And many who had believed came confessing and telling their deeds. Also many of those who had practiced magic brought their books together and burned them in the sight of all. And they counted up the value of them, and it totaled 50,000 pieces of silver."** These people cleaned house and put an immediate end to their sorcery. May the ladies spark a similar revival and clean closet. Maybe they could have a bonfire of immodest clothing. And may God greatly bless them for it.

In verse 3 of our story, **"David sent and inquired about the woman."** This was very bad. The fact that David already had a number of wives should have kept the story from starting. But the story should have ended when David got word that Bathsheba was married to Uriah. Every married person today should wear a wedding ring at all times to preclude improper relationships. Bathsheba also could have stopped it cold here. She should have declined David's invitation and refused all further inquiry. It is a foolish thing to think, "Well let's just see where this goes."

Verse 4 tells us, **"Then David sent messengers, and took her; and she came to him, and he lay with her... and she returned to her house."** There was grieving in heaven and rejoicing in hell! It almost sounds as casual as if she was out running errands and then returned to her house. **"This is the way of an adulterous woman: she eats and wipes her mouth and says, 'I have done no wickedness.'"** (Proverbs 30:20)

This was certainly a consensual affair. Of course David initiated, but Bathsheba **"came to him."** So casually does adultery or fornication begin, as if they had said, "Hey lets go bowling." But we fail to think of the broader consequences. We terribly hurt the one person who has loved us more than anyone else in the world: the one we're married to. (We can't assume that word will never get out.) We have branded a stinging memory in our consciences for the rest of our life. We have both grieved and angered the God who has so loved us all these years. Who knows how many financial collapses are a judgment for an extramarital affair? Or accidents or sickness? Consider this true story:

Mitchell (not his real name) and I used to work together years ago. He was an incurable joker and cut-up. He was a lot of fun. I remembered that when he was a teenager, he lured a girl into giving up her virginity.
But 14 years later, Mitchell was not the same. He was no longer cheerful and joking. He was depressed and heart-broken. He told me the most important thing in the world to him was his 5 children. But his children had recently been taken away and given to another family. You may be thinking, "Well I know someone who had an affair, but nothing bad ever happened to them." You mean, not yet. The blade of the guillotine is still poised over their neck.

I don't understand folks who tamper with sex before marriage. Why should they damage their future for a little fun now. They may as well hang a sign from their neck notifying future prospects, USED BODY – REDUCED PRICE – CHEAP. How can someone live with the thought that they have cheated that wonderful person they hope to marry some day. After committing the act, how do they bring themselves to pray again to a holy God? How can they have the heart to ever go to church again ? How does the adulterer ever face their wife or husband again? How would they ever talk to their child about being Godly or pure? Surely their conscience would jeer at them, "Sure, tell your kids to be pure, you hypocrite." It might be continually on your mind, "Will I get punished for this? Well, I'm a Christian. surely God wouldn't be too hard on me." Maybe you never heard the scripture, **"Judgment must begin at the house of God." And "that servant which knew his lord's will, and prepared not himself, neither did according to his will, shall be beaten with many stripes."**

The consequences begin mounting in the next verse: **"And the woman conceived; so she sent and told David, and said, 'I am with child.' "** It's as if she was saying, "So fix this."

Initially, David just plans to have an afternoon fling. Rank has its privileges, Right? No harm done. But a few days later, things began getting complicated. He hadn't planned for this; it was not part of the deal. So David hatches this plan beginning in verse 6. David orders General Joab to send Uriah, Bathsheba's husband, to Jerusalem from the battlefront. After several months of deployment, Uriah would be glad to get a little time at home. David questions Uriah about the progress of the war and sends him to his house with a big plate of food from the king's table. When Uriah departed, David must have breathed a sigh of relief. Problem solved.

Apparently there were some folks close to the king who knew what was going on. One of them reported to David, **"Uriah did not go down to his house."** His stubborn problem was not going away. David calls in Uriah and asks him why he didn't go home (to his beautiful wife). Uriah's answer had to sting deep in David's heart, **"The ark and Israel and Judah are dwelling in tents, and my lord, Joab and the servants of my lord are encamped in the open fields. Shall I then go to my house to eat and drink, and to lie with my wife? As you live and as your soul lives, I will not do this thing."** This is a man after David's own heart. David was exactly like him years ago. Remember it had troubled David that he lived in a house of cedar, while the ark abode in tents. This Uriah was a strongly principled man. It's interesting that Uriah was not an Israelite, but a Hittite, one of the seven nations that occupied Canaan before Israel. God could have said, "I have not found such great righteousness, no not in Israel."

Unbelievably, David goes to further devious means to cover up his sin. But *"He* who *covers his sins* **will not prosper, But whoever confesses and forsakes them will have mercy."** (Proverbs 28:13) Adam and Achan both covered their sins (with fig leaves), and they sure didn't prosper. Sadly, confessing his sins did not even enter David's mind. Instead, he gets Uriah drunk and gave him another meal fit for a king, but that night he went out and slept at the king's gate again instead of going home. What a contrast to the many men in the military who seek out illicit sex in every port and duty station! **"Righteousness exalts a nation, but sin is a reproach to any people."** Uriah had more honor drunk than most men do sober.

In verse 14, David writes Uriah's death warrant and sends it with him back to the front lines. It was worded to general Joab, **"Set Uriah in the forefront of the hottest** battle, and retreat from him, that he may be struck down and die.**" Uriah carried the letter and faithfully delivered it to Joab. If ever Joab was to question or disobey an order from king David, this should have been it. But he becomes co-conspirator and assigns Uriah to the place where he knew the enemy had some valiant men. Israel's own soldiers, being pre-instructed, retreated from Uriah, leaving him unprotected, and he was killed. The conspiracy gets bigger and bigger. Such a military does not deserve divine protection! When David was told the news, his cold-hearted reply was sort of like, "Well everybody's got to die sometime." Here's another one who **"Eats and wipes his mouth and says, 'I have done no wickedness.'"**

At the end of this grievous and shameful chapter, we read, **"When the wife of Uriah heard that...her husband was dead, she mourned for her husband."** At least somebody mourned for noble Uriah. (verse 26) David brings her to his home, marries her and they have their child.

This dark chapter of David's life ends with an ominous note. **"But the thing that David had done displeased the Lord."** David would pay dreadfully for his double crime, but Bathsheba also pays a heavy toll: besides the blackness of her guilt, she suffers the painful grief of the loss of her husband and later the anguish of the death of her baby. The wages of sin is death. It is never a good deal.

David is also terribly grieved at the loss of this beloved baby. But he would pay much more. By the time he finishes paying for his crime, it looks like he never again has a happy day.

THE AFTERMATH

It looked like David had committed the perfect crime. He covered it up. When Bathsheba turns up pregnant, people will assume Uriah became the father while he was home briefly. But **"the eyes of the Lord are in every place, beholding the evil and the good."** (Proverbs 15:3 KJV) God knew it, and He revealed His secret to His servant the prophet, Nathan. He confronts the king by telling a story.

A rich man and a poor man lived near each other. The rich man had many flocks and herds, but the poor man had only one little ewe lamb, which was like a daughter to him. David could relate. One day a traveler came to the rich man and he declined to cook one of his own lambs for the guest's dinner. Rather he took the poor man's lamb and prepared it for the dinner instead. David was greatly angry against the rich man. He said, **"As the Lord lives, the man who has done this deserves to die! And he shall restore fourfold for the lamb, because he did this thing and because he had no pity."** (II Samuel 12:4-6) Like a thunderbolt to his heart, Nathan gives him the word of the Lord: **"You are the man! Thus says the Lord God of Israel: I anointed you king over Israel and I delivered you out of the hand of Saul. I gave you your master's house and your master's wives into your keeping, and gave you the house of Israel and Judah. And if that had been too little, I also would have given you much more! Why have you despised the commandment of the Lord, to do evil in His sight? You have killed Uriah the Hittite with the sword; you have taken his wife to be your wife, and have killed him with the**

166

sword of the people of Ammon. Now therefore, the sword shall never depart from your own house; and I will take your wives before your eyes and give them to your neighbor, and he shall lie with your wives in the sight of this sun. For you did it secretly, but I will do this thing before all Israel, before the sun. "

David is reeling with the blow of Nathan's words. Completely broken, he says to Nathan, **"I have sinned against the Lord."** Probably in a much milder tone, Nathan says to David, **"The Lord also has put away your sin; you shall not die. However, because by this deed you have given great occasion to the enemies of the Lord to blaspheme, the child also who is born to you shall surely die."**

Soon their baby becomes sick. David prayed and fasted for seven days for the child, but the baby dies. With his own words, David judged that the rich man should repay four-fold. It was the correct judgment. According to Exodus 22:1, **"If a man steals an ox or a sheep, and slaughters it ...he shall restore...four sheep for a sheep."** I don't think it registered in David's mind that he would pay a fourfold penalty.

I suspect he was thinking as a lot of us do, that God would surely go easy on him since he was such a nice fellow. We would say, "I attend church regularly, I give faithfully. God knows I love Him." David may have been thinking about when he put his life on the line in defeating Goliath; risking his life in numerous battles, defending God's people; refraining twice from killing Saul, because he was God's anointed. It was David with whom God had those special moments of prayer after he expressed a desire to build a house for God. God was highly pleased and gave further promises to David to extend his kingdom many generations, saying that his house shall be established forever. Surely God knew how David loved him. Isn't that enough for God to go easy on him? Not a chance. In fact all the above is plenty reason for God to give him even sterner judgment. For **"Judgment begins at the house of God."** (I Peter 4:17) To whom much is given, much is reasonably expected. **"And that servant who knew his master's will and did not...do according to his will, shall be beaten with many stripes. But he who did not know, yet committed these things deserving of stripes, shall be beaten with few."** (Luke 12:47,48)

The damage David caused was severe. As Nathan pointed out, his sin has given **"great occasion to the enemies of the Lord to blaspheme."** It appears that a lot of people had initially come to David to serve under him not just because he was a phenomenal success in warfare, but because he was a good man. Now when they hear of his moral collapse, many of his friends must have gone back and walked with him no more. (See John 6:66)

David, who once had a sterling reputation now has a terrible blemish from which he would never recover. He has a fly in the ointment. **"Dead flies putrefy the perfumer's ointment, and cause it to give off a foul odor; so does a little folly to one respected for wisdom and honor."** (Ecclesiastes 10:1) God surely forgave him, but history has not to this day. See the ever widening ripple effects of David's sin, which encourage others to go and do likewise. David had once set the standard for righteousness, but now as a result of his actions, many have a damaged view of Godly people and ministers. They are now more prone to be suspicious of people who seem to be righteous. Some of that damage will strike close to home for him.

TAMAR'S TRAGEDY

Some time later, one of David's sons, Amnon, falls in love with the half sister, Tamar. She was a virgin and was very beautiful. He didn't want to marry her, he just wanted to have sex with her. He got heartsick with desire, but could see no way to get what he wanted, since she was a king's daughter. But Amnon's cousin, Jonadab, came up with a plan for Amnon to get his wish. So Amnon pretended to be sick, staying in bed. As planned, David came to visit him and Amnon requested of him that Tamar be sent to wait on him. David agreed and sent Tamar. While they were secluded in his room, he forces her. Afterward, we're told that he hated her and harshly put her out of his house. Tamar fled to her home, weeping. When her full brother, Absalom, found out, he tells her not to take it to heart, and she lived desolate in her brother's house. David also hears about it, but does nothing. However, Absalom is not forgetting.

AMNON

Two years later, Absalom is planning a sheep-shearing party out of town in Baal Hazor. He invites his brothers and his father. Perfectly normal. David thanks Absalom, but declines. As expected. Absalom acts disappointed and asks his father if Amnon can come instead, being the eldest son. Sounds reasonable. So David sends Amnon to attend. As predicted. At the height of the party, Absalom has his assassins kill Amnon. No one else knew it was coming. The rest of the family flees for their lives back to Jerusalem. But Absalom wanted only Amnon killed for what he did to Tamar, his sister. Absalom flees the country. Again, David did nothing. It is disturbing to see at the end of II Samuel 13, that David **"longed to go to Absalom. For he had been comforted concerning Amnon, because he was dead."** He allows a rape to go unpunished and now a murder.

It is to be feared that David was a permissive parent, not holding his children accountable for their sins. It is a very great wrong to withhold correction and punishment from a child. Proverbs 23:13 gives this unpopular advice, **"Do not withhold correction from a child, for if you beat him with a rod, he will not die. (He'll just sound like it.) You shall beat him with a rod and deliver his soul from hell."** If you don't like this, just remember: this is the Manufacturer's instructions.

What has happened to David? Once a champion of justice, he is now permissive and soft on crime. This kind of judicial system is a festering cancer that can destroy its host. Shortly after becoming king, Joab murders Abner, the newly appointed army commander. David never prosecuted. Both were David's cousins. Later in David's reign, Joab also kills Amasa, another official appointed by David after the Absalom rebellion. And again, David only gives Joab a verbal reprimand. So he was also permissive and lenient toward his relatives. So David has allowed two major crimes by his own children and two by a cousin. However, David executed swift and fair justice to all other criminal actions.

It's hard to say which of the two sins of David were worse: his adultery-murder double crime or his miscarriages of justice as king and his neglect of correction and punishment toward his children. Both sets of failures had far-ranging destructive consequences.

Now Israel's first two kings, Saul and David, started off promising, but later collapsed into dismal failures. It is a syndrome that we should be extremely wary of in other arenas of life. How many marriages start off sweet and romantic, but turn sour in the end? How many times does someone start off on fire in his new job, having strong company loyalty, good work ethics and relationships, but eventually loses momentum and drive or even integrity. Let's face it, life is a marathon. We should have an eye for being steady for the long haul. We should resolve to keep the love in our marriage, to be unwaveringly loyal to our God and render good service to our fellow man. Let us be wary that we do not get a fly in the ointment.

It was a painful loss when his baby died; it hurt badly when his daughter Tamar suffered her tragedy; it was a double hurt when his first-born son was assassinated by his own brother. I can't picture David smiling ever again. Life has really weighed him down. But he has made only three payments on his sin. One more is still due.

ABSALOM

For three years, Absalom remains in exile. David finally brings Absalom back home to Jerusalem in an apparent reconciliation. All during this time, Absalom had been a much favored son to David. There is nothing in the Biblical record of any goodness or virtue in Absalom. The record does state that he was very good looking. **"Now in all Israel there was no one who was praised as much as Absalom for his good looks.**

171

From the sole of his foot to the crown of his head there was no blemish in him." (II Samuel 14:25) This could be the reason Absalom was in high favor with David. It is certainly a common mistake that a beautiful child is more loved than the plainer ones. A person's beauty far outshines any shortcomings of virtue such as being selfish, dishonest or lazy. No matter how bad the beautiful child is, some parents continue to dote upon them with lavish kindnesses. Commonly a child's beauty becomes their downfall. But it would be the parents' fault. Compounding Absalom's problem was the fact that he was a king's son. He would have been continuously waited upon, spoiled and never required to work. He literally got away with murder. We'll be seeing more of his poor character shortly.

"After this it happened that Absalom provided himself with chariots and horses, and fifty men to run before him." (II Samuel 15:1) Today he'd be driving a late model Mercedes with an escort of big black SUV's everywhere he went. At taxpayer expense.

In the following verses, we see him making a play to win the hearts of the people. Hours every day over a long period of time, he intercepted citizens on their way to king David for a ruling on some civil matter. He would converse with them in a friendly manner and enquire about their case. He would say they have a good case, but that the king has no one to hear their case. He would then say that if he were king, he would get them the justice they seek. So he slandered his father, the king, lied to the people and made empty promises to them. He gave each of them a sort of hug and a kiss. It is reported that this **"stole the hearts of the men of**

Israel.” His good looks probably helped his plan. (Not to mention his chariot and fifty soldiers.)

When the time seemed ripe, Absalom launches his conspiracy. He goes to Hebron, the former royal city, where he assembles his rebellion against David. He travels with two hundred armed men, apparently upgrading from his original fifty. He also sends for the famous wise man, Ahithophel, to be his counselor. Absalom sends messengers throughout all Israel to come at a set time and shout, “Absalom reigns in Hebron!” So Absalom wants to win the throne of Israel through his pompous self-serving, his trickery of the people and of course, good looks. The shocking thing is that the people of Israel let him get away it! Hitler won over Germany with similar strategy, except that he was not good looking. Let us who are voting Americans be well informed of the candidates, seeing through the fog of slanted media.

It is also surprising that David let this happen. As wise and as well informed as David was, he should have seen this coming. I have to wonder if God allowed this conspiracy to develop and to keep David from realizing what was happening, because He was allowing the fourth payment for David’s sin to come due.

If David was aware of this, it would explain his strange decision to vacate the palace and Jerusalem with all his servants.

As David flees the impending invasion by Absalom, we see that he “went up by the ascent of the Mount of Olives, and wept as he went up; he had his head covered and went barefoot.” This is a solemn preview of the Son of David, who also ascended the Mount of Olives, weeping with “strong cryings and tears.”

- Both were being betrayed by someone close to them.
- Both went with greatest possible humility.
- At the top of Mt. Olive, David worshiped God; when the Son of David came to the top of Mt. Olive, he went a little farther, and prayed half the night.
- No doubt David's weeping were for his own sins; Jesus wept and interceded for the sins of mankind.
- David's enemies sought to kill him; Jesus's enemies also sought to kill him: both the hordes of hell and the wicked Jews.
- Both factions had intended to kill them in Jerusalem, which kills the prophets and stones those who are sent to her, for it cannot be that a prophet should perish outside of Jerusalem.

As the terrible, woeful chapter 15 finally comes to an end, we find ominous words, **"So Hushai, David's friend, went into the city. And Absalom came into Jerusalem."** One man slinks into the city under cover of darkness, solemn-faced, coming from a band of fugitives, weeping as they fled. At the other end of town, a king's parade arrives in spectacular fashion, with an army of about twenty to thirty thousand men. Oddly, the entourage finds neither resistance, nor cheering crowds. There were probably few people in sight. The one man had a mission assigned to him: stop the king and his murderous army.

As David's forlorn and weary band continues to flee eastward, support is steadily rallying to him. Ziba, the servant of Mephibosheth comes to David and his people with a vast supply of food, water and donkeys for carrying the women and children. Desperately needed supplies! Remember Mephibosheth is the crippled, poor guy whom David brought in to his house, taking him to be as his own son. Ziba remembers this from years ago and comes to repay David. **"Cast your bread upon the waters, for you will find it after many days."** (Ecclesiastes 11:1) Solomon penned these words and it is probable that he was in the group who got the food.

One other notable incident during the fleeing of the people is when Shimei came near to David's caravan and cursed David long and loudly. (Apparently assured that David was in no position to retaliate.) He falsely accused David of murder and insurrection against Saul. This went on and on until Abishai, one of David's top thirty mighty men, asked for David's permission to go take his head off. David says No. **"So let him curse, because the Lord has said to him, 'Curse David'...it may be that the Lord will look on my affliction, and that the Lord will repay me with good for his cursing me this day." (II Samuel 16:10-12) "Never take your own revenge, but leave room for the wrath of God."** Jesus would have counseled, **"Bless them that curse you...that you may be sons of your Father in heaven."** This incident may have reminded Abishai of another time he wanted to kill an enemy of David: Saul. David and Abishai had gone down to Saul's army camp in the middle of the night and stealthily crept to where Saul was sound asleep, surrounded by an army of sleeping soldiers. Abishai asked David to let him spear Saul to the ground. That time as well, David said, No. **"For who can stretch out his hand against the Lord's anointed and be guiltless?"** (I Samuel 26:9) So the very man Shimei accused David of murdering is the man whom

David saved alive. Too bad David didn't let Abishai go over and tell that story to loud-mouth Shimei. There's nothing like being wrong at the top of your voice. But David was not interested in exonerating himself. He would await the Lord's vindication. Now this looks more like the David we're accustomed to hearing about! It also looks like the Son of David, who, when facing his accusers, opened not his mouth.

Meanwhile, in Jerusalem, Hushai is pondering his mission impossible. He decides to present himself to Absalom, the king pretender. Hushai finds him surrounded by his courtiers and friends, most notably, Ahithophel, the great wise man. In II Samuel 16:16, Hushai bows to Absalom and says, "Long live the king!" A little suspicious, Absalom says, **"Is this your loyalty to your friend? (David) "Why did you not go with your friend?"** Hushai gives a perfect response: **"No but whom the Lord and this people and all the men of Israel choose, his will I be, and with him I will remain. Furthermore, whom should I serve? Should I not serve in the presence of his son? As I have served in your father's presence, so will I be in your presence."** Absalom and everyone around him believed Hushai.

Absalom and his army had just walked into Jerusalem and took the throne of Israel. But once he got there, he had no idea what to do. He asks Ahithophel, "Give advice as to what we should do." Now it was said of Ahithophel, **"Now the advice of Ahithophel, which he gave in those days, was as if one had inquired at the oracle of God."** (v.23)

Will the wise Ahithophel counsel Absalom to hold court to give justice for all the Israelites he had met recently? Remember Absalom had promised them that if he were king, he would get them justice. But whoever performs all the promises made during the campaign? Does Ahithophel give wise counsel to convene all the top heads of Israel and appoint a cabinet of advisors and other key leaders? No. But what he does advise is incomprehensible! **"Go in to all your father's concubines** (have sex with them), **whom he has left to keep the house; and all Israel will hear that you are abhorred by your father. Then the hands of all who are with you will be strong."** Is this the oracle of wisdom by the great Ahithophel? It appears rather to be an answer to David's prayer in II Samuel 15:31: **"O Lord, I pray, turn the counsel of Ahithophel into foolishness!"** Well Absalom sure liked the advice to go have sex with all those good-looking women! **"So they pitched a tent for Absalom on top of the house, and Absalom went in to his father's concubines in the sight of all Israel."** He had sex with ten of David's concubines in one extended session. This was not only multiple cases of adultery, but vile cases of incest. A sin that **"is not even named among the Gentiles – that a man has his father's wife."** (I Corinthians 5:1) If David's sin with Bathsheba was an occasion to the enemies of the Lord to blaspheme, how much more would this horrid crime be an occasion for the enemies of Israel to be utterly nauseated.

Now a battle for the throne of Israel is about to ensue. We know that "victory belongs to the Lord." Who shall we suppose He will give victory to? Absalom? With his list of sins:

- Murdered his own brother, Amnon;
- Deceiving the people of Israel about getting them justice;
- Slandering David's administration about not hearing the cases of the people;

177

– The public incest on the rooftop.
Or to David, who -
- Served the people of God in defending them against Goliath and the Philistines,
- Who would not avenge himself against Nabal's greed and insults,
- Refused to kill Saul, God's anointed,
- Kept peace with the house of Saul, after his death,
- Took care of Mephibosheth,
- Wants to build a house for God and dedicates all his wealth to it,
- Would not punish Shimei for his slandering and cursing;
- Who wrote so many of the Psalms honoring God.

With this contrast, it's a wonder that God restrained his anger against Absalom for even a few days. He was as vile to God as a roach that needed to be stomped.

In chapter 17, Ahithophel further counsels Absalom to give him twelve thousand men to immediately pursue after David and kill him. It sounded good to Absalom, but he calls for Hushai and asks his advice. After he hears what Ahithophel advised, he says, **"The advice that Ahithophel has given is not good at this time."** Hushai had just been with David and saw what a disarray his forces were in. He would not be prepared for a large, immediate attack. So he counters Ahithophel's advice by recommending that Absalom gather all Israel into a huge army to come in a few days and wipe out David and his men. He presented his case extremely well and convinced Absalom and all the men with him. So Hushai accomplishes his mission to stop the twelve thousand man army, and defeating the counsel of Ahithophel. No doubt, he had been specially inspired by God with the proper words. God works defeat for Ahithophel as well as to gain time for David to recover. Defeat for Ahithophel, because he conspired with Absalom against God's anointed king and for David's safety. Even though God laid the whip hard on David, it was only a prescribed, limited judgment. (As He sometimes does with us.) But woe to those who try to add judgment or insult on the victim over and above what God had prescribed!

As pre-arranged, Hushai sends two spies back to inform David of the large army being gathered in a few days. So David retreats into a defensible area and starts getting an army organized.

In chapter 18, David appoints three generals over the army of soldiers who have rallied to his support: Joab, Abishai and Ittai the Gittite. Very likely, some of the phenomenal mighty men of David were present in his army. This is much like the army who served under David years earlier. They had never been defeated. Joab and his brother Abishai, cousins of David, had also never been defeated as generals. The size of their army is not given. The forces of Absalom met the forces of David and the battle occurred in the woods of Ephraim. Numbers are not given, but Absalom's army was probably much larger, since he had recruited soldiers from all Israel.

"So the people went out into the field of battle against Israel. And the battle was in the woods of Ephraim. The people of Israel were overthrown there by the servants of David, and a great slaughter of twenty thousand took place there that day. For the battle there was scattered over the face of the whole countryside, and the woods devoured more people that day than the sword devoured." (II Samuel 18:6-8) It wasn't even a close contest. It seems that the victory for David was helped along providentially, with such an overwhelming victory and the fact that the woods **"devoured more people than the sword did."**

Absalom was found abandoned in the woods, hanging by his very long hair in tree branches. Even his mule abandoned him. He was promptly executed by getting impaled with ten spears. A cursed death for a man responsible for the death of over twenty thousand of his countrymen and tried his best to kill his own father. It is a fearful thing to fall into the hands of the living God.

David may have been the only one to mourn his death. He bewailed him as he wept, **"O my son Absalom – if only I had died in your place!"** David remembered God's judgment on him for his sin with Bathsheba, as spoken by Nathan the prophet. He would pay four-fold for his crime. First, his baby died; then his lovely daughter, Tamar was violated; then wicked Amnon, his son, was murdered by his own brother; and now Absalom's rebellion and brutal death. David felt guilty for all four tragedies. For the sins of the father came upon the children.

It may be that David never had another happy day the rest of his life. It's hard for spirits to rise when such leaden weights are upon the soul. Oh the wages of sin! They can exact a heavy toll on us. The time to think about that is before we succumb to temptation. Sin is never worth the price. Before buying something, it's a good idea to check the price. Just ask Eve and Adam. Or how about Cain, who lamented, **"My punishment is greater than I can bear."** ? Consider whether Gehazi would have pursued after Namaan for the gold if he knew it would make him a leper the rest of his life. Surely Judas' conscience stung him so severely upon betraying Jesus, that he did not want to live another day. The memory of sin normally does not let one look back on it and reflect, "I sure had a good time!"

Yes **"the wages of sin is death, but the gift of God is eternal life, through Jesus Christ our Lord."** God knew we would all be sinners, but He made a way for us to be cleared of our sin. **"If we confess our sins, He is faithful and just to forgive us our sins and to cleanse us from all unrighteousness."** (I John 1:9) He is faithful to forgive. We may fail to confess, but when we do, he never fails to forgive. God gave up His Son, Jesus, to death by crucifixion so that He *could* forgive us. He can *justly* forgive, since the death of Jesus pays for all our sins. We cannot possibly merit a gift of such immeasurable value. We must simply accept this gift of God freely, or we shall not have it at all. The greatest gift we can give God is to accept *His* gift. I pray that you will do so.

SOLOMON

Solomon's birth would have made tabloid news. His father was David, the popular king of Israel. He was also a war hero. And his music would have made the top 40 with his many Psalms. Almost anything celebrities do makes it into the tabloids. God pity them. People don't value obscurity and privacy until it is taken from them by becoming a celebrity. With our warped values of today, celebrities become superheroes if they do something bad. Like getting divorced or having an affair. But this chapter isn't supposed to be about David. How'd we get into this? As you probably know, one of the best known stories of the Bible is the affair of David and Bathsheba. We all know they had an affair, although they were both married. Boy, was David ever married! He had about five wives at the time of this incident. It is surprising and very disappointing that Bathsheba agreed to this very shameful sin. She was already married to her own war hero, Uriah. He was also a principled man and a gentleman. Well you probably know the story, Bathsheba turns up pregnant and David plots to cover it up. But **"he who covers his sins will not prosper."** David plots to get Uriah killed and ends up marrying Bathsheba. Then the baby dies. Definitely tabloid material. When David's friend, Nathan the prophet confronts him with his double sin, guilt finally hits him and he repents. Very sincerely. But you won't read anything like that in a tabloid. David mourns not just the loss of his baby, but his terrible guilt and the fact that he has offended his great friend, God. **"For I acknowledge my transgressions...against You, You only, have I sinned, and done this evil in Your sight. Create in me a clean heart, O God...restore unto me the joy of Your salvation."** Surely God was very pleased with David's deep repentance. David fasted and prayed for the life of his sick baby for seven days. His baby died anyway. God surely mourned with David over this, for He is near to those who are of broken heart.

David was probably never more right with God than in the aftermath of this incident. This could have a lot to do with what happened next.

In II Samuel 12:24, David and Bathsheba have another baby, Solomon. In the same verse we see God's response to this new baby, **"Now the Lord loved him."** What a marvelous start for a baby to be found in the high favor of God when he is just beginning life! Isaac was a long promised son to Abraham and Sarah. What a mighty prince he became! An angel announces Samson's birth. John the Baptist was announced in prophecy and by an angel. Isaiah prophesied, **"For unto us a child is born, unto to us a Son is given."** This same baby was announced in advance to both parents, one by an angel, the other in a vision. What manner of child will this be! Baby Solomon, having the high favor of God, is also in this elite group. This should be interesting.

Maybe you have high aspirations for your child, boy or girl. It is really nice when both parents prepare the way and pave the road to greatness for their baby. You could try putting in a formal request for an angel to announce your child's birth. Or you could seek greatness for your child in the usual way: pray for the physical and spiritual development of your child. Every day. At length. I'd suggest a minimum of ten minutes per day for each child. This would be for the rest of your life. And maybe for a few years before they are born. And don't forget: *God* defines their greatness, not you.

Another thing Solomon has going for him is that his mother does not have to work. If we assume that King Lemuel, in Proverbs 31, is actually King Solomon, it makes the first nine verses of that chapter a description of some excellent parenting by his mother Bathsheba. "Lemuel" means "belonging to God".

Proverbs 31:1 **"The words of Lemuel, the utterance which his mother taught him."** This is giving due credit to a Godly mother and her advice.

V. 2. **What, my son? And what, son of my womb? And what, son of my vows?**

Here is a woman who made a vow before God to have a child. Women who ache in their heart for a child are more likely to deeply love that child and make the best of that child when he arrives. Consider Rachel, who so ached for a child that she cried out in desperation to her husband, "Give me children, or else I die!" Then God gave her Joseph! Hannah ached for a child a long time and finally made a vow before the Lord that if He would give her a male child, she would give him to the Lord all the days of his life. Then God gave her Samuel! Let not mothers be discouraged who wait and pray a long while for a child. It may be that God has a great son (or daughter) in store for them. Not one prayer for that child will be lost.

V. 3. **Do not give your strength to women**

This is an allusion to Proverbs 5:8, 9 which cautions

184

a young man to stay far from the lips of an immoral woman, lest they give their honor (wealth and property) to others. The young man is rather counseled to rejoice with the wife of his youth and to always be enraptured by her love.

V. 3 **Nor your ways to that which destroys kings.**
What is it that can destroy kings or top executives? We find out in the following verses.

V. 4 **It is not for kings, O Lemuel, it is not for kings to drink wine, nor for princes intoxicating drink.**
Alcohol can destroy the lives of even a strong man or a high-ranking man. A wise man will completely abstain from this notorious destroyer.

V. 5 **Lest they drink and forget the law, and pervert the justice of all the afflicted.**
Alcohol degrades the mental faculties. It renders a man less capable of making the right decisions, whether it's settling a complex legal case or treating a patient with subtle symptoms.

V. 6 **Give strong drink to him who is perishing, and wine to those who are bitter of heart.**
Alcohol for medicinal purposes is marginally acceptable. My worry is that everyone who wants a drink can find an excuse for it. But please don't mortgage your future competence for your present comfort.

V. 7 **Let him drink and forget his poverty, and remember his misery no more.**
This may provide temporary relief, but when sobriety returns, so will the memory of his troubles. The drinking will likely only worsen his poverty and add to his list of troublesome memories. How much better to abstain from the treacherous drink and

instead turn to an understanding heavenly Father, casting all our cares upon Him who cares for us.

V. 8, 9 Open your mouth for the speechless, in the cause of all who are appointed to die.

Open your mouth, judge righteously, and plead the cause of the poor and needy. Public advocates and social workers are commended here. All of us should in some degree be eyes to the blind, ears for the deaf, feet for the lame, hands for the helpless, a supply for those who lack and a voice for those who don't know what to say. Those who do so, God will surely be an advocate for them, a helper in every way.

We need kings trained up by a Bathsheba. We have enough who appoint themselves to be the hammer of the law, who use their power to feather their own nest, and who indulge themselves at the expense of the people or the company.

It was good that Solomon was well-groomed for the throne of Israel. And he did justice to his upbringing. He did quite well for a judge who never got a law degree. He never took a course in economics or business management, but he ran an entire nation skillfully. His parents did give him a good heart. If your parents were not able to put you through college, but trained you up in the way of righteousness, love of neighbor and the fear of God, you have a great deal to thank them for.

We're told very little about Solomon's upbringing. But even before Solomon was born, God spoke to David telling him he would have a son who was to be named Solomon. So God names him. At the same time, God tells David that he would not be allowed to build the new temple, which he wanted to do. He said Solomon would build it. Then God says Solomon would be *His* son. Sort of the way old Jacob told Joseph that his two sons, Ephraim and Manasseh, would become Jacob's sons. So David knows he has a very special son, whom God has big plans for. David probably spent a lot of quality time with his son.

In I Chronicles 22:11, David gives his son some good exhorting just before he rose to power, **"Now my son, may the Lord be with you; and may you prosper, and build the house of the Lord your God, as He has said to you. Only may the Lord give you wisdom and understanding, and give you charge concerning Israel, that you may keep the law of the Lord your God. Then you will prosper...Be strong and of good courage; do not fear nor be dismayed."** Solomon would later became extremely intent on getting wisdom. This talk with his father David may be where the desire for wisdom was first triggered in Solomon.

As David was nearing the day of his death, he gives Solomon a charge with these words, **"I go the way of all the earth; be strong, therefore, and prove yourself a man. And keep the charge of the Lord your God: to walk in all His ways, to keep His statutes, His commandments, His judgments, and His testimonies, as it is written in the law of Moses that you may prosper in all that you do and wherever you turn; that the Lord may fulfill His word which He spoke concerning me, saying, 'If your sons take heed to their way, to walk before Me in truth with all their heart and with all their soul,' He said, 'You shall not lack a man on the throne of Israel.' "**

David's final words are reminiscent of God's words to Joshua. **"Only be strong and very courageous, that you may observe to do according to all the law which**

187

Moses my servant commanded you; do not turn from it to the right hand or to the left, that you may prosper wherever you go. This Book of the Law shall not depart from your mouth, but you shall meditate in it day and night." Having received such wisdom and sage advice, Solomon was equipped with fine guidelines to navigate through the hazards of life.

SOLOMON BECOMES KING

I thank God that Solomon became king rather that vile Absalom, evil Amnon or self-serving Adonijah. Solomon did not rally the troops and garner support or build an allegiance to take the throne of Israel, as his half brother Adonijah tried. He did not slaughter all the males in the family and all the prominent men close to the throne, which was the usual method of gaining power. He simply believed the word of God spoken to his father, David, that he would be king. We also should try more often, just believing God and letting Him do His job.

Solomon started as king of Israel with no experience at any kind of leadership. Yet he demonstrated exceptional wisdom and good judgment from the outset. At the tender age of about 20, he became ruler of all Israel, commander in chief of Israel's impressive military forces, a one man chief justice of the nation's legal system, master architect and chief superintendent of the construction of an elaborate temple complex and organizer of the worship order of the priests and Levites. He did a superb job of managing all this, having had no experience of leadership in any of those fields. This kind of workload would normally require about a dozen top quality chief executives. He was absolutely phenomenal! It does not seem humanly possible. Here's how he did it.

SOLOMON'S WISDOM

In I Kings chapter 3, soon after he is inaugurated, we read in verse 3, **"And Solomon loved the Lord, walking in the statutes of his father David."** He put God first in his life as we also are exhorted to do by our Lord Jesus, **"Seek first the kingdom of God and His righteousness, and all these things shall be added to you."** (Matthew 6:33)

In verse 4, we see that Solomon, probably with a large crowd goes to Gibeon, where the tabernacle and the altar were set. There, after Solomon offers a thousand burnt offerings to the Lord, a wondrous experience occurs.

At Gibeon the Lord appeared to Solomon in a dream by night; and God said, "Ask! What shall I give you?" (V. 5) Solomon's reply was lengthy, but he requested only that God would give him an understanding heart to judge his people and that he may discern between good and evil. God was very pleased with his reply. God responds in v. 11, **"Because you have asked this thing, and have not asked long life for yourself, nor have asked riches for yourself, nor have asked the life of your enemies, but have asked for yourself understanding to discern justice, behold I have done according to your words; see I have given you a wise and understanding heart, so that there has not been anyone like you before you, nor shall any like you arise after you. And I have also given you what**

189

you have not asked: both riches and honor, so that there shall not be anyone like you among the kings all your days." I don't know that God has ever made such an offer to any man who ever lived! Equally astonishing is the noble response of Solomon. He asked for nothing but the ability to do his job well. When Jabez presented his request to God, he said, **"Oh that You would bless me indeed, and enlarge my territory, that Your hand would be with me, and that You would keep me from evil, that I may not cause pain."** So God granted him what he requested. (I Chronicles 4:10) So Jabez, along with some material requests, also asked for some noble things. But Solomon requested nothing for himself.

We learn an interesting principle of prayer in God's response to Solomon: that He sometimes grants us our petition because we did not ask for it. He gave Solomon riches and honor *because* he did not ask for it.

Not only did Solomon ask for a very good thing, he requested it with a very good motive: to serve his people.

We can do the same thing. For example, in my routine of praying, I sometimes have financial concerns I want to bring up before God. But when I have a lot of other more worthy things to pray for, like missionaries, spiritual needs of my friends, etc., I sometimes run out of time to cover the financial issues, leaving room for God to supply my needs without my asking for it. At times I resolve to keep all dollar signs from littering my prayers, as if "filthy lucre" is unworthy of occupying such holy ground. Let the Lord decide if He wishes to bless me anyway.

Would God give us wisdom in the same way He gave it so liberally to Solomon? That would be asking a hard thing, as Elisha when he requested a double portion of

190

Elijah's spirit. But we have good news on the subject. In James 1:5-7, the word of God gives us a magnificent promise: **"If any of you lacks wisdom, let him ask of God, who gives to all liberally and without reproach, and it will be given to him. But let him ask in faith, with no doubting, for he who doubts is like a wave of the sea driven and tossed by the wind. For let not that man suppose that he will receive anything from the Lord."** God's been wanting to give this to you anyway, so He's glad to grant it. Liberally. This does not mean He will make you shrewd and crafty in business or that you'll know how to pick stocks. But His wisdom will make you wise to know Him and understand His counsels, to know how to preserve the love in your marriage, to become skilled in personal relationships or to give wise advice to people.

In Solomon's case, God gave him a very broad wisdom in a wide range of subjects. [I Kings 4:29-34ff] It makes me wonder how that much wisdom and knowledge can fit in a single human head. He became world famous for his wisdom. **"Men of all nations, from all the kings of the earth who had heard of his wisdom, came to hear the wisdom of Solomon."** Most of us would be glad if just our wife would acknowledge our wisdom. "Nice idea, honey." May God give us such preachers today that people flock to hear him. For most of us, it might work better to request wisdom in just one field. "God, please make me wise to do my job extremely well." **"But this one thing I do...I press toward the mark for the prize of the high calling of God in Christ Jesus." "But seek that you may excel to the edifying of the church."** May the best and wisest men of today be His preachers!

SOLOMON AND THE TEMPLE

It is phenomenal how much Solomon kept meticulous attention to all the many aspects of the temple construction. He wrote to King Hiram of Tyre requesting large cedar trees from Lebanon be cut down and transported to Jerusalem. Old king Hiram was so struck by the wisdom in Solomon's letter that he said, **"Blessed be the Lord this day, for he has given David a wise son over this great people!"**

Solomon organized over 150,000 men to quarry large stones, cut to size in the mountains and delivered to the temple site. Thousands of others of various trades were employed in the temple construction, all under Solomon's orders. In the seven years the temple was being built, Solomon ordered that no noise, such as hammering or chiseling be allowed in the temple complex. The temple was to be treated as holy ground so as not to disturb the praying of God's people. This reminds me of Jesus and His care of the same holy ground: **"And He found in the temple those who sold oxen and sheep and doves, and the money changers doing business…He drove them all out of the temple."** We can imagine how noisy and clamorous it was! **And Jesus said to them, "It is written, 'My house shall be called a house of prayer, but you have made it a den of thieves.' "** God help us to restore reverence to our churches today!

We are told in I Kings 6:38 that Solomon was seven years in building the temple. And in the following verse (I Kings 7:1), that he spent thirteen years building his own house, or rather, palace. He also built a summer home which was also like a palace. So Solomon was like a lot of us today, doing a fine work for God, but a much greater work for ourselves.

When the temple was finally complete, Solomon dedicates it with the second longest prayer in the Bible. With the top leaders from around the country and thousands of people present, they sacrificed innumerable sheep and oxen and the ark of God was transported to be placed in the new temple as its permanent home. God expresses his pleasure at the magnificent work of the people over the past seven years: **"And it came to pass, when the priests came out of the holy place, that the cloud filled the house of the Lord, so that the priests could not continue ministering because of the cloud; for the glory of the Lord filled the house."** May the houses of the Lord all over America be likewise filled with the glory of God, as He expresses His pleasure at the abundant labors and reverence of His people! May He respond to the unceasing prayers of his church, and light again the fires of His Pentecost! May we be miraculously transformed from a church that is **"wretched, miserable, poor, blind and naked"** to a church that is eaten up with a zeal for the Lord of Hosts! This can happen in a church of ten as well as in a church of ten thousand. This kind of revival can happen in any denomination. It will happen when He chooses. But it is more likely to happen in churches who are much into the word of God, who pray without ceasing and who separate themselves from a corrupt, worldly society.

SOLOMON'S MARRIED LIFE

He married Pharaoh's daughter, ill advisedly. It appears that the marriage was more for political reasons than for love. **"Now Solomon made a treaty with**

Pharaoh king of Egypt, and married Pharaoh's daughter." (I Kings 3:1)

This was like Samson, who declined to marry a woman of Israel. **"Now Samson went *down* to Timnah, and saw a woman in Timnah of the daughters of the Philistines."** Samson's troubled life is already going downhill. He has no business keeping company with ungodly idolators. **"So he went up and told his father and mother, saying, 'I have seen a woman in Timnah of the daughters of the Philistines; now therefore get her for me as a wife.' "** Apparently, he was not much of a Bible reader. **"Then his father and mother said to him, 'Is there no woman among the daughters of your brethren…that you must go and get a wife from the uncircumcised Philistines?' "** Apparently, they *were* Bible readers.

The strongest man and the wisest man make the same mistake. Let us beware of making the same mistake as these two men. They also both fell the same way: from the cajoling of their lovers. Delilah and Solomon's wives.

It was expressly against the Scriptures to marry outside of their faith as Israelites. But Solomon did so many times over. He ends up having 700 wives and 300 concubines! What was he thinking? How can he possibly give a proper amount of love and attention to that many women? Most of us can barely satisfy one woman. Let us choose our spouse wisely and from the household of faith. If a man does nothing else well in life, let him marry well.

Lessons to learn from this:
- **Make a decision early in life not to ever veer away from following the Lord.** There are a lot

of ways to fall away from God. And any one of them can bring disaster on our lives.

– **Be obedient to all the teachings of God's Word.** e.g.: Do not be unequally with an unbeliever.
– **Stay in the word of God every day.** Solomon probably did so for many years. But I suspect he got out of the habit and started skipping days more and more. Finally the influence of his pagan wives became stronger than the word of God in his heart. **"Nor shall you make marriages with them. You shall not give your daughter to their son, nor take their daughter for your son." (Deut. 7:3) "Neither shall he multiply wives for himself, lest his heart turn away."** (Deut. 17:17) It is as if these verses were written personally for Solomon. If he had read these scriptures recently before one of his wives begged him to build her a shrine for her god, it would probably have been enough of a deterrent. Or maybe he would have declined dating additional women entirely.
– **Choose your friends from the household of faith.**
– **Try not to marry several hundred wives.**

SOLOMON'S PRAYER

Solomon's prayer is the second longest in the Bible. The first is in Nehemiah (Eight Levites are named as leading this prayer.) This was part of a worship service consisting of 3 hours of Scripture reading and 3 hours of prayer and worship. The third longest is Jesus in the upper room. All three were in Jerusalem. We may conclude that great men can be associated with great praying.

At the end of Solomon's prayer service, they had a super offering: 22,000 bulls and 120,000 sheep. They also had dinner on the grounds - for 14 days. We are told that "all Israel" attended. That was a pretty nice church dedication service.

Now let's consider Solomon's prayer of I Kings chapter 8. His actual prayer begins in verse 23 and ends at verse 53. Consider these elements of this historic prayer:

a. In v. 23 – He declares God to be the only God. An important point with Israel surrounded by false gods.
b. V. 24, 25 – God is a promise keeper.
c. V. 26 – God's prophetic word will always be fulfilled.
d. V. 27 – God inhabits the heavens and beyond.
e. V. 28 – God hears our prayers.
f. V. 30 – God hears from heaven and forgives.
g. V. 32 – God judges justly.
h. V. 33, 34 – God rewards confession and repentance.
i. V. 35, 36 – God chastens His people as a father his children.
j. V. 37-39 – God is sovereign over all nature and all nations.
k. V. 39 – He knows the heart of every man.
l. V. 40 – God's people are to properly fear Him.
m. V. 41-43 – God so loves the nations of the world.
n. V. 44-45 – God maintains the cause of His people.
o. V. 46-50 – God forgives and restores.
p. V. 51 – God is possessive of His people whom He has redeemed.
q. V. 52 – God is continually attentive to the prayers of His people.
r. V. 53 – God's people are to be a separated people.

His prayer is a theological masterpiece! Not only

was his prayer effectual before God, it was extremely edifying for all in attendance. It ranks among the greatest prayers in the Bible. Those who like to recite the "Our Father" ought to also memorize and recite this one regularly. Well…maybe read it regularly.

SOLOMON AS A TYPE OF CHRIST

Psalm 72 is a prophetic psalm. According to the last verse, it is also a prayer of David for his son, Solomon. Now keep in mind that David dies shortly after Solomon becomes king. He sees virtually nothing of his reign. Psalm 72 is David's prayer for the success of Solomon's reign. But as with many prophets of old, they wrote as moved by the Holy Spirit, sometimes not even knowing what they wrote. I suspect that was the case with David here. In David's mind, he was praying, prophesying of the reign of Solomon, who probably was not yet king. Yet many of the events prophesied came to pass during Solomon's reign. But they are also prophecies of the coming reign of Jesus Christ in His millennial kingdom.

This psalm describes the character of Solomon and his reign although Solomon was a feeble and faulty preview of the perfect and eternal Christ.

- V. 1 **Give the king your judgments, O God,** Solomon was renowned for his wise judgments. In His coming kingdom, Jesus will judge with perfect equity.
- V. 1b **And Your righteousness to the king's son.** Solomon was somewhat righteous, most of his life. Jesus will remain perfect in righteousness throughout his reign.

- V. 2 **He will judge your people with righteousness, and your poor with justice.** True for both.
- V. 4 **He will bring justice to the poor of the people; he will save the children of the needy, and will break in pieces the oppressor.** Characteristic of both reigns.
- V. 7 **In his days, righteousness will flourish, and abundance of peace.** Peace prevailed all throughout Solomon's reign. He was the only king of Israel who had no wars. The peace of the millennial kingdom will be so thorough that the wolf shall lay down with the lamb and the leopard shall lie down with the young goat. And maybe the Democrats will cease squabbling with the Republicans.
- V. 8-11 **He shall have dominion also from sea to sea, and from the River to the ends of the earth... 11. The kings of Tarshish and of the isles will bring presents; the kings of Sheba and Seba will offer gifts. Yes all kings shall fall down before him; all nations shall serve him.** David predicts that Solomon's kingdom will extend fully to the original limits of the Promised Land. This is seen in I Kings 4:21. We also know that Jesus will reign over all the nations of the world in the millennial kingdom.
- V. 12-14 **He will deliver the needy when he cries, the poor also and him who has no helper. He will spare the poor and needy, and will save the souls of the needy, He will redeem their life from oppression and violence; and precious shall be their blood in His sight.** May God make

us His instrument in performing this.

- V. 17 **His name shall endure forever; His name shall continue as long as the sun. And men shall be blessed in Him; all nations shall call Him blessed.** Both the name of Jesus Christ and Solomon have endured to this day and will continue. But Jesus has the name that is above every name, before whom every knee shall bow and every tongue shall confess that He is Lord!

Consider also these ways in which Solomon is a type of Christ:

a. Both Solomon and Christ are sons of David. Solomon was David's immediate son; Jesus Christ was his last prophesied Son.

b. Solomon was the wisest man of his time; Jesus is the wisest of all time.

c. Solomon was the richest man of his time; according to Revelation, Jesus has received "power and riches and wisdom and might and honor and glory and blessing".

d. Both have a long reign of peace. Solomon reigned 40 years with no war; Jesus will have a 1000 year reign of peace.

e. Both Solomon and Jesus reign in Jerusalem.

f. Solomon built the temple of God; Jesus builds the church of God.

g. Both were chosen by their fathers. According to Bathsheba, David said, "Assuredly, Solomon your son shall reign after me and he shall sit on my throne." And Jesus' Father in heaven said, "This is My beloved Son in whom I am well-pleased."

h. Solomon built the temple; Christ cleansed the temple. And Christ inhabits the temple of our heart.

THE QUEEN OF SHEBA

One particular incident in Solomon's life makes a fascinating preview or allegory of the coming King: when the Queen of Sheba visited king Solomon. This is recorded in I Kings chapter 10. Never before in history and never again since, was there such a vast exchange of royal revenue. (The exchange was about 20% of Israel's gross national product.)

The location of Sheba is not known exactly, but the distance is roughly 1300 miles, mostly through rough wilderness terrain. We don't know how long it took her to make the trip. Probably something like two to four months. Let's just ponder this for a moment: she made a long, uncomfortable round trip to hear Solomon. Apparently she was also seeking God. Like the Ethiopian eunuch. Verse 1 tells us **"When the queen of Sheba heard of the fame of Solomon *concerning the name of the Lord*, she came to test him with hard questions."** She did not come to meekly sit and listen, she was planning to be a little confrontational. "She came to test him." I get the impression she wanted to be convinced to believe in God, but over every challenge and objection she could throw out. She wanted to be thoroughly convinced like some people today.

Jesus Himself likens the queen of Sheba seeking Solomon to men seeking Christ. **"The queen of the South will rise up in the judgment with the men of** this generation and condemn them, for she came from the ends of the earth to hear the wisdom of Solomon; and indeed a greater than Solomon is here."

In verse 2, she arrives in Jerusalem with a caravan of **camels "that bore spices, very much gold, and precious stones."** This was like the wise men who came bearing gold, frankincense and myrrh. Both groups came to see the king of Israel. But baby Jesus didn't have much to say. It is safe to say that both groups put a high value on the king they planned to see. Both groups came a very long way, as did the eunuch of Acts. The question is, how far are we willing to go to find God, get answers and to receive Jesus Christ? **"And you will seek Me and find Me when you search for Me with all your heart."** (Jeremiah 29:13) If we have to work at finding Him, we will value a relationship with Him much more.

At the end of v. 2, the queen of Sheba comes to Solomon and **"she spoke with him about all that was in her heart."** This is a perfect picture of how we should come to God, opening our heart entirely to Him.

In v. 3, we find that nothing is hidden from the understanding of the king. Just as God knows all the thoughts, intents and motives of our heart.

At the end of v. 5, the queen of Sheba is completely disarmed. **"There was no more spirit in her."** She was no longer critical or skeptical. She sort of surrenders. So must the one seeking God also surrender.

V. 6 tells us that after coming to the king, she now believes everything she had been told. Solomon's wisdom exceeded everything she had imagined. It could have been said of Solomon as it was said of Jesus, **"Never a man spoke like this man!"** How marvelous is the wisdom of the first and second Solomon!

V.7 illustrates that the unbeliever is transformed when they come and see. In utter amazement, the queen of Sheba exclaims, **"Indeed the half was not told me. Your wisdom and prosperity exceed the fame of which I heard."** As we're told in Corinthians, **"Eyes have not seen, ears have not heard and neither has it entered into the heart of man the things that God has prepared for them that love Him."**

V. 8 tells the good fortune of the men who attend Solomon day to day and hear him. How much more is there joy indescribable for those who come to God and are born again!

V.9 **"Because the Lord has loved Israel forever, therefore He made you king."** And blessed be God who gave Jesus to the church to be our Head. He gave us the one who loved us and gave Himself for us.

V.10 **"Then she gave the king 120 talents of gold, spices in great quantity, and precious stones."** We also have much to give God, our king. To Him, we are like gold, spices, precious stones. Each of us has so much beauty, love, personality, talent, etc. But we tend to feel so insignificant. Even so, we are greatly loved by God. God sooo loves the world – the people, that is.

V. 13 **"Now King Solomon gave the queen of Sheba all she desired, whatever she asked, besides what Solomon had given her according to the royal generosity."** So he gave her two categories of gifts: a large royal sum and all else she desired. This neatly parallels what God gives the new believer. First the great, unimaginable gift of everlasting life and a place in heaven. But He also gives us numerous little desires of our heart throughout our life. **"Delight yourself also**

in the Lord and He will give you the desires of your heart." (Psalm 37:4)

When we are saved, born again, we have a Friend for life. I wonder if Solomon and the queen of Sheba kept up a friendship and correspondence between them. Maybe they texted every day. We should certainly commune with our God every day and hear from His word every day. We should try to grow in our relationship with Him.

Today, the greatest possible exchange of gifts is between you and God. We all know how much God plans to do for us. But can you tie a big red bow around yourself?

CONCLUSION

God appeared twice to Solomon and spoke to him on two other occasions: once just after his inauguration, again during temple construction in which the word of the Lord came to him and a third time after the completion of all Solomon's construction work. (I Kings 6:11 and 9:2) On a fourth occasion, God rebuked him for his idolatry. (I Kings 11:9ff) In addition to these personal encounters, Solomon also witnessed close up, the cloud of the glory of the Lord filling the temple at the dedication. With all this going for him, his failure is all the more inexcusable. To whom much is given, much may be expected. I can imagine that Solomon may have rationalized his idolatry like this, "I'm still worshiping God faithfully. I'm just also attending my wife's church with her. Sure I sing along with their people and say their prayers to the lady god they worship just to go along with them. But I still worship You, Lord. I'm just trying to keep peace in the family." But **"I am the Lord your God, you shall have no other gods before Me. You shall not bow down to them nor serve them."**

Have you been raised in a Godly home and in a good church? Were you blessed to keep company with very saintly people, many of whom pray for you? Were you sent to get a quality education in a Christian school or college? Were you privileged to have a dating relationship with a virtuous woman? To whom much is given, much can be expected.

Solomon ran so well earlier in life, but his wives hindered him. How could such a wise man make such a foolish mistake? **"The fear of the Lord is the beginning of wisdom; and a good understanding have all those who do His commandments."** Maybe Solomon was more worried about the clamoring of his wives than the retribution of God.

Solomon's inexplicable collapse into idolatry was a "fly in the ointment". (He actually wrote this proverb.) When David had his affair with Bathsheba and had Uriah killed, Nathan the prophet, rebuked king David with these words, **"By this deed you have given great occasion to the enemies of the Lord to blaspheme."** (II Sam. 12:14) This was Solomon's parents! No doubt he knew all about the matter. He likely grew up hearing people blaspheme God and his so-called holy people, as a result of his parents' sins. Maybe young Solomon sometimes thought to himself, "I would never do such a sinful thing and cause disgrace to God's name and His people!" But Solomon would do even worse.

Therefore let him that thinks he stands take heed

lest he fall. Peter would agree. "Lord I would never deny You."

May God preserve you.

DANIEL

Daniel confronted and rebuked two separate emperors and rose to the presidency under a third, in a different empire. Hungry lions would not touch him; he spoke with angels, he had visions of heaven and he was given visions detailing the rise and fall of empires to the end of the world. What manner of man is this?

In the New Testament, we have the "disciple whom Jesus loved". In the Old Testament, we have Daniel, the greatly beloved of God. This is said only of Daniel. Who is this man? In this chapter on Daniel, we will investigate and analyze the character traits of this man. He is not a popular folk hero like David or a wealthy man and father of many nations like Abraham. He was a little on the reclusive side and turned down the offer of more wealth than we ever dreamed of.

While others take vacations on cruise ships, Daniel takes trips to heaven. Instead of a cruise ship that indulges every pleasure and fine food, Daniel fasted three weeks and had terrifying visions of heaven that left him weak and sick for days. I don't recommend a visit to heaven for your next vacation.

May I introduce you to Daniel, man of God.

CHAPTER 1

"But Daniel purposed in his heart that he would not defile himself with the portion of the king's delicacies, nor with the wine which he drank.; therefore he requested of the chief of the eunuchs that he might not defile himself." (Daniel 1:8)

Earlier in chapter one, we see Daniel and his three friends heading off to college. Sort of. He's now living away from Dad and Mom for the first time. Probably. They get a scholarship to the University of Babylon. In a way. So this passage talks to young men starting off to college.

In recent years, over one quarter of all college students in the United States drop out in their first year.[1] It's not that college is so hard. There are other contributing factors. It seems that it's a common tendency among these students to throw off all restraint as soon as they can get out from under the "tyranny" of their parents. Barely 18, three years below the legal drinking age, young college students quickly fall for the lifestyle of "frat" parties and binge drinking. It's not surprising that church attendance in this group also drops off to about half by their third year of college.[3]

But not so for Daniel. We are given a few insights into his character. First, notice in v. 8 the words: "Daniel purposed". Instead of drifting with the tide of popularity, he formed his own life principles. Rather than a spineless jellyfish drifting aimlessly with the tide, he was more like the amazing salmon, who determines his goals and, overcoming all obstacles, finds his way there. Establishing life purposes is particularly important for a young man. Before launching out into life, he should have his moral compass well calibrated and his rudder working.

In this opening round of analyzing Daniel's character, I can see how someone could easily think that the main point is eating healthy food. But that would not be right. Although a healthy body would be a nice side effect. More than pursuing the pleasures of this world, he was determined to abstain from sin and defilement. Where did he get this sterling value? Probably from his "tyrannical" parents.

> **My son, keep your father's command, and do not forsake the law of your mother. Bind them continually upon your heart; tie them around your neck. When you roam, they will lead you.** (Proverbs 6:20-22)

This is one of those priceless jewels of the Bible, well able to take a man a long way in life – like Daniel.

In the same verse, we find the words, **"therefore he requested of the chief of the eunuchs that he might not defile himself."** He respectfully acknowledged the authority of the chief eunuch. He did not take up a holier-than-thou attitude and refuse the king's vile food. Although he was one of the highly favored "scholarship" students at the king's college, he did not talk down to this palace servant, a eunuch. He probably spoke as respectfully to him as he would have to the emperor. As we will see later, he showed respect to men of all ranks. This may be part of why Daniel had special favor with the eunuch. I wouldn't be surprised if the other honor students were not very respectful toward this eunuch. But the main reason why Daniel was well-liked is found in verse 9. **"Now God had brought Daniel into the favor and goodwill of the chief of the**

eunuchs." We shall find that such goodness and mercy shall follow Daniel all the days of his life. No value can be put upon such divine blessings. Worth more than all the wealth of the world is God's love upon a person. Did God arbitrarily chose to bless Daniel? He would have the right to, but remember Daniel first chose to obey the laws of the Bible by not eating forbidden food or drinking strong drink, alcohol. It seems that God gave him favor with a key person in his life because he *first* purposed to obey God.

Now at first the eunuch was hesitant to give Daniel his request. Maybe he thought Daniel was anorexic and would start getting thin. And the king would hold him responsible. So Daniel proposes a test: let him and his friends eat healthy vegetables and drink water for ten days and then compare them with the rest of the students. So at the end of the ten days, Daniel and his friends looked healthier than the others. So the eunuch allowed them to change their diet.

Now think about this: Daniel never drank alcohol in his life. So he never had damage to his brain cells and neurons, which alcohol can destroy or damage[2]. He retained his full faculties all his life. It's a good thing he did, because he would become a top minister of two world empires and would need all the help he could get. He had a definite edge on all the guys that drank wine all their lives.

So how did Daniel do in academics? We find the answer in v. 17: **"As for these four young men, God gave them knowledge and skill in all literature and wisdom..."** Sure Daniel and his three friends all studied. And yes, their brains were not damaged by the alcoholic wine. But probably the most significant benefit they had is that **"God *gave* them knowledge"**.

We are not told that any of the other students were given knowledge, only the four Hebrew, Jewish boys. God honors those who honor Him. And they certainly honored God. Probably in many more ways than we're told in this chapter. No doubt they were praying young men. They probably did not share in the dirty jokes of the other young men. They purposed not to defile themselves. Not with their food and not with their words. And surely not with women. They were raised with good morals in God-worshiping families. And they kept those values when they left home.

No wonder they found favor with the great Emperor Nebuchadnezzar upon their graduation. **"Then the king interviewed them, and among them all none was found like Daniel, Hananiah, Mishael, and Azariah; therefore they served before the king. And in all matters of wisdom and understanding about which the king examined them, he found them ten times better than all the magicians and astrologers who were in all his realm."** They aced their first interview and got top jobs.

DANIEL 2

One night, Emperor Nebuchadnezzar had a disturbing dream. He was so troubled he could not get back to sleep. So he calls in all his experts and this is what happened:

And the king said to them, "I have had a dream, and my spirit is anxious to know the dream. Then the Chaldeans spoke to the king in Aramaic, "O king, live forever! Tell your servants the dream, and we will give the interpretation." The king answered and said to the

210

Chaldeans, **"My decision is firm: if you do not make known the dream to me, and its interpretation, you shall be cut in pieces, and your houses shall be made an ash heap."** I have the feeling the king and his advisors had issues. He goes on: **"However, if you tell the dream and its interpretation, you shall receive from me gifts, rewards, and great honor. Therefore, tell me the dream and its interpretation." They answered again and said, "Let the king tell his servants the dream, and we will give its interpretation." The king answered and said, I know for certain that you would gain time, because you see that my decision is firm: If you do not make known the dream to me, there is only one decree for you! For you have agreed to speak lying and corrupt words before me till the time has changed. Therefore tell me the dream, and I shall know that you can give me its interpretation."**

He was probably as much fun to work for as Pharaoh, when he said make bricks and from now on get your own straw.

V. 10 continues, **The Chaldeans answered the king and said, "There is not a man on earth who can tell the king's matter; therefore no king, lord, or ruler has ever asked such things of any magician, astrologer or Chaldean. It is a difficult thing that the king requests. and there is no other who can tell it to the king except the gods, whose dwelling is not with flesh." For this reason the king was angry and very furious, and gave the command to destroy all the wise men of Babylon.** This man has got some anger issues. This is what happens when you don't have a system of checks and balances.

So the decree went out and they began killing the wise men; and they sought Daniel and his companions,

to kill them. In the midst of this mayhem, we read in v. 14, **Then with counsel and wisdom Daniel answered Arioch, the captain of the king's guard, who had gone out to kill all the wise men of Babylon: he answered and said to Arioch the king's captain, "Why is the decree from the king so urgent?" Then Arioch made known the decision to Daniel.**

Can you believe what Daniel does next? Remember now, His Royal Highness is having a temper tantrum. He has just ordered the execution of all the wise men of Babylon, which included young Daniel. But Daniel just calmly walks into the great throne room and asks the emperor for a little more time. Poor Daniel! Nobody told him that that's exactly what got him so mad in the first place! **"I know for certain that you would gain time."**

And he was right. They were stalling so they could come up with some kind of response that would keep them from getting executed. Anybody else, Nebuchadnezzar would probably rage at him and order him to be executed.

Daniel is getting some early experience in facing a raging lion. It's equally astonishing that Nebuchadnezzar says to Daniel, "Sure kid, take all the time you need." Or words to that effect.

So Daniel and his friends spent the entire night coming up with the correct answer. Meanwhile, it appears that the other not-so-wise men had their executions suspended, pending Daniel's success. They must have been sweating bullets that night. Except they didn't have bullets in those days. Although Daniel's life was also in danger, it is clear that he mainly wanted to help the distressed Nebuchadnezzar and to save the lives of the other wise men.

In Dan. 2:18, we find that the 4 young Jewish boys spent the night seeking their God for answers. Now remember, Daniel has never had a vision before. This is all new to him. All he knows is: he's got a big problem and he's going to God for help.

V. 19 **Then the secret was revealed to Daniel in a night vision.** Daniel does not hasten off to Ariel with the great news. He tarries in prayer to glorify and thank his God first. Like the one leper. Listen to this magnificent prayer.

"Blessed be the name of God forever and ever, for wisdom and might are His.

And he changes the times and the seasons;

He removes kings and raises up kings;

He gives wisdom to the wise, and knowledge to those who have understanding. He knows what is in the darkness, and light dwells with Him.

I thank you and praise you, O God of my fathers; you have given me wisdom and might,

And have made known to me what we asked of you,

For you have made known to us the king's demand."

This prayer by a young man ought to be etched in gold on a back drop of silver. It should be hung in great cathedrals, next to Mary's Magnificat and Hannah's prayer. Most of *our* prayers should be taped to the refrigerator next to the grocery list. They would look a lot alike, with our usual "grocery list" of requests. A man's prayer is probably the best gauge of his Godliness. Unfortunately.

It's touching that near the end of his prayer, he credits his three friends with the revelation God sends. **"What we asked of you".** He does not hurry back

213

to the king with the exciting news, even though we already saw that Daniel had direct access to the king. In v. 24, he first goes to Captain Arioch and immediately tries to stop the execution of the other wise men. Then he says, **"Take me before the king, and I will tell the king the interpretation."** So he includes Arioch in delivering the good news. We can be sure that Arioch deeply appreciated Daniel deferring to him like this. It's always a good policy to deflect credit to others for some good, wherever possible. It's like casting your bread upon the waters, for it will come back to you after many days. (Eccles. 11:1) Also the less credit we get for whatever reason, the more God will be inclined to bless you over and above.

V. 25 Then Arioch quickly brought Daniel before the king, and said thus to him, "I have found a man of the captives of Judah, who will make known to the king the interpretation." It probably passed through the king's mind that Daniel came to him on his own the day before. But now Arioch is taking credit for it. Nebuchadnezzar graciously drops it and gives attention to Daniel.

V. 26 Then the king answered and said to Daniel, "Are you able to make known to me the dream which I have seen, and its interpretation?" It would be so easy to take credit for something that looks like he deserves it. "Yes, O king, I sure can." was ready to just roll off his tongue. But deeply imbedded character restrained him and gave him his carefully worded response,

"The secret the king has demanded, the wise men, the astrologers, the magicians, and the soothsayers cannot declare to the king."

In saying this, he exonerates the wise men from any plot the king may have suspected, thus strengthening the case to save their lives. Now Daniel honors God.

But there is a God in heaven who reveals secrets, and he has made known to King Nebuchadnezzar what will be in the latter days.

Notice Daniel does not say, "He has made known to me", but **"He has made known to King Nebuchnezzar."** So Daniel bypasses himself in his explanation, as if he is just the insignificant messenger between God and the king. This was not just quick thinking in a show of humility. He probably truly regards himself as a lowly servant, so that his language flowed naturally. Or maybe he didn't regard himself at all. For humility is not belittling one's self, but forgetting one's self. In a very humble attempt to deflect credit for the revealing of the dream, Daniel says in v. 30,

"But as for me, this secret has not been revealed to me because I have more wisdom than anyone living, but for our sakes who made known the interpretation to the king.

Translation: I'm no better than anybody else. God just did this for me and my friends.

Finally, Daniel gives the king a detailed description of the dream which Daniel had the night before, which was apparently identical to the dream Nebuchadnezzar had two nights before.

In v. 36, we find that the interpretation is given not by Daniel alone, but by all four Jewish young men, each probably giving a pre-arranged portion of the explanation. Maybe each one gave an interpretation of one of the four empires to come. It would be just like Daniel to share the honor of the interpretation. All four did get substantial promotions.

We will mercifully not get into the fascinating prophetic dream itself and its fulfillment. That would fill another entire book.

As if this incident is not already full of enough shocking things, look what happens when Daniel concludes his discourse. In v. 46, we read, **Then King Nebuchadnezzar fell on his face, prostrate before Daniel and commanded that they should present an offering and incense to him.** Obviously, the king wasn't paying very good attention when Daniel said, "there is a God in heaven who reveals secrets" and that Daniel has no more wisdom that other people. Well Daniel tried. How embarrassing. The emperor bowing down to you!

The king answered Daniel, and said, "Truly your God is the God of gods, the Lord of kings, and a revealer of secrets, since you could reveal this secret." What a mighty God we serve! Oh, that our lives could similarly cause others to glorify God!

This incident concludes with the king promoting Daniel to ruler over the entire province of Babylon. In the last verse, we see Daniel petitioning on behalf of Shadrach, Meshach and Abed-Nego with similar promotions over Babylon. You may be thinking, we all need a friend like Daniel. But rather, let's all *be* a friend like Daniel.

Notice the timing of Nebuchadnezzar's dream. It happened shortly after Daniel becomes one of the Emperor's wise men. It seems that God orchestrated Daniel getting a job close to Nebuchadnezzar for such a time as this. For God will do nothing, but He will reveal His secret to his servants, the prophets. And only to His prophets. Similar providential timing brought Joseph before Pharaoh and Mordecai before

Emperor Ahasuerus. All three of these men had humble positions in life. But through God's sovereign working, He raised up these men to running the greatest world power of their time. None of the three had the slightest idea this would happen. All three were foreigners and they certainly had no plans to seek such power. But God would have His lights shining in every place, high and low. Joseph saved several nations from likely starvation; Mordecai saved the Jews from a likely genocide and Daniel may have been instrumental in the Jews being allowed to return to Israel and become a nation once again.

Why did God choose to raise these men out of obscurity to the most exalted office possible? Because they were highly intelligent? Not really. Nothing is written about any of them being exceptionally smart. On the contrary, it is written that not many wise men after the flesh…are called. None of them sought the high position. Men who have an obsession for power are probably most unfit for it.

So was there a common attribute among these men that would explain why God chose them? Who can say? However, what we can see is that all three had a willingness to do good at every opportunity. They seemed to have no thought about being rewarded for it, paid for it or even acknowledged for it. Remember that Jesus counseled us not to advertise our good deeds:

Therefore, when you do a charitable deed, do not sound a trumpet before you as the hypocrites do in the synagogues and in the streets, that they may have glory from men.

Mordecai never mentioned that he had saved the life of the emperor. Joseph was never rewarded or even remembered for the care he provided for the prisoners.

For them, doing good was its own reward. Daniel was called out in the middle of the night to help Emperor Belshazzar in a terrifying situation. When he offered a great reward to Daniel for his service, Daniel replied basically, keep your money. Elisha would have been proud of him.

All these men faithfully adhered to a strong moral code without wavering. The point is: God chose and still chooses a good man. Preferably a man who thinks little of himself. For it is the humble who shall be exalted.

DANIEL 4

We do not hear at all about Daniel in chapter 3, so we pick up his story in chapter 4. We have the same two main characters: Daniel and Emperor Nebuchadnezzar. I have to wonder if in those days, the more important you are, the longer a name you get. I just thank God that we're never told Nebuchadnezzar's middle and last name.

This is the same Nebuchadnezzar we had back in chapters 1 and 2. I say this because he is almost unrecognizable in chapter 4. In chapter 2, he is a perfect grouch, unreasonable, demanding, threatening and clinically paranoid.

Some of you might work for a Nebuchadnezzar. Some of you ladies might be married to one. It takes an act of God to reason with him. And that's exactly what is about to happen. But in chapter 4, he is much more reasonable about getting help with difficult problems. There was no more of his threatening to cut people in pieces and turning their houses into an ash heap if they can't figure out his problem. In chapter 2, he was a godless egotist. In chapter 4, he is a God worshipper and a reasonable man. What could have happened to change this emperor so drastically? You're not going to believe it.

Notice that the entire chapter is a letter from Emperor Nebuchadnezzar to every nation on earth. This may be the single greatest act of evangelism in history. In this letter, he glorifies God, the Most High God, he confesses his own sins and he honors God's man, Daniel. At the very end of his letter, he writes:

Now I, Nebuchadnezzar, praise and extol and honor the King of heaven, all of whose works are truth, and His ways justice. And those who walk in pride He is able to put down.

This looks more like something Daniel would write. But how could this be from Nebuchadnezzar? No mention of raising taxes. No threatening to chop people in pieces. What we do know is that he's been around Daniel for a long time. How blessed is that person whose Godly qualities can be seen in the people he has spent time with. Many pastors are like that.

In this chapter, we pick up more qualities of Daniel, as seen through the eyes of a world emperor, and as moved by the Holy Spirit, the author of the Scriptures. In verse 5, Nebuchadnezzar begins his astonishing tale:

I saw a dream which made me afraid, and the thoughts on my bed and the visions of my head troubled me.

So he has another dream, but this time he remembers it. Same routine: he calls in all the "wise" men to give him the interpretation. Nobody has a clue. But nobody got chopped to pieces either. Finally, Daniel comes to see if he can help. Daniel comes highly recommended. Nebuchadnezzar writes, "in him is the Spirit of the Holy God." No doubt, Daniel's holy life style contributed to Nebuchadnezzar's good opinion of God. "Hallowed be thy name." God give us men who have such a good testimony with people around them. In his letter, he tells about the dream which he had, and told to Daniel:

I was looking, and behold, a tree in the midst of the earth, and its height was great.

The tree grew and became strong; its height reached to the heavens, and it could be seen to the ends of all the earth. Its leaves were lovely, its fruit abundant, and in it was food for all.

The beasts of the field found shade under it, The birds of the heavens dwelt in its branches, and all flesh was fed from it.

I saw in the visions of my head while on my bed, and there was a watcher, a holy one, coming down from heaven. He cried aloud and said thus, "Chop down the tree and cut off its branches, strip off its leaves and scatter its fruit. Let the beasts get out from under it, and the birds from its branches. Nevertheless leave the stump and roots in the earth, bound with a band of iron and bronze, in the tender grass of the field. Let it be wet with the dew of heaven, and let him graze with the beasts on the grass of the earth. Let his heart be changed from that of a man, let him be given the heart of a beast, and let seven times pass over him. This decree is by the decision of the watchers, and the sentence by

the word of the holy ones, in order that the living may know that the Most High rules in the kingdom of men, gives it to whomever He will, and sets over it the lowest of men.

In v. 18, Nebuchadnezzar expresses his confidence in Daniel to interpret the dream. Back in v. 9, he expressed the same confidence in Daniel and says **"no secret troubles you."** But he was mistaken, for in v. 19, we are told that Daniel **"was astonished for a time, and his thoughts troubled him."** But he was troubled only because of what it meant to the emperor. He felt bad for him. Daniel expresses his wish that the bad news would be for his enemies, rather than for him. But he faithfully delivers the bad news to Nebuchadnezzar in a lengthy, detailed explanation. Just as little Samuel delivered the bad news to old Eli, though it made him afraid. A prophet or a preacher who delivers only the good news is not worth his salt. The truth is: if we would deliver the bad news as we should, then the good news will be better accepted.

Daniel is not hesitating here because he's afraid to say it. Rather, he is struggling to find a way to save his friend from the disaster being predicted. He does his best to accomplish this with his counsel at the end. He is far from gloating that this evil dictator is getting a terrible punishment he deserves.

Daniel reluctantly gives the bad news: Nebuchadnezzar is the great tree in the dream. It is decreed by angels that he will be "chopped down". He will then be put out to pasture with the beasts to eat grass for 7 years. Daniel tactfully omits the part where he will be given the heart of a beast. But he elaborates on the part at the end when he says in v. 26,

> **And inasmuch as they gave the command to leave the stump and roots of the tree, your kingdom shall be assured to you, after you come to know that Heaven rules.**

There is some good news at the end. In closing, Daniel speaks words that would enrage most kings,

> **Therefore, O king, let my advice be acceptable to you; break off your sins by being righteous, and your iniquities by showing mercy to the poor. Perhaps there may be a lengthening of your prosperity."**

Excellent advice. Surely that was God's full counsel to him. Not some watered down facsimile of truth. This is rather like King Ahab when another man of God soundly rebuked him. After the murder of Godly Naboth over his vineyard, Elijah confronted him and pronounced his doom. It shook Ahab so badly, that we are told in I Kings 21: 27:

> **So it was, when Ahab heard those words, that he tore his clothes and put sackcloth on his body, and fasted and lay in sackcloth, and went about mourning.**

Then in v. 29, God responds,

> **See how Ahab has humbled himself before Me? Because he has humbled himself before Me, I will not bring the calamity in his days. In the days of his son I will bring the calamity on his house.**

In speaking the hard words to Nebuchadnezzar, Daniel probably had in mind mitigating the punishment he would be getting. He makes a valiant attempt to turn a man from his sins and lead him to salvation. Daniel, the prophet and master statesman never shined brighter than he did at that moment. How about you? Have you spoken the hard words needed by someone you know? John the Baptist rebuked another king, Herod, for his adultery, and it cost him his life. What would it cost us? A frown? God give us some men!

DANIEL 5

In this chapter, Daniel interacts with Emperor Belshazzar, ruler of the Babylonian empire. He seems to spend a lot of time around emperors. But he was not the kind of guy who courted their favor. All that our holy record shows is that he came only when called. He never showed up at parties to boost his popularity. He wouldn't have cared for Washington. So when King Belshazzar "made a great feast for a thousand of his lords", Daniel was not invited. Apparently they had learned that he was not the partying type.

Now we have to wonder what was the occasion for the party? It seems that Belshazzar didn't need a reason. It was probably a lifestyle for him – and them. But here's the disturbing thing: they decided to throw a party while their city, Babylon, was under siege by the Medes and Persians. They were in dire straits. With the attacking Persian armies penetrating into the heart of the Babylonian empire and besieging the capital, it looks like they should have been giving serious attention to national defense. Maybe they were thinking, "let's eat, drink and be merry, for tomorrow we shall die." Well that's exactly what happened.

V. 1 "Belshazzar the king made a great feast for a thousand of his lords, and drank wine in the presence of the thousand."

"It is not for kings, O Lemuel, it is not for kings to drink wine, nor for princes intoxicating drink; lest they drink and forget the law and pervert the justice of all the afflicted." (Proverbs 31:4,5)

Alcohol is the gateway for sin to enter in. In the multitude of it, there is no lack of sin. Verse two illustrates this.

V. 2 While he tasted the wine, Belshazzar gave the command to bring the gold and silver vessels which his father Nebuchadnezzar had taken from the temple which had been in Jerusalem, that the king and his lords, his wives, and his concubines might drink from them.

So Belshazzar, with his reason being seriously impaired, gets cocky and wants to drink from God's holy drinking cups. These were not supposed to touched by anyone but the holy priests of Israel. When Uzzah broke a similar law in touching the ark, he died instantly. Too bad Belshazzar never read his Bible. Just for fun, he is foolishly tampering with a deadly time bomb – with a short fuse. People can do some really dumb things when they drink. Just ask Herod.

V. 3 Then they brought the gold vessels that had been taken from the temple of the house of God which had been in Jerusalem; and the king and his lords, his wives, and his concubines drank from them.

224

Here is the husband giving his wives forbidden fruit and they will quickly be cast out of their Eden. The cup of their iniquity is nearly full. First, the lords were in serious neglect of their duties at a critical time. Second, they were all drunk. Third, they handled the holy cups, which was a capital offense. And now they hasten their ruin in verse 4.

V. 4 They drank wine, and praised the gods of gold and silver, bronze and iron, wood and stone.

If he didn't read the Bible, he should have at least read a little history. It wasn't very long before, that his father Nebuchadnezzar suffered the loss of his sanity for seven years by divine decree and then later was restored to his throne. His father spoke with great reverence of the God of Israel.

And surely it made headlines when Shadrach, Meshach and Abed-nego were un-harmed by the fiery furnace. Some of those same lords must have surely been there. He probably didn't like to hear about those kind of stories. Some **"people are destroyed for lack of knowledge."** (Hosea 4:6) The fiery furnace was a clear message from the Holy God of Israel that He alone was God and not some giant gold statue. All this was common knowledge and should have worked some wise restraint in Belshazzar. But he was living a reckless life, ignoring all the warning signs.

Well that was the last straw. Their cup of iniquity was full. Time's up.

V. 5 In the same hour the fingers of a man's hand appeared and wrote opposite the lampstand on the plaster of the wall of the king's palace. And the king saw the part of the hand that wrote.

This probably shocked him into being completely sober. He was more terrified than he had been in his entire life. He's lucky Gabriel didn't suddenly appear before him in his full glory. The sight of such an apparition may have killed him. Listen to what happened to him just seeing a few fingers.

V. 6 Then the king's countenance changed, and his thoughts troubled him, so that the joints of his hips were loosened and knees knocked against each other.

Can you imagine what it will be like for him when he stands before the Living God? So Belshazzar calls all his wise men and as usual, they have no idea what the hand wrote, much less what it means. Eventually the queen spoke to Belshazzar and reminded him of Daniel. In verse 13, Daniel is finally brought in.

The king spoke and said to Daniel, "Are you that Daniel who is one of the captives from Judah, whom my father the king brought from Judah? I have heard of you, that the Spirit of God is in you, and that light and understanding and excellent wisdom is found in you.

He continues in v.16

And I have heard of you, that you can give interpretations and explain enigmas. Now if you can read the writing and make known to me its interpretation, you shall be clothed with purple and have a chain of gold around your neck, and shall be the third ruler in the kingdom."

Whether or not "third ruler in the kingdom" meant the next emperor after Belshazzar or the number three ranking man in the current administration, it was a phenomenal offer. But Daniel wasn't interested in the slightest. He could have responded, "Thanks, but my clothes are fine, and I've already got a job." Blessed is the man who is immune to such temptations. Daniel replies, **"Let your gifts be for yourself, and give your rewards to another; yet I will read the writing to the king, and make known to him the interpretation."** I wonder if anyone had done this before: render a service to the emperor without being paid for it.

Now he delivers the bad news. He begins with a recounting of the terrible judgment on his own father, Nebuchadnezzar. Belshazzar already knew about that, but didn't like to think about it. He did not want a God to hold him accountable for his actions. In verse 22, he drives his point home:

> **"But you his son, Belshazzar, have not humbled your heart, although you knew all this. And you have lifted yourself up against the Lord of heaven. They have brought the vessels of His house before you, and you and your lords, your wives and your concubines, have drunk wine from them. And you have praised the gods of silver and gold, bronze and iron, wood and stone, which do not see or hear or know; and the God who holds your breath in His hand and owns all your ways, you have not glorified.**

Daniel gives God's view of the events. Belshazzar's view was, "Aw, we were just having a little fun." But it was a deadly mistake. It is more dangerous to fail to take God seriously than to fail to take a rattlesnake seriously. It is a fearful thing to fall into the hands of the living God.

> **Now Daniel concludes with the interpretation: (V. 24) Then the fingers of the hand were sent from Him, and this writing was written. And this is the inscription that was written: MENE, MENE, TEKEL UPHARSIN.**
> **This is the interpretation of each word. MENE: God has numbered your kingdom, and finished it. TEKEL: you have been weighed in the balances, and found wanting; PERES: your kingdom has been divided and given to the Medes and the Persians.**

True to his word, Belshazzar delivers the gold chain and purple clothing and declares Daniel to be the third ruler in the kingdom. In the very next verse, Belshazzar is killed and Darius the Mede takes the kingdom. In Daniel chapter 5 is a historically momentous event: the overthrow of the Babylonian empire by the Medo-Persian empire. The actual event is covered in only two verses. The other 29 verses detail the hand writing on the wall, Belshazzar's sins and the interpretation of the writing on the wall. We can see that in heaven's eyes, sin, preaching and judgment are far more significant than the rise and fall of empires.

II Chronicles tells an almost identical story. Amon was another son whose father, Manasseh, king of Judah, was severely judged for his terrible sins and suffered imprisonment and deportation to Babylon. When Manasseh humbled himself, God restored him to his throne in Judah. But Amon did not learn the lesson his father got: that there is a God who holds us accountable for our actions. Amon became as evil as his father had been. After being king for only two years, he was assassinated. For the wages of sin is death.

We will all be held accountable for our sins, but I believe we will also be held accountable to learn from the mistakes of others. Especially when the judgment strikes very close to us.

DANIEL 6

This man who was diligent in his business often stood before kings. He was discovered by the first world emperor, Nebuchadnezzar. Daniel served him for his entire 43 year reign. He also served under his son, Belshazzar and under Cyrus and Darius, emperors of the Medo-Persian empire. He served in the top offices of each administration. This is truly amazing! It would be like a man serving in the top federal office for multiple U.S. presidents in both the Democratic and Republican parties. We'd have to conclude, the guy must be really good.

So far, what stands out most is that Daniel was completely faithful to God. He was also a man of unshakeable integrity. He is a princely man and holds up well under pressure. He is estimated to be about 75 to 80 years old in this account. He is still holding a high political office. Very likely he is promoted to the position of being over the whole realm (like a prime minister) by the end of this chapter. It seems he wanted to keep working as long as he could be useful. A fine quality.

Verse one begins soon after Emperor Darius receives the kingdom. He begins to set up his government.

V. 1 It pleased Darius to set over the kingdom 120 satraps, to be over the whole kingdom; and over these, three governors, of whom Daniel was one, that the satraps might give account to them, so that the king would suffer no loss. Then this Daniel distinguished himself above the governors and satraps, because an excellent spirit was in him; and the king gave thought to setting him over the whole realm.

Now this is impressive: to be the most qualified and trustworthy man in high public office. But instead of his colleagues' congratulations and back-slapping, he gets resentment and back-stabbing.

V. 4 So the governors and satraps sought to find some charge against Daniel concerning the kingdom; but they could find no charge or fault, because he was faithful; nor was there any error or fault found in him.

Sounds like cutthroat U.S. politics. But what a fine testimony for the man of God! This is like Zecharias and Elisabeth of whom we read, **"they were both righteous before God, walking in all the commandments and ordinances of the Lord, blameless."** But they didn't have a committee of guys trying to dig up dirt on them like Daniel had. May God help us go and do likewise.

V. 5-8 Then these men said, "We shall not find any charge against this Daniel unless we find it against him concerning the law of his God." So these governors and satraps thronged before the king, and said thus to him, "King Darius, live forever! All

the governors of the kingdom, the administrators and satraps, the counselors and advisors, have consulted together to establish a royal statute and to make a firm decree, that whoever petitions any god or man for 30 days, except you, O King, shall be cast into the den of lions. Now O king, establish the decree and sign the writing, so that it cannot be changed, according to the law of the Medes and Persians, which does not alter."

Now what kind of government statute is that? Nobody's allowed to pray for a month? I would guess that none of them were praying men. They present it as a unanimous decision by all the top officials in the empire. I really doubt that. Darius should have laughed at such foolishness. He later regretted not taking some time to think it over. Without giving it much thought, he signs the decree.

Life is not fair. Daniel had done nothing to offend any one of them. But these top officials are out to kill him. The same thing happened to Jesus.
Why do the nations rage, and the people plot a vain thing? The kings of the earth set themselves, and the rulers take counsel together... against His Anointed." (Psalm 2:1,2)

Remember back in chapter 2, a similar group of counselors were being executed? At that time Daniel saved their lives. Yes, life is not fair, but this story is not over.

In verse 10, we see a very courageous man.

Now when Daniel knew that the writing was signed, he went home. And in his upper room, with his window opened toward Jerusalem, he knelt down on his knees three times that day, and

231

prayed and gave thanks before his God, as was his custom since early days.

Daniel knew the consequences of praying. We need to beware of the consequences of not praying. We see that he prayed toward Jerusalem, as taught in I Kings 8:29. He prayed on his knees, not sitting back in his easy chair. He prayed three times that day as he did every day. Maybe he spent as much time praying as he did eating. He could have prayed with his windows shut and nobody would know. But he fearlessly prayed in the same manner he always did, knowing it could cost him his life. Maybe we could fearlessly pray as we always do, even when we are eating in a public place. It probably won't cost us our life.

In verse 11, the snoops came and found Daniel praying. I wish they would have been so deeply moved that they too would have knelt down and prayed with Daniel. Like Saul among the prophets. But these guys were hard cases, you know – politicians.

Verse 13 tells us that these tattling little children reported to the king **"That Daniel, who is one of the captives from Judah, does not show due regard for you, O king, or for the decree that you have signed, but makes his petition three times a day."**

V. 14 **And the king, when he heard these words, was greatly displeased with himself, and set his heart on Daniel to deliver him; and he labored till the going down of the sun to deliver him.** In verse 15 they come to nail the lid onto the coffin. **Then these men approached the king, and said to the king, "Know, O king, that it is the law of the Medes and Persians that no decree or statute which the king establishes may be changed."** Then we are told the outcome: **So the king gave the command, and they brought Daniel and cast him into the den of lions. But the king spoke, saying to Daniel, "Your God whom you serve continually, He will deliver you."**

You may recall that when Herod spoke as rashly as Darius wrote, John was beheaded. Jephthah could also sympathize. It would not be bad praying to say, "God please preserve me from my enemies and from my own words."

Then a stone was brought and laid on the mouth of the den, and the king sealed it with his own signet ring and with the signets of his lords, that the purpose concerning Daniel might not be changed. There was another Godly man who was falsely accused and had a stone rolled over his grave and sealed. In both cases, wicked men thought to thus put away the blameless, but God would justify His greatly beloved. Thus God over-ruled the seals and caused both stones to be removed. In the same way, when we were dead in our own sins, and our eternal fate sealed, He comes to roll away our reproach and gives to us a new life. The most evil of men and the most ravenous of lions cannot harm us when God saves us. But He does not save us because we were so righteous. For "you who once were alienated and enemies in your mind by wicked works, yet now He has reconciled." For us, the heavy stone is our own sins. But God is pleased to remove for us what we cannot do by ourselves. We are not able to remove the guilt of our own sins. But "if we confess our sins, He is faithful and just to forgive us our sins and to cleanse us from all unrighteousness." (I John 1:9)

In Daniel 6:18, Darius must have felt like the disciples on the night after they buried Jesus. In mourning. Then as the ladies did on Easter morning, **"the king arose very early in the morning and went in haste to the den of lions."** And he had as big a surprise waiting for him as the ladies who went to Jesus's tomb.

The king cries out, **"Daniel, servant of the living God, has your God, whom you serve continually, been able to deliver you from the lions?"**

V. 21 **Then Daniel said to the king, "O king, live forever! My God sent His angel and shut the lions' mouths, so that they have not hurt me, because I was found innocent before Him; and also, O king, I have done no wrong before you." Now the king was exceedingly glad for him, and commanded that they should take Daniel up out of the den. So Daniel was taken up out of the den, and no injury whatever was found on him, because he believed in his God.**

Maybe the courage of Shadrach, Meshach and Abednego in a similar circumstance inspired Daniel and helped him through his trial. And now both incidents are recorded for us,

> **For whatever things were written before were written for our learning, that we through the patience and comfort of the scriptures might have hope.** (I Cor. 15:4)

Oh, I forgot to mention, all those bad guys (you know, the politicians) were cast into the lion's den. And everybody loved that happy ending – including the lions.

V. 2 **In the first year of his reign (Darius's), I Daniel, understood by the books the number of the years specified by the word of the Lord through Jeremiah the prophet, that He would accomplish seventy years in the desolations of Jerusalem.**

Daniel has been studying the scriptures, which were on scrolls in those days. He read in Jeremiah where the Lord said Jerusalem would be in desolation for seventy years.

> **And this whole land shall be a desolation and an astonishment, and these nations shall serve the king of Babylon seventy years.** Jeremiah 25:11 (605 B.C.)

Several years after Jeremiah wrote those words, Jerusalem fell to the Babylonians. (At least twice.) Now Daniel is reading the prophecy somewhere around seventy years later. He realizes: this is about to be fulfilled. This moves him to prayer. What follows is a monumental prayer of the magnitude of Solomon's prayer of dedication of the newly built temple in Jerusalem. When he finished leading the prayer, with thousands of believers present, we are told,

> **Fire came down from heaven and consumed the burnt offering and the sacrifices; and the glory of the Lord filled the temple.**

The prayer of Daniel chapter 9 is probably much longer than the 10 minutes that we have recorded. In the same way, we're told that Jesus' prayer in Gethsemane was at least three hours long, but all we have recorded is:

> **Oh my Father, if it is possible, let this cup pass from me;**

nevertheless, not as I will, but as you will.

Notice in Daniel's prayer that his confessions are genuine. He is not just voicing right sounding words. He is not just a good man pretending to be humble, so as to add humility to his list of qualities. All throughout the book of Daniel, he is humble. Sometimes circumstances contributed to his humility. He was frightened, he was sick, he fasted and put on sackcloth and ashes. These can help humility along. Just as we should covet earnestly the best gifts, we should covet earnestly the best fruits. And humility should rank high on the list.

We should pray for humility. When we do, I can just picture God smiling and thinking, "I've got just the plan." Several times, I have missed the turn to my house in my own neighborhood. I probably prayed for humility that morning. You probably have your own list of "answered prayers". Watch for humility throughout Daniel's prayer.

V. 3, 4 **Then I set my face toward the Lord God to make request by prayer and supplications, with fasting, sackcloth and ashes. And I prayed to the Lord my God, and made confession, and said, O Lord, great and awesome God, who keeps His covenant and mercy with those who love Him, and with those who keep His commandments.**

Scripture says he prayed and made confession. As nice a guy as Daniel is, we wouldn't expect his confession to take very long. But he spends 12 of the next 16 verses of his prayer confessing sins. Too many of us pray, "O God, I'm sorry for my sins. Please help me with ...." Then the grocery list of requests. Confession is an uncomfortable subject we'd rather avoid. But nothing opens heaven's door like itemized, in-depth confession.

v. 5, 6 We have sinned and committed iniquity, we have done wickedly and rebelled, even by departing from Your precepts and Your judgments. Neither have we heeded your servants the prophets, who spoke in Your name to our kings and our princes, to our fathers and all the people of the land.

Pure confession. No excuses. No sharing blame. We should try it some time. In the following verses, he recounts the judgments that have befallen his people, agreeing that they were fully deserving of it. Rather than lessening their guilt, he aggravates it in pointing out that the judges and the prophets also declared their guilt and God's just punishments. He says they disobeyed in spite of the fact that Moses thoroughly forewarned them. And after all the guilt and disaster that was brought upon them, they still did not even confess their guilt before God. He says if they had but turned from their iniquities at any time, they would have come to understand His truth. For sin cripples our spiritual understanding. **"Harlotry, wine and new wine take away the understanding."**

In verses 17-19, his prayer hits a crescendo of intensity. His words become the effectual, fervent prayers of a righteous man. Even as Jesus, in the days of His flesh prayed with strong crying and tears.

Now therefore, our God, hear the prayer of your servant, and his supplications, and for the Lord's sake, cause Your face to shine on your sanctuary, which is desolate.

237

O my God, incline Your ear and hear; open Your eyes and see our desolations and the city which is called by Your name; for we do not present our supplications before You because of our righteous deeds, but because of Your great mercies.

O Lord hear! O Lord forgive! O Lord, listen and act! Do not delay for Your own sake, my God, for Your city and Your people are called by Your name.

I hope this sounds like your prayers, because it sure doesn't sound like mine.

For God's eyes run to and fro throughout the whole earth, to show Himself strong on behalf of those whose heart is loyal to Him. (II Chronicles 16:9)

Now watch God do exactly that for Daniel.

V.21 While I was speaking in prayer, the man Gabriel, whom I had seen in the vision at the beginning, being caused to fly swiftly, reached me about the time of the evening offering.

So it comes to pass that **"while he prayed, the heaven was opened."** (Luke 3:21) When he prayed, angels were moved to action. **"Being caused to fly swiftly."** Notice as soon as *Daniel started* praying, the answer was on the way. May it be so when you pray. In Daniel 10:12, in a different vision, another angel who looked like lightning, says,

Do not fear, Daniel, for from the first day that you set your heart to understand, and to humble yourself before your God, your words were heard; and I have come because of your words."

Again, our prayers move angels into action.

In the next two verses, Gabriel tells Daniel,

"I have now come forth to give you skill to understand. At the beginning of your supplications the command went out, and I have come to tell you, for you are greatly beloved; therefore consider the matter, and understand the vision."

Notice these fringe benefits of praying:

1. The angel announces that Daniel is greatly beloved. The man or woman deeply in prayer to God is specially beloved of God. We have seen that Daniel had a lifestyle of regular prayer.

2. Also as a result of his praying, his understanding skills have improved. "I have come to give you skill to understand." This also applies in the New Testament: "If any of you lacks wisdom, let him ask of God who gives to all liberally…and it will be given to him." It's also interesting that Daniel did not specifically ask for wisdom or understanding, but it was given to him anyway. So this gift of immeasurable value is given to Daniel because he came to talk to God. He didn't come to get anything. He didn't complain about anything. He just poured out his heart to his Friend.

3. Our prayers move heaven.

It's my opinion that this precise prayer of Daniel sparked the re-birth of the nation Israel. The return of Israel happened between the end of chapter 9 and before the beginning of chapter 10. Even though the return of the Jews to Jerusalem was prophesied to occur, God may have been just waiting for someone to ask.

We're not told that anyone else prayed for the reviving of Jerusalem. Now notice that he's praying for the re-establishing of a city 500 miles away in complete ruins. He labored in prayer for something that had no direct bearing on his own life. It was entirely for other people and for God's honor. And the city was in utter ruins. It was the equivalent of praying, "O God, please restore Hiroshima." He was asking for something very big and very far away. And it would very greatly revive the honor of God. But is anything too hard for the Lord? I bet God loved it! Finally, a big prayer request! I wonder if God gets tired of answering prayers like, "Dear God, please help me find my keys."

In the last verse of this book, an angel gives these comforting words to Daniel:

But you, go your way till the end; for you shall rest,

and will arise to your inheritance at the end of the days.

These are very sweet words to the soul who has labored much of their life in serving their Master. The prospect of rest is pleasant indeed. It also confirms to us that there is an inheritance for the saints awaiting us in the land of glory. Blessed are those who have laid up treasure in heaven. For eyes have not seen nor ears heard, neither has it entered into the heart of man the things that God has prepared for them that love Him.

JOHN THE BAPTIST

THE GREATNESS OF JOHN

Jesus commended John the Baptist as being the greatest man that ever lived, up to his time. (Matthew 11:11) He says John is more than a prophet. Other than Jesus Christ, he is the only man in the New Testament who was prophesied about in the Old Testament. It's interesting to note that not one Old Testament prophecy was made of the apostle Paul or Peter or John. Only John the Baptist. The prophecy correctly predicted him as the fore-runner of the Messiah. In the last two verses of the Old Testament, we read: (Malachi 4:5,6)

"Behold, I will send you Elijah the prophet before the coming of the great and dreadful day of the Lord. And he will turn the hearts of the fathers to the children, and the hearts of the children to their fathers, lest I come and strike the earth with a curse."

You may be thinking, "but the prophecy says "Elijah". Yes, but that is a prophetic name for John. Let me explain. First of all the prophecy in Malachi was written about 430 B.C. Secondly, Elijah lived from about 900 B.C. to about 850 B.C. So Elijah sort of died 400 years before. I know: "Sort of?" OK, just give me a minute. To complicate a bit further, Elijah didn't exactly die. He was caught up alive into heaven by a whirlwind. Seriously. If that's not bad enough, Jesus said that John the Baptist is Elijah, but not really because John was born in about 1 B.C. Here's what Jesus said on this:

For all the prophets and the law prophesied until John.
And if you are willing to receive it, he is Elijah who is to come. (Matt. 11:13,14)

I can imagine you thinking, "Well that really cleared things up." Well prophecy can get a little confusing in places. I think that's just to make it more fun.
The key here is that John and Elijah have such striking similarities that John is almost like a return of Elijah. Consider this:

a. John and Elijah both wore a leather belt. (II Kings 1:8 and Matt. 3:4)
b. John was clothed with camel's hair. II Kings 1:8 in the ESV Bible states that Elijah "wore a garment of hair, with a belt of leather about his waist." Both men intentionally denied themselves comforts and pleasures of life.
c. It is said of John that he ate locusts and wild honey. Elijah once fasted 40 days without eating a thing.
d. Both spent a lot of time in solitude in the wilderness.
e. Both men fearlessly confronted a king about his sins.
f. Elijah's life was threatened and John was arrested and imprisoned for telling a king that he was not allowed to marry a divorced woman. John was later executed by being beheaded.

g. The public ministries of both men were also very similar. They each single-handedly turned much of the entire nation of Israel back to God.

h. John gave his life willingly for the preaching of righteousness. However, Elijah never did exactly die. (II Kings chapter 2.)

And they that be wise shall shine as the brightness of the (sky) and they that turn many to righteousness as the stars for ever and ever." (Daniel 12:3)

Getting back to the prophecy that Elijah would come back to earth, Malachi 4:5 says, **"Behold I will send you Elijah the prophet before the coming of the great and dreadful day of the Lord."** Now you probably remember that Jesus applied this prophecy to John the Baptist as being the forerunner of Jesus's coming. But it also applies to the second coming of Jesus, as Revelation tells us. His second coming culminates in chapter 19, when He returns and destroys the Antichrist and his army. Now all that period surrounding the second coming is certainly "great and dreadful", so Elijah's "second coming" seems to fit the second coming of Christ. The first coming of Jesus would be more like "sweet and mild". So the prophecy seems to apply to another period of time.

We all have a choice. We can accept the sweet, loving, gentle Jesus who gave his life as a ransom for many. Or we can face the glorious, mighty Jesus whose second coming is dreadful and terrible.

Shortly before the second coming of the Lord, we find two witnesses appearing on the scene. We are not given their names. We have no clue where they came

243

from. Most of the world will not care where they come from; they just want to know how to get rid of them. Prophecy experts believe they are a return of Elijah and Moses. Some think one of them might be Enoch. There is an excellent case for both views. And the time of the two witnesses certainly fits the description of the **"great and dreadful day of the Lord"**. In fact they did a lot to help *make* it dreadful. So if Elijah returns near the second coming of the Lord, it seems less likely that John the Baptist is a literal return of Elijah in Jesus's day.

As Jesus said, he was the greatest man ever born, up to his time. (Luke 7:28) Now think about that. He is counted greater than Joseph, who was like the prime minister of Egypt for about 80 years. Joseph died at 110, John died at about 32. So he became great on the basis of what he did in only the last 3 years of his life. Much of the greatness in a man's life is in the preparation. He is counted greater than Moses, who performed numerous miracles in his life, including the spectacular dividing of the Red Sea. Moses also spent the first 80 years of his life preparing, or rather being prepared for the final 40 years of his life. John did no miracle at all. Moses was part of the royal family of Egypt (by adoption). John had no special pedigree, except that he had godly parents, Zecharias and Elisabeth.

John is counted greater than King David, who reigned over Israel for 40 years. In all his life, David was unbeatable in battle. But only because God was with him. John never served in the military and never held public office. There is no record that John ever built anything or even owned a house. And he easily beats Nebuchadnezzar, who conquered the entire settled world of his time.

JOHN'S FAMILY

Admittedly, John did have a huge head start over these other men. The angel Gabriel prophesied of John, **"For he will be great in the sight of the Lord, and shall drink neither wine nor strong drink. He will also be filled with the Holy Spirit, even from his mother's womb."** (Luke 1:15) Very likely this happened when Mary came to visit Elisabeth where we read, **"And it happened that when Elisabeth heard the greeting of Mary, that the babe leaped within her womb and Elisabeth was filled with the Holy Spirit."** (Luke 1:41)

It would be nice if every Christian mother who is filled with the Holy Spirit while expecting, that their child would also be filled with the Spirit and grow into a Christian believer.

Maybe even more significantly, John's parents were an older couple and were exceptionally Godly. Scripture tells us, **"And they were both righteous before God, walking in all the commandments and ordinances of the Lord blameless."** (Luke 1:6) For the most part, we reproduce after our own kind. Godly parents produce Godly offspring. It didn't hurt that both Elisabeth and her husband, Zechariah, were both of the family of priests in the tribe of Levi. No wonder the neighbors said, **"What kind of child will this be?"**

Zecharias was both a priest and a prophet. Remember he was one of those who were selected for the high honor of serving as the Temple high priest at one time. While in the temple, tending the altar of incense, the golden candelabra and the show bread, the angel Gabriel appeared to him. After he got up off the floor (not really), Gabriel tells him that they will be having a boy, whom they were to name John. Gabriel prophesies, **"You will have joy and gladness, and many will rejoice at his birth."** (Luke 1:14) Certainly quite a few rejoiced with the couple at the birth of John, but many rejoiced at his birth when long after, he entered his public ministry.

Now that's some quality parents! What kind of parents do your children have? What's on your resume? They raised their child not to ever drink. It's a safe assumption that they did not drink either. It is also a significant point that he was raised as an only child. This gave a lot of time for Elisabeth and Zacharias to give John personal attention and nurturing. If a couple has several children, it would be time well invested to give quality attention to each one. I would guess that Elizabeth told her child about the time cousin Mary visited, and she spoke prophetic things. Maybe she related to him the words she spoke, prophesying things she may not have understood herself:

> **"Blessed are you among women, and blessed is the fruit of your womb. But why is this granted to me that the mother of my Lord should come to me?"**

Maybe little John said, "Wow, Mom! That's going to be a great baby!" "And, my John, she also stayed with us for three months until you were born. She took such good care of me. I was having a hard time getting around at my age, being about to have a baby. She was such a saint!" (Of course, I'm ad-libbing.)

It's probably a pretty safe assumption that elderly Zacharias likewise told his little boy all about the angel in the temple and his going mute for 9 months. It might have been too much of a burden to put on a little child to tell John the words of the prophecy he spoke just

246

after his birth. Maybe he told him later in life as a man. He had spoken by the Holy Spirit,

"And you, child, will be called the prophet of the Highest; for you will go before the face of the Lord to prepare His ways, to give knowledge of salvation to His people by the remission of their sins, through the tender mercy of our God, with which the Dayspring from on high has visited us; to give light to those who sit in darkness and the shadow of death, to guide our feet in the way of peace."

We are told Zacharias spoke as he was moved by the Holy Spirit. For he gave the general character of John's ministry before he even knew he would be a prophet. Luke chapter one concludes, **"So the child grew and became strong in spirit, and was in the deserts till the day of his manifestation to Israel."** Very similar to the early years of Jesus. So John remained in solitude until he began his ministry at about the age of 29 or 30. Almost nothing is told of these formative years of both men. It may have been like Samson that **"the Spirit began to move him at times in the camp of Dan."** Early in Ezekiel's life, the Spirit transports him in the spirit to Jerusalem. In his vision of chapter 8, Ezekiel is shown various abominations being done by the elders of Israel and other worshippers, as the Spirit says repeatedly to Ezekiel, **"Have you seen this, O son of man?"** He is shown the false idols set up in the temple. The vision continues until Ezekiel sees angelic beings begin to slaughter the sinful residents of Jerusalem. Finally Ezekiel cries out in horror, **"Ah, Lord God! Will you destroy all the remnant of Israel?"** The

Spirit was moving Ezekiel as He had moved Samson in the camp of Dan. This was preparing Ezekiel for the ministry.

WHAT MADE JOHN THE BAPTIST SO GREAT ?

PRAYING PARENTS

John was the only child of Zechariah and Elisabeth. They were well advanced in years when he was born. Luke 1:7 tells us "they both were now well stricken in years". It is my personal opinion that these parents had wanted and prayed for a child for many years. Finally, after those many years, consider what the angel said to Zechariah in Luke 1:13, "Fear not, Zechariah: for your prayer is heard; and your wife Elisabeth shall bear you a son." We can suppose that over those many years, every prayer spoken by this couple to have a child counted for something. Like your prayers. Not one prayer was wasted or lost. Imagine those many thousands of prayers being stored up and poured into the baby when it arrived! "The effectual, fervent prayers of a righteous man avails much." (James 5:16) If they had prayed only 500 times for a baby and then gave up, we probably would never have heard of John the Baptist. But God withheld from granting their petition for many years, probably to get more and more prayers stored up for the coming child. Every single prayer counted to make this child great. Surely God remembered all their thousands of prayers, their yearning and longing and tears.

Maybe God let Joseph sit in prison for 13 years for the same reason: to store up Joseph's prayers in order to make him great. All those years, Joseph probably felt he was about to burst with the potential of what he knew he could do. Who knows how many times in life the answer to our prayers are delayed so that more prayers are stored up for a glorious unveiling?

It could be that God has you where you are to give you time to prepare yourself for your future by investing much prayer. It's my guess that you probably do more praying when there's not much else to do. When a man is free to do whatever he wants, he probably does far less praying. Even when he wants to pray, there is so much distraction that it's hard to spend time in prayer at all. Commonly our best praying is done while others sleep.

It would be a safe assumption that even after John was born, his parents continued to pray for his moral development, his walk with God, his development of a holy life. We can feel confident that his parents prayed about every lesson they taught, every habit they encouraged and every quality they instilled in their son. Every building block of John's life was cemented into place by much prayer. That's how to raise a child.

JOHN LIVED A LIFE OF SELF-DENIAL

He held no worldly ambitions. He had no interest in making money, buying a house, getting himself a late model camel or whatever. John was not interested in luxuries or entertainment. No good cooking. No home comforts. No designer clothing or shoes. According to Matthew 3:4, John led a very simple life of self denial and devotion to God. **"And the same John had his clothes of camel's hair."** Normally, camel's hair is used for making stiff bristle brushes. This is the equivalent of wearing clothes made of burlap sack material. **"And a leather girdle about his loins (waist)."** This would be like taking a leather basketball and cutting it in half to make some underwear. **"And his food was locusts and wild honey."** Can you imagine trying to get supper together? First you have to fight the bees, then you have to catch enough locusts for supper. Pretty humble food. It's doubtful that anybody ever came by for supper. Everything about his life was self-denying. He did nothing for his own pleasure or comfort.

Now this is vital: because he did not reward himself, God rewarded him. How? With His own glorious presence and power in his ministry. Remember what God said to Abraham when he declined to accept the spoils of battle? **"I am your...exceeding great reward."** (Genesis 15:1) We can be sure that God was John's exceeding great reward also.

So every person should ask the question: will I reward myself? Or will I let God reward me? Remember when Jesus said, **"But when you fast, anoint your head, and wash your face; so that you appear not unto men to fast, but unto your Father which is in secret: and your Father, who sees in secret shall reward you openly."** I suspect that most of us can't get past the first four words: **but when you fast.** (Matthew 6:17,18)

In the same chapter, in v. 5, Jesus says, **"And when you pray, you shall not be as the hypocrites are: for they love to pray standing in the synagogues and in the corners of the streets. Verily I say unto you, They have their reward."** The implication is that since they have their reward, God will not be rewarding them for their prayers. This really hits me, because sometimes I tell people, "I've been praying for you." My boasting makes them have a high opinion of me. If that's the only reward I get, it's pretty lousy. No reward from God.

Now let's look closely at John's personal life. John probably did the least good for himself and the most good for man than anyone who ever lived. In consideration of what Jesus said, **"If any man will come after me, let him deny himself, and take up his cross and follow me"**, John followed this pretty closely.

JOHN WAS A MAN OF SOLITUDE

There is no record of John having any other brothers or sisters. As a child, he probably grew up somewhat alone. He was filled with the Holy Spirit. Other kids were nothing like John. I imagine that even as a child, he spent a lot of time alone with God.

The more alone he was, the closer he felt to God. As he grew into adulthood, the more he wanted solitude; the more he felt the need to be with God. Alone. It soon wasn't enough that he walk from home to a quiet area to pray and be with God, and then come home at night. Perhaps he had glow of God's presence on him as Moses had. (The people close to Moses actually saw his face glow with the glory of God.) Maybe John felt the glow of God's presence fade from his soul every time he would come back to town and be surrounded by people and activity again. Maybe he wanted to go and be with God and never feel like he has to leave. So we read, **"And the child grew, and waxed strong in spirit; and was in the deserts till the day of his showing unto Israel."**

251

It seems that a lot of people today are afraid to be alone at all. If they're the last person in the house, they can't stand it. They have to call someone on the phone or turn on the TV or a radio. But men destined for greatness value time alone. Whether it's to do some good thinking or to tarry in the presence of God, good men value solitude. **"And in the morning rising up a great while before day, He (Jesus) went out and departed into a solitary place and there prayed."** (Mark 1:35)

"And Isaac went out to meditate in the field at the eventide." (Genesis 24:63) I would just guess that he spent that time both praying and thinking.

JOHN WAS PATIENT

There was hardly any question in John's mind that he had a special calling of God on his life. People being called to the ministry can usually tell early on. So picture John as a child and as a teenager. He hears his parents talking about the Old Testament prophets and the great works of God. He hears the preaching in the synagogues every Sabbath. He thinks of things he'd like to add to what is said. But he keeps quiet. He begins to feel like God might want him to preach. But he keeps it to himself. Surely the Spirit of the Lord began to move him in those times. Then he gets into his twenties. He wants so much to get started in what he knows God wants him to do – preach. But still, he holds back. Luke 1:80 tells us, "and the child grew, and waxed strong in spirit, and was in the deserts till the day of his showing unto Israel." There was so much he wanted to do for people with his preaching, but he knew better than to launch into his ministry before God called him. He continued to do the important thing – pray in preparation for his future. He was in the deserts so he could pray and seek God and prepare without distraction. That is the way to greatness. Finally, somewhere in his late twenties, God was ready to show him to Israel.

If you recall, Moses had a similar sense of God's calling on his life. He knew he was Hebrew when he was growing up. If you remember, his mother helped raise him and surely told him who he was. It grieved him to see his own people treated so harshly by the Egyptians. I feel sure he sensed that God was calling him to do something about it. But he didn't wait for God to call him. Rather, he prematurely took matters in his own hand. He went out and saw an Egyptian beating a Hebrew. He killed the Egyptian. Then Pharaoh sought to kill Moses and the Hebrews rejected him as a leader. Not a good start in the ministry.

But John was patient. He waited for God's perfect timing. It helped that he had good parents. They certainly knew the importance of being patient for God's timing.

THE CHARACTER OF JOHN'S MINISTRY

Just as prophecy foretold the character of Jesus and the nature of his ministry as thoroughly as the apostles who walked with him, so it is with John. This prediction about John the Baptist is found in Malachi 4:5,6

"Behold I will send you Elijah the prophet before the coming of the great and dreadful day of the

Lord. And he shall turn the hearts of the fathers to the children and the hearts of the children to their fathers, lest I come and strike the earth with a curse."

We've looked at this verse before, but notice that the end of the passage describes the subject of his preaching. John addressed a terrible shortcoming of his generation: fathers neglecting their children. The fathers were physically there in the home, but their heart was not very much toward the children. They left that for the mother. Maybe they figured it was enough that if they spent the whole day providing for them, they were exempt from caring and interacting with the kids. But this flaw and gross neglect was so serious that it was the number one sin that this "Elijah" would preach about. It was the foremost reason why God was going to **"strike the earth with a curse."** Why was this such a serious sin? First we see that it directly led to the hearts of the children turning away from the fathers. That would be a flagrant violation of the fifth commandment: **Honor your father and your mother.** Tragically, this neglect which was started by the fathers, all but destroys one of the sweetest joys and strongest satisfactions of life: fathers cherishing their children and being so proud of them and children loving and admiring their Daddy. Who can calculate the damage caused by the loss of this? The development of normal love in the child's heart is crippled. Much of the wisdom and protection of the father is lost. And Daddy has a big empty spot in his heart all his life. Daddy's who won't take their son fishing or attend his daughter's recital have deprived themselves and their children. Proverbs cautions: the child left to himself brings his parents to shame. If they can't find acceptance and appreciation at home, they'll look for on the street. If the father would but love his child, it would surely prevent a multitude of sins.

But John's preaching addressed a wide range of issues. When soldiers were present, he counseled them, **"Do not intimidate anyone or accuse falsely, and be content with your wages."** Good advice for any man. To tax collectors, he said, **"Collect no more than what is appointed for you."** I wish somebody would make a sign out of this and hang it at all the IRS collection centers. To folks living comfortably, he encourages, **"He who has two tunics, let him give to him who has none, and he who has food, let him do likewise."** I really like how John makes it clear what we're supposed to do. This may be partly why he was a very popular preacher.

All this was how he preached to the people. But the general thrust of his preaching was to prepare the nation for imminent arrival of the long-awaited Messiah. John was humble enough to declare that the one coming after him (and very soon) was mightier that he was and that he was not worthy to loose his sandal strap. He preached like no one had ever preached before. He stated things that seemed strange and were never heard of previously. Like, **"He will baptize you with the Holy Spirit and with fire."** Remember that in John's time, the Holy Spirit was never before heard of. **"We have not so much as heard whether is a Holy Spirit."** They knew only of the "Spirit of the Lord". And what does John mean by "baptism"? A totally new concept. John was way ahead of his time. And the people had a lot of catching up to do to be ready for the Messiah, of whom it was said, **"Never a man spoke like this man!"** Fortunately, John came to prepare the people to be ready for the Messiah. **"For this is he that was** spoken of by the prophet Isaiah, saying "the voice of one crying in the wilderness, Prepare ye the way of the Lord, make his paths straight." (See Isaiah 40:3)

Maybe the greatest impact John made was preaching the baptism of repentance. Somehow his preaching powerfully influenced an entire nation to repent. They came to realize what their sins were; to feel bad about their sins, to feel the guilt of sin; to see sin as exceedingly sinful and to want to be rid of the guilt of sin. Hearing John preach, they felt the heavy burden of sin and wished to get rid of it. So John effectively gave them the answer to their griefs: repent and be baptized for the remission (removal) of sins. They would have been glad to sing:

My sins were washed away
And my night was turned to day
Heaven came down and glory filled my soul!

They weren't ready for the preceding line in the above hymn:

When at the cross my Savior made me whole,

In Matt. 11:10, Jesus says, **"For this is he of whom it is written, 'Behold I send my messenger before your face, who will prepare your way before you'."**
Jesus is quoting Malachi 3:1, the last book of the Old Testament.

Earlier in the book of Matthew, it is said of John the Baptist, **"then Jerusalem, all Judea, and all the region around the Jordan went out to him."** So these are two verses predicting the nature of John's ministry and preaching. A third verse, **Luke 3:21 says, "when** *all* **the people were baptized, it came to pass that Jesus also was baptized."** Gabriel foretold, **"And he will turn many of the children of Israel to the**

Lord their God." This was a phenomenal revival! He made such an impact on Judea and Israel in general, that **"they reasoned in their hearts whether he was the Christ or not."** (Luke 3:15) At first, they thought that John might be Jesus Christ; later they thought that Jesus might be John the Baptist. There may have even been some family resemblance since they were cousins. After John's decease, Jesus asked his disciples, **"Who do men say that I am?"** (Mark 8:38) To which the disciples reported, **"John the Baptist, but some say Elijah."** It was quite a compliment that the people thought he was a lot like Elijah.

But John never did miracles. Elijah was connected to seven miracles, including raising a dead child back to life. What so moved the people is that there was a strong anointing on his preaching. His words went deep into their hearts. Some may have said of John what was said of Jesus, **"no man ever spoke like this man!"**

JOHN PREACHED PURELY TO PLEASE GOD, NOT PEOPLE

May God give us some preachers like that today! John traveled around Judea a little, preaching basically one message: that the predicted Messiah was about to arrive. But generally, he preached and stayed in an area near the Jordan River in Judea (southern Israel). It was mostly uninhabited, a desert region. Not a place recommended for starting a church. He had to live off the land. He did not waste his time making a living and taking care of a home. He never married or had kids. His life was totally committed to serving God.

John had no interest in comforts and had no appetite for popularity. He was not swayed with the tides of public opinion. He did soften his message to avoid criticism. He did not cater to the rich man, nor look down on the poor. His sole thought when he preached was to win people to God. He did not care to entertain, educate, compliment, or impress.

As far as we know, he never took up an offering or had any sponsors. He did urge the people who had two coats to give one to the person who had none.

When the influential Pharisees came from Jerusalem to hear him, he addressed them as a generation of vipers! This was not an insult; it was an accurate rebuke. He preached what people needed to hear, not what they wanted to hear. **"He who rebukes a man will find more favor afterward than he who flatters with the tongue."**

This kind of boldness cost him his life. At one point, sinful King Herod came out to hear him preach. It was probably public knowledge that Herod had married the woman who used to be married to Herod's brother, Phillip. John very well knew the consequences when he told Herod that it was a sin to marry his brother's ex-wife. Herod needed to hear that. Sometimes we need to preach the bad news, not just the good news.

Proverbs puts it this way, **"faithful are the wounds of a friend"**. Translation: it is a faithful friend who will tell you what you need to hear, even if it hurts. We should value a friend who will tell us our faults for our own good. They're worth gold to us. Our cheap friends will tell us:

- take care of yourself,
- look after number one,
- treat yourself to something nice;
- do whatever makes you happy

and other baloney like that. Jesus had a friend like that and He said to him, **"Get thee behind me, Satan."**

We don't know how Herod himself took John's hard words, but we do know how his wife took it when she found out what John said about their marriage. She blew a gasket! She put enough pressure on her husband the king to put John in prison. Then when she had the chance, she got John the Baptist beheaded. (Conniving women!)

John wasn't just criticizing Herod, he was warning him for his own good.

"Cry aloud, spare not, lift up your voice like a trumpet and show my people their transgression, and the house of Jacob their sins." Isaiah 58:1

This was how the prophets of the Old Testament preached. And none did it better than the last of the Old Testament prophets, John the Baptist.

I have to wonder how the beheading of John the Baptist affected Herod's lovely step daughter, or Herodias. I wonder if they ever had nightmares of the bloody head of John on a platter. We're not told what impact it had on Herod or on his public approval ratings. We do know that about three years later, he was struck by an angel and was eaten by worms and died. Then he went to the place where the worm dies not and the fire is not quenched. The only surprising thing here is that he didn't die sooner. It seems that God gave even wicked Herod time to repent, for He takes no pleasure in the death of the wicked.

BARNABAS

In Acts 6, it's surprising that Barnabas was not chosen to be one of the original seven deacons. He was a notable member of the early church, among the first to sell land and donate the proceeds to the apostles for general distribution to the fledgling church. This was just one example of his good works in the early days. At the first mention of Barnabas in Acts 4:36, his actual name, Joses, was changed to "Barnabas" by the apostles, which means "Son of Encouragement". He was the only one we know of who was so honored with a new name. Apparently he was well known early on, for being an encouragement. How did he do so? Maybe with words of exhorting for the new believers, possibly for hospitality to the many out of towners who had flocked to Jerusalem, probably for his generosity in supporting the many new believers, but most likely in all these ways. What would you have been named in those days? Wise Counselor? Helper? Angel? Too many today might have been named "Pew warmer", "Spectator", "Complainer" or "Sleeper", as Jonah: **"What do you mean, O sleeper?"** So why wasn't he selected as a deacon? (Actually, they weren't called "deacons" until much later.) Probably for the same reason none of the apostles were. The apostles wisely declined to do the good work of caring for widows of the early church, because they did not want to leave the ministry of the word to serve tables. It seemed reasonable to decline to do a good work, if it kept them from doing a better. It also made sense to allow others to take over widow ministry since there were some who were well qualified to handle it, and keep themselves in the preaching business, which few were qualified to do.

When the apostles first presented the idea of seeking out seven other men of good report, they gave their reason for declining the job themselves, **"But we will give ourselves continually to prayer and to the ministry of the word."** In other words, they were saying they just didn't have the time for such widow care. It would cut into their prayer time. The early apostles understood that prayer was the absolute, number one priority of the church. I wonder if the words haunted James, John and Peter, **"Could you not (pray) with Me one hour?"**, and drove them toward steady, unceasing prayer. The apostles carefully guarded their prayer time against any distractions. Prayer is the ministry that activates all other ministries.

Thank God for the many in our churches who are doing substantial, good things for the church, such as facility maintenance, helping with church dinners, visiting sick and shut-ins. But prayer time should not be cut short in deference to the other things. For without prayer, the effectual good of other activities is diminished. The church needs more believers who will go "a little farther" with Jesus into Gethsemane. The pastor of one of the most successful churches of modern times is reported to pray for five hours most days. When asked how he could find time to pray so much with all he had to do, he replied that he had so much to accomplish, that he'd never get it all done if he *didn't* pray five hours per day.

We will soon discover what an excellent man of God Barnabas was. Where did such a man come from? His character is not just an anomaly of Jewish society. Maybe we should ask, "What did he come from?" He was one of those blessed souls who happened to live in Jerusalem in the days following the crucifixion, resurrection and ascension of Jesus Christ. He wasn't far away when Pentecost struck the 120. He was surely somewhere in town when Peter preached and 3000 souls were added to the church. He may have been in the number. If he missed church that day, maybe he was in the crowd of several thousand who were saved a few days later, when the crippled man was healed. He probably heard the news of the phenomenal prayer meeting of Acts 4:31, **"And when they had prayed, the place where they had assembled together was shaken; and they were all filled with the Holy Spirit, and they spoke the word of God with boldness."** We can be certain Barnabas was present in the events of v. 32-37: **"Now the multitude of those who believed were of one heart and one soul; neither did anyone say that any of the things he possessed was his own, but they had all things in common. And with great power the apostles gave witness to the resurrection of the Lord Jesus. And great grace was upon them all. Nor was there any among them who lacked; for all who were possessors of lands or houses sold them, and brought the proceeds of the things that were sold, and laid them at the apostles' feet; and they distributed to each as anyone had need. And Joses, who was also named Barnabas by the apostles (which is translated Son of Encouragement), a Levite of the country of Cypress, having land sold it, and brought the money and laid it**

262

at the apostles' feet." Maybe the most wondrous days in all history! This may be as close as we've ever come to heaven on earth. Out of such a lush, fertile, rich environment came the likes of Barnabas.

PARTNERS WITH PAUL

Of course, Paul's original name was Saul, and somehow he came to be known as Paul. So these two name changers ended up being game changers as missionaries. We don't know exactly how Saul's name was changed, but the word "Paul" means small and it could be a nick-name he picked up for being short of stature, the way we might call somebody "Shorty".

Well Shorty was quite a grouch at first. He was widely known as a persecutor of the early Christians, especially around Jerusalem. Since business was doing so well, he decided to branch out to Damascus. On his way there, he got the surprise of his life! He had a personal encounter with the glorified Jesus Christ. The dazzling brightness of what he saw was probably as bright as Jesus appeared in the transfiguration. It actually injured his eyes, similar to the way a welder's white hot arc is so bright that unprotected eyes would get flash burns. It takes several days for eyes to heal from flash burns. So Saul went from blind to seeing in three days, two different ways. First, his eyes heal. Now if this had happened today, his doctor might have advised wearing a welder's helmet the next time he visited with Jesus. Second, Saul is completely reborn spiritually as a result of meeting Jesus.

Amazing grace, how sweet the sound
That saved a wretch like me,

I once was lost, but now I'm found,
Was blind, but now I see.

Saul's conversion was so dramatic and so complete, that no one could believe the change in him. He was suspected of impersonating a Christian as an undercover ploy. He was a totally different person. It's as if he was born again. In explaining the spiritual rebirth, Jesus said, **"Except a man be born again, he cannot see the kingdom of God."** In and around Damascus, Saul slowly became accepted as a genuine Christian. By their fruits you shall eventually know them. Saul was also outspoken in preaching the salvation of Jesus Christ. For this, he became hated by many unbelievers in Damascus. When they plotted to kill him, he escaped and went to Jerusalem. But there also, Christians were afraid to associate with him. Finally, in Acts 9:27, Barnabas takes Saul to the apostles and makes the case that he is truly a believer. Barnabas had heard of Saul's conversion in Damascus and how he had preached boldly in Damascus and had to flee for his life. From that point on, he was accepted by the Christian church. So he singlehandedly saves Saul from being an outcast again. Once a man has spent a lifetime building a bad reputation, it's hard to live it down. For those who have genuinely changed their life in trying to follow God, it sure can help to have a friend like Barnabas. In being an advocate for the questionable Saul, he did a very great service to him. He likewise did a very great service to the church in giving them such a gifted, chosen man, who would become as great a leader in the church as Peter and James. I have to wonder if Saul was so extremely grateful, that he labored all the more to validate Barnabas's defending him. If you are a Barnabas, where is the one who is crippled with a bad reputation or poor self-esteem, whom you can restore with a few well-placed words?

Many years ago, early in my Christian years, I got roped into assisting with a third and fourth grade children's Sunday school class. So I went with my friend, feeling completely out of place, and tried to help in some little ways. After about a month, the guy who was the main teacher just stopped showing up. The other two ladies pleaded with me to teach the lesson the next Sunday. I could see they were in a bind, so I reluctantly agreed. I stumbled and stammered my way through the lesson, completely unsure of myself. It was poorly done, but the kids didn't care. And the ladies were relieved that at least somebody filled the vacancy. I was very upset to find out that being the teacher was a lifetime appointment. I had no training, no coach, no nothing. I stuck it out for a couple of months, having a terrible struggle every week putting the lesson together and delivering it. The only bright spot was I came to love the kids a little. Then I got disenchanted and quit the class. Feeling guilty, I started visiting other churches, looking for where I might fit in better. (Looking for a church with an active singles fellowship.) I remember what a frustration the next three months were to me. I was restless and dissatisfied. Finally I started going back to my home church, but still wanting to avoid my children's class. I also wanted to avoid anybody who would make me feel guilty. So I started coming to church about an hour early and sitting alone in the sanctuary, reading my Bible. I usually ended up dozing as much as reading. After about a month of this, something happened that completely changed my life.

The event lasted about eight seconds. I was reading in the sanctuary one Sunday morning and heard someone walking in toward me. I did not turn around and look, not wanting to encourage the person to talk to me. Then Margaret Casey, the Sunday School director, quietly came and sat on my pew about ten feet away. I glanced up, expressionless, and she spoke ten words to me. All she said was, "Woody, why don't you go back and teach those children?" After a momentary pause, I replied with, "OK, I will". Then she quietly got up and left. It was like somebody lit a match and started a bonfire in my heart.

For the next 20 minutes, as I sat waiting for church, I repented to the Lord of my neglect of what He wanted me to do. He grew a strong resolve in me that would drive me into caring for children and eventually into the ministry. It became a great joy to me. The ministry would still be a burden to me. But I must say, His yoke is easy and His burden is light. As you can see, I still remember her name, forty eight years later. I still feel greatly indebted to her. She willingly became God's instrument of encouragement. Someone needs to go and do likewise.

Well it wasn't long before Saul in his usual hot-headed way got into heated arguments with some Hellenist Jews. They became so angry at Saul that they plotted to kill him – again. But this wasn't entirely the Hellenist's fault. In Acts 11:20 and 21, other believers spoke with some Hellenists and **"a great number believed and turned to the Lord"**. Fortunately, his Christian brothers saved his life by escorting him out of town and sending him home. The whole region has a collective sigh of relief. But Saul is dejected. He must have been thinking, "What am I doing wrong?" Both before and after his conversion, he faithfully tried to serve God by doing right. Before his conversion, he was just plain wrong; after his conversion, he went about doing the right thing, but in the wrong way. Some people in this predicament just can't see what they're doing wrong. It would take a wise man (or woman) to gently show Saul what he needed.

It seems that Saul was unable to recover from the discouragement he faced. It is not clear how long he remained at home in Tarsus. Estimates range between 5 and 10 years. What a tragedy! Maybe he felt like Moses, who tried to start a revolution to rescue the enslaved Israelites, but was rebuffed by the Israelites and charged with murder by the Egyptians. Discouraged, he fled across the Arabian desert for forty years. What a tragedy! Another man who went about doing the right thing, but in the wrong way. An encourager was urgently needed.

Nearly two full chapters of Acts pass by before we hear of Saul again. He is right where we left him, and probably still dejected.

A great revival was breaking out in Antioch, where Saul had been saved. Acts 11:21 tells us that great numbers **"believed and turned to the Lord."** 450 miles away, news of this reached Jerusalem. A similar revival occurred in Samaria not long before this. Acts 8:14 tells us, **"Now when the apostles who were at Jerusalem heard that Samaria had received the word of God, they sent Peter and John to them."** Now the church at Jerusalem responds the same way. **"They sent out Barnabas to go as far as Antioch."** Apparently, he rated very highly in Jerusalem. (Acts

267

11:22) The Jerusalem church wanted to encourage the new believers in Antioch, so they sent Barnabas, the Encourager. We see the result of Barnabas's visit: **"When he came and had seen the grace of God, he was glad, and encouraged them all that with purpose of heart they should continue with the Lord. For he was a good man, full of the Holy Spirit and of faith. And a great many people were added to the Lord."** They sure sent the right guy!

Three times now, Barnabas steps up when there is a great need in the church:

- Just after Pentecost, he sold his land and gave all the proceeds to supporting the new believers.

- He helps Saul get started in the ministry when he was ostracized.

- He is sent to help the large numbers of new believers in Antioch who needed encouragement, strong preaching and discipling.

This sending by the Jerusalem church sort of made Barnabas the first missionary. He was the number one choice to send to distant Antioch, far from Israel, his home country. How did he come to be such a highly valued, gifted man? I have the feeling that when Barnabas gave the proceeds of his land sale to the Lord's work, that it was about all he had to give. But unlike the rich, young ruler, who went away sorrowful, he gave it all, and thus had treasure in heaven and came and followed Jesus. It may be that by thus emptying his heart, God decided to fill up the corresponding void with an anointed empowering for the ministry. This heavenly treasure brought him more joy and fulfillment in life than he ever dreamed of! How about you? Do you crave for success in the ministry? Do you yearn to have the power of God in your life? Do you feel like there's one thing you lack? See if the Lord may touch something in your heart that needs to go, in order to make room in you for greater fullness, the way the apostles left their boats, or how Matthew left his business. Whatever you put on the altar, you can be sure to receive **"a hundredfold now in this time and in the world to come, eternal life."**

In Acts 11:24, Barnabas is said to be **"a good man, full of the Holy Spirit, and of faith."** This is a rare commendation of Scripture. I can think of only one other man in the New Testament who was similarly honored: Stephen. He was said to be **"full of faith and power, (and) did great wonders and signs among the people."** It is also said that men **"were not able to resist the wisdom and Spirit by which he spoke."** Stephen and Barnabas were much alike. Fortunately, Barnabas didn't become the second martyr.

Barnabas was in the middle of all the glorious revival at Antioch. It was probably reminiscent of the phenomenal revival in Jerusalem following Pentecost. Maybe he never felt such fulfillment as he did in his preaching and encouraging at Antioch in those days. But abruptly he leaves town and heads for the coast. He travels 2 to 3 weeks to a city in south central Turkey. ("Asia" in New Testament times.) What was he doing? Was he taking a vacation from the stressful work at Antioch? Was he heading to a waterfront resort to take a much needed break? Was he doing a preaching tour from city to city? None of the above. He went to one city, tracked down one man, and convinced that man to walk two weeks with him back to Antioch, with no plans to come back. Who was that man? No less than Saul of Tarsus. A man so dis-liked that people would have crossed the street to avoid contact with him. I wonder if Barnabas was the first man in several years to show any kind of friendly interest in him. No doubt, Saul still felt indebted to Barnabas for taking up for him in Jerusalem. Now I know I'm being terribly conjectural with this, but please humor me. At least I'm admitting it. Let's imagine that these two old friends were glad to see each other. Saul had to be wondering what in the world Barabas was doing almost a thousand miles from home - and wondering how he even found him. Imagine them sitting down to dinner that night talking old times. Imagine Saul listening to Barnabas's exuberance in telling him all the great things going on in the Jerusalem and Antioch churches, with thousands of men and women coming to Christ, rejoicing greatly and taking their bread together from house to house. After a good while together, I can just see Saul warming up to what he was hearing. I suppose the fire began to burn again, as with Samson when **"the Spirit of the Lord began to move him at times in the camp of Dan."** Saul's depression began to clear up like thinning clouds in a long overcast sky.

Barnabas's gentle encouragement began to soften Saul's hard heart. There was nobody else in the world who was in a better position to bring this man back. The details are not important. What we do know is that Saul came back to Antioch and back to God as a different man. Imagine the transformation in Saul as they traveled back to Antioch. By the time they got there, he couldn't wait to preach again. A lot of ministers know how this feels.

In Acts 11:26, Saul starts going to church again. Maybe Saul wondered if he would even be able to preach again after being out of it for so long. But he would find out that **"the gifts and calling of God are**

without repentance." Saul may have quit on God; but God didn't quit on him. The verse implies that both Barnabas and Saul began preaching to "a great many people." Barnabas is the kind of guy who more and more would have stepped aside and had Saul do the preaching. This went on for a year. And nobody wanted to kill him. The long years had changed this man. Just as 40 years changed the impetuous Moses. Have you fallen away from the ministry? Have you quit from discouragement? Maybe you feel like you have been driven from the ministry. **"The gifts and calling of God are (still) without repentance."**

At the end of chapter 11, a widespread famine was prophesied to strike the region. It is very heartwarming to see that the Antioch Christians **"determined to send relief to the brethren in Judea."** Apparently Judea was more vulnerable to suffering in a famine. So with Antioch being in a good position to help financially, they decided to send help without being asked. It's possible that Antioch knew about the coming famine before Judea did. In Acts 11:30, we once again find Barnabas stepping up to do a great service for the church. Saul and Barnabas were asked to deliver the relief funds, since they were highly trusted. So now Barnabas is branching out into the courier business. I wouldn't be surprised if God intentionally had Saul be a part of giving the financial aid to people in need. It may go a long way in giving Saul a tender heart.

Wealthy America is in the position of well-to-do Antioch. It was a providence of God that Antioch got early notice of the need. We also are thoroughly aware of needs around the world and have the means to help. I'm happy to be part of a country that regularly sends aid to nations in need. But it is important that we also help individually as we have ability. Some of us may also need a more tender heart. So now for the fourth time, Barnabas helps with a great need in the church. What a fine, polished tool in the hand of God, easily moved at the impulse of the Spirit!

BARNABAS AND PAUL AS MISSIONARIES

Acts 13 begins the final stage of Jesus' mandate to evangelize the world:

"But you shall receive power when the Holy Spirit has come upon you; and you shall be witnesses to Me in Jerusalem, and in all Judea and Samaria, and to the ends of the earth." (Acts 1:8)

These were the last words of Jesus before His ascension. It seems to me that we ought to occupy ourselves with that command until otherwise notified. By the time Acts 13 begins, Jerusalem, Judea and Samaria had been well evangelized. Now the Holy Spirit determines that it's time to head for the ends of the earth with the gospel. (Acts 13:1-3) The church is ministering to the Lord in prayer and fasting. Thank God they had ears to hear what the Spirit says to the churches. May God also give us today such hearing and discernment.

The Bible gives us the list of prominent men who were instrumental in launching the first missionary endeavor. Notice who is at the top of the list: Barnabas. Our man! This is now the fifth time he leads the church in a major new work. But it wasn't his idea. He had no interest in being in charge, in getting attention or being famous. Notice in v. 2, the Holy Spirit chooses him, **"The Holy Spirit said, "Now separate to me Barnabas and Saul for the work to which I have called them."** Again, the Holy Spirit seems to put honor on Barnabas by mentioning him first.

So off they go on their first missionary journey. They can expect great things from God since it was initiated by the Holy Spirit and the Antioch church waited on the Lord in fasting and prayer and they laid hands on them as they were sent away. They put a great deal of reliance on God in all this. We also have a hard-working Barnabas and a humble Saul. This is looking very good. We're not told, but the Antioch church was probably praying daily for them, praying without ceasing. It's interesting that no mention is made of financial support. I guess the writer told about only the most important element of support.

From the outset of their travels, they went first to the Jews with the gospel. Remember Jesus had commanded the disciples to go to the lost sheep of the house of Israel. Even in foreign countries like Cyprus, their first stop was to Jews. It seems like a wise strategy, for a Jew already has a good foundation laid for their faith. On this, Paul later commented, "It was necessary that the word of God should be spoken to you (Jews) first." (Acts 13:46) They would much more readily grow into solid Christians than people who know almost nothing about God and the Bible. In their travels and preaching, it isn't long before Paul becomes the more prominent speaker of the two. It seems that this transition happened gracefully, since nothing is said about it. At first Barnabas was like a mentor to Paul, but as he began to surpass Barnabas in preaching ability, I feel sure that Barnabas must have smiled for being so proud of him. It soon became "Paul and Barnabas". John the Baptist also humbly bowed to the rising popularity of

Jesus. "He must increase, but I must decrease." May God grant like grace to senior pastors who have rising stars in their church. They need all the encouragement we can give them.

Later in their first trip, Paul and Barnabas face severe persecution in Lycaonia, in southern Turkey. Furious Jews and Gentiles hunted down Paul and nearly killed him by stoning him. Laying on the ground, nearly dead, guess who was there to "pick up the pieces" and to help Paul get up and keep going? That's right – our man. This was exactly what happened to Paul twice before and it resulted in him quitting the ministry. This time he stays with it. Pretty good chance it was Barnabas, the encourager, that made the difference.

After the long missionary trip together, in which Paul and Barnabas shared a lot of glorious victories, miracles and life-threatening dangers, they return to Antioch like heroes. They also travel together to Jerusalem and were well-received. Then it was back to Antioch. The friendship and kindred spirit and shared experiences should have made them best pals, like David and Jonathan. But that's not what happened.

THE FEUD OF PAUL AND BARNABAS

It all started in Acts 15:36 where Paul says to Barnabas, **"Let us now go back and visit our brethren in every city where we have preached the word of the Lord, and see how they are doing."** Great idea! But I wish he had worded it, "Let's pray about going back and visiting..." The last time they went out, it was the Holy Spirit's idea. This time there is no clear mandate from the Lord. There is also no mention of "ministering to the Lord", prayer or fasting. It seemed like a good idea to Paul and he was ready to go with it. The same way we usually do.

In v. 37 and 38, a disagreement comes up. **"Now Barnabas was determined to take with them John called Mark."** Mark had gone with them on their previous journey, but after a while he left and went back home. Notice it says Barnabas was **"determined"**. He felt strongly about this. **"But Paul insisted that they should not take with them the one who had departed from them in Pamphylia and had not gone with them to the work."** Notice Paul **"insisted"**. He also felt strongly about it. Neither one had to feel strongly about the matter. It might have been wise to keep their feelings in neutral until they discussed it. To make matters worse, in v. 39 **"the contention became so sharp that they parted from one another. So Barnabas took Mark and sailed to Cyprus, but Paul chose Silas and departed, being commended by the brethren to the grace of God."** This event shook the early church like an earthquake. How could this have happened? First, they did not wait on God for His instruction. But even though this was a failure on their part, God blessed the outcome anyway. God knows how to make all things work together for good to them that love God. Just as He made the wrongful separation of Joseph and his brothers work out for good.

Let's also consider this: the two men were very different. Paul was highly driven and motivated; he would not shy away from an argument; he was a little hot-headed; everywhere he went, people wanted to kill him. Barnabas was a kindly, caring person; very giving and encouraging; forgiving. He was named "The son of Consolation". Radically different people. But God

275

picked these two men to bring the gospel to the Western world. They had a balance of qualities that worked well together in spite of their differences.

The truth is: both men had a good case. And the way things worked out was very good. Now there were two missionary teams spreading the gospel. Encouraging Barnabas was just right for fledgling Mark. Paul and Silas were also a good team. Silas was a strong Christian and he was tough. He did not quaver when persecution arose. But I don't think that was the way God intended for it to happen. **"The wrath of man works not the righteousness of God."** They could have achieved two missionary teams peaceably. No problem though, God is accustomed to working through man's faults and failures.

It is a sad story. It appears that Paul and Barnabas never saw each other again. It's also sad that there was no peacemaker in Antioch to reconcile these two brothers and help them keep the friendship even though they disagreed on one point. A relatively minor point. Was there no one to help Paul and Barnabas see the other's point of view? Why couldn't someone help them see that their difference in views was a result of their different temperaments? It's very possible that no one had the nerve to step in and help these two great men, as Nathan confronted King David. These men needed a Godly Elihu to mediate their differences.

If Paul and Barnabas had ever met again, I think they would have made amends as surely as Esau and Jacob.

Some good lessons to learn here are:

a. No matter how prominent or gifted a man may be, he is still a man **"subject to like passions"** as the rest of us.

b. **"If it be possible, as much as lies in you, live**

peaceably with all men." (Written by Paul) I wonder if Paul was remembering his sharp words with his old friend, and had painful regrets.

c. **In everything by prayer...** No matter how obvious it is how to act on a matter, commit it to prayer first.

d. **The wrath of man works not the righteousness of God.**

e. **Blessed are the peacemakers; they shall be called the children of God.**

f. In some things, we don't need to be strongly opinionated.

g. Believe in younger people to become something better in later life. Years later, Paul wrote, **"Aristarchus my fellow prisoner greets you, with Mark, the cousin of Barnabas (about whom you received instructions: if he comes to you, welcome him.)"** (Colossians 4:10) Thank God for Barnabas!

I do not agree with those who fault Barnabas in the disagreement. Some say proof that he was wrong is the fact that after they separated, Barnabas is never heard from again. If you'll pardon my Greek, that's baloney. What it is proof of is that Luke, the writer of Acts, did not travel with Barnabas, but with Paul. That would be like saying the apostles, Bartholomew, Matthew, Thomas, Simon and Jude never did any good because we do not hear about them after Pentecost.

Bibliography

1. Introduction, *Matthew Henry Commentary,* Vol. II, p. 548

1. Daniel, p. 207 Education Initiative, College Drop Out Rate By Year, October 29, 2023

2. Daniel, p. 209 Brad Landers, PHD, Ohio State University, Wexler Medical Institute, "How Alcohol Abuse Affects Your Brain", March 16, 2021

3. Daniel, p. 207 – Culture / Lifeway Research, January 15, 2019 - Church Attendance

4. Jacob, p. 17 Website: caregiveraction.org.statistics, *"Caregiving in the U.S.",* November 2009 1

www.ingramcontent.com/pod-product-compliance
Lightning Source LLC
Chambersburg PA
CBHW020437130626
46549CB00001B/184